THE RIGHT TIME TO SPEAK

ANETA WEINREICH

SYDNEY JEWISH MUSEUM
holocaust and australian jewish history

Community Stories

עַתָּה בּוֹא כָתְבָהּ עַל לוּחַ אִתָּם וְעַל סֵפֶר חֻקָּהּ
וּתְהִי לְיוֹם אַחֲרוֹן לָעַד עַד עוֹלָם

Now go, write it before them on a tablet,

and inscribe it in a book,

that it may be for the time to come

for ever and ever.

(Isaiah 30, 8)

I would like to give special thanks to:

Joseph Weinreich
In particular I give thanks to my husband and best friend, Joseph,
for writing this entire book in longhand as I dictated it—
and for steadfastly sitting with me, day after day, encouraging and
enabling me to write it. He has been my rock for forever.

Michelle Weinreich Roth
My daughter Michelle has provided me with remarkable strength
throughout this book process. She was involved in every aspect
of it, even from her home in New York City. When necessary, she
travelled to Sydney to sit with me for countless hours, reviewing
the book, pictures, and documents, and meeting with editors and
designers. We've also 'face-timed' nearly every day to ensure that the
book is everything I wanted. Michelle is truly unique in the world.

Thank you for your invaluable assistance
in helping to shape my book:
Lilian Weinreich Ezekowitz, Henry Weinreich, Peter Roth,
Jacqui Wasilewsky, Audrey Larsen, Rabbi Cantor Yehoshua Niasoff,
Adam Benedykt Bisping, Yehiel Lehavy, Edward Baral, Ilona Vaskó,
Anna Körmendi Ottóné, Anna Tanczer, Lucy Nguyen, Lee Ung,
Sue Robbins, Susie Zeilic, Joel Tuch, Bibi Pfefferbaum, Ita Buttrose,
Rex Dupain (son of Max Dupain) and Kim Taylor.

Thank you also to:
Yad Vashem, Jerusalem; Israeli Embassy, Budapest, Hungary;
Hungarian Consulate, Budapest, Hungary; Polish Consulate,
Kraków, Poland; Galicia Jewish Museum, Kraków, Poland;
United States Holocaust Memorial Museum;
The Vatican, Rome, Italy; The Ghetto Fighters Museum, Israel.

In Memoriam, Elżbieta Kołodziej

With thanks to my Mother, Franka Baral (top),
Bronka Porwit (centre left), Ilonka Nemes (centre right)
and Dr Yahya Shehabi.

They saved my life. They will always be remembered.

CONTENTS

1

SURVIVAL

❖

I opened my eyes and looked up, blinking. Above me stood a doctor with a concerned expression on his face. I was lying in a hospital bed after being rushed to an intensive care unit when my husband Joseph and daughter Lilian saw my desperate situation. I was suffering from a severe form of pneumonia following an operation which had caused my lungs and large airways to swell. Three doctors and other medical staff had been working on me. It was difficult to breathe, there were pains in my chest and I continually wheezed and coughed.

Dr Yahya Shehabi leaned over and introduced himself. He smiled and told me to relax. I knew instantly that he would help me.

'I'll make you better and get you out of here on your feet,' he said gently. 'But it will take me a couple of days. Can you be patient?'

I tried to smile and reached out my hands to grasp his. We clasped hands to seal our agreement.

That afternoon Dr Shehabi also spoke to my devoted husband, reassuring him that I would be fine. I could see some relief on Joseph's face. But he knew that other medical people had been pessimistic about my chances, preparing the family for the worst. After all, I was in my early 80s and very sick. Some of the other doctors were convinced that I would die.

In the days that followed I saw Dr Shehabi watching how Joseph cared for me and how my children rushed to my side from New York. He told us he was reminded of his own father, an Arabic-speaking Palestinian, who had told him that it's such moments of powerful human connection in our lives that make us who we are.

The doctor treated me as if I were his own mother. I saw how much he appreciated my family's gratitude to him for what he was doing for us, hour by hour, day by day. My case became far more than just a regular two-week block of duty. I became aware, under his care, that what was keeping us all going was my conviction, my will to survive and our mutual faith and hope.

Over the 11 traumatic days that I was connected to the machine that helped me breathe but prevented me from speaking, we bonded. Those days were a roller-coaster of ups and downs. I was so gravely ill that Dr Shehabi was astonished I could tolerate my situation without sedation. He had never seen this before. He could sense my steely determination, and I watched the other staff silently observe the growing relationship between us: a Palestinian doctor and a Jewish family whose common goal was to keep me alive and help retain my sanity. They wanted me to improve each day.

When they removed the breathing tube, I was able to communicate with my doctor for the first time since we'd met. My voice was gravelly and weak, since I was exhausted and found speech very difficult. But even with the barest minimum of words, from the beginning, we understood one another.

We all learned from this crisis of mine. After a slow and tedious rehabilitation at the Wolper Hospital in Sydney's Eastern Suburbs,

I returned home. We then invited Dr Shehabi and his wife to share coffee and cake at our home. I am a very private person, but this meeting acknowledged the way that suffering makes sisters and brothers of us all. I was proud that he had seen the strength of the love between Joseph and me, and our children Lilian, Michelle and Henry. Dr Michael Ezekowitz, my future son-in-law, consulting from Philadelphia around the clock, would not allow the first team to give up on me and opted for aggressive treatment together with Dr Shehabi. Over those 11 anxious and gruelling days in the hospital, Dr Shehabi became an honorary member of our family.

This was not the first time I had narrowly survived. But it was the first time I had ever been silenced. I knew after this experience that I had to speak out so that people would hear me. This was the moment I decided to write my story.

I was born in the historic city of Kraków, the ancient capital of Poland, known as 'the City of Kings', with its stately old buildings, theatre, the famous Jagiellonian University that attracted so many scholars and artists, and its large, well-to-do bourgeois families. On 1 September 1939 when Nazi Germany invaded Poland, I was nearly ten years old. My whole world was about to implode.

At a doctors' Intensive Care Foundation conference at the Sofitel Hotel in Melbourne, 24 May 2013. Aneta's case was one of the lecture topics. From left: Joseph, Dr Yahya Shehabi, Henry and Aneta Weinreich.

2

MY HAPPY CHILDHOOD

◈

When I was born at our home in Kraków at 20 Na Groblach Street, at midnight on 24 December 1929, no one could have imagined that, 37 years later, far away in Israel, I would meet up again with the midwife who helped Dr Neumuntr bring me into the world.

In Tel Aviv I was sitting with Joseph at my favourite place to have coffee and cake, Roval Restaurant, when Auntie Ela, my father's sister, suddenly became very excited. She rose to greet a lady in her early sixties who was approaching our table, then introduced us.

'It's Pola Pogacz, your midwife!' We fell into each other's arms. 'You were such a blessed child,' Pola cried. She remembered my parents well, especially my mother, and we were able to catch up on years apart.

I was named after my father's mother, Antonieta (Yiddish name: Jenta) and still have a clear picture in my mind of the big, bright apartment we rented when I was a child, in the heart of Kraków, at 4 Morsztynowska Street. My maternal grandparents, Matias and Lieba Feuer, had originally lived there before they bought a house in the centre of the city at 16 Floriańska Street. When we moved in, I was delighted to find the rooms led on to balconies, one of which could be reached from the bedroom my brother Marcel and I shared. Another adjoined the bigger room in which my parents slept, and there was a tiny one off the kitchen, next to a small room for our housekeeper, Kasia. The rest of the apartment consisted of a sitting and dining room and a bathroom. We were an up-to-date family and owned the latest appliances, a fridge and a phone. I can even remember our telephone number: 206-274.

As my father's fur business prospered, my parents were able to give us a very happy childhood. Our German nanny, Aniela Plonka, spoke to us in her own language, insisting that we should always be clean and tidy. I loved the stories she read us, particularly a book about balloons, *Hazi Bratzi Luftballon* and *Struwwelpeter*.

To lull us to sleep, she taught us to recite the following:

Ich bin klein	I am small
Mein Herz ist rein	My heart is pure
Soll niemand drin wohnen	So nobody should live there
Als der liebe Gott allein	Except my Dear Lord

As a child, I recited this simple little prayer every evening. It would also give me great comfort when I was in the hospital in 2012, and the strength to overcome my ordeal with all those tubes. I recited it over and over again in my head, hoping that God was listening and would help me recover.

Marcel (Hebrew: Moshe, English: Martin) was also born at Na Groblach Street on 21 March 1932. My Auntie Ela told me years later that she and Hela Pfefferbaum, a distant relative, kept my mother company throughout her pregnancy, only being asked politely to leave by the doctor and midwife when my brother was about to be born.

I was delighted to have someone to share my toys and accompany me on walks with my nanny. Marcel had a very strong personality from the beginning, wanting everything his way. Later in life, he came up with many original ideas. It was evident even then that he had the talent to become a force in the business world.

There are many details of my childhood that I remember vividly—and these are such sweet memories. The Kraków apartment's balconies became our playground. On the floor below us lived the Orthodox Grienfeld family, and my brother and I used to play with their daughters, Mimi and Thea. On the balcony, we would send toys down to them in a basket, on a pulley operated by Marcel.

Once my brother sprinkled pieces of bread across the balcony next to my parents' bedroom, then hid behind the door until pigeons flew in to eat. Emboldened, they ventured into the bedroom itself. He quickly shut the door, trapping them inside. They flew round the room, desperate to get out. When our nanny discovered what we were up to, she of course released them.

I also remember Marcel buying a chicken at the market and locking it in our bedroom. It flapped around the room soiling the parquet floor and the furniture. This time when Aniela discovered what we were doing I, as the eldest, was made to clean up most of the mess. I don't know what happened to the chicken.

Aniela taught us to speak German. Sometimes this was hard, but even today I'm grateful for what we learned from her. She was insistent on *Ordnung*: tidiness, order, organisation and discipline.

My second brother, Janek (Hebrew: Jakob, English: Jim) was born after we had moved to Apartment 12A at 4 Morsztynowska Street, on 24 July 1935. Soon he joined us in our bedroom. We welcomed him and I learned, under the watchful eye of Aniela, to change his nappies, even though I was only six. As my husband Joseph writes down these memories in longhand for me whilst I speak the words, he laughs and says, when we had our own children, *he* was the main nappy-changer. 'But you had the experience!' he says.

As the youngest, Janek was spoiled by everyone: grandparents, uncles and aunts—and of course Marcel and I indulged him too.

As siblings we learned to understand each other's idiosyncrasies and personalities. We really related well and our happy times together established a solid base upon which trust was built. It was strong as steel and bonded us together. We could 'read' each other without words.

We loved visiting a nearby pet shop and looking at the animals. We were also devoted to our tropical fish in their little tank. Once we were allowed to buy a tiny white mouse, which we carried home in a box. We decided that she could live between the outside windowpane and the inner one, and watched her scurrying about, attracted by the food we put out. One morning when we opened the inner pane to put in more food, the mouse jumped out and escaped. A few days later she was spotted in the kitchen. Then she disappeared forever.

Our fox terrier Bijou lasted longer. Wild and messy, he trotted around our bedroom, barking. I chased him and tried to calm him down, even putting him into my doll's pram. But he was too noisy and energetic for an apartment. Finally my parents gave him away.

When I was growing up, it was fashionable for little girls to wear bows in their hair. I was a meticulous child, and always made sure that my bow matched the colour of my dress. Even then I had a sense of fashion, of how clothes should be matched with accessories.

My mother, Franka, was always stately and up-to-date in the way she dressed. She loved the latest fashions that my father, Samek, brought home from his business trips to London. From an early age, I wanted to look as good as she did in her smart suits, hats and beautiful dresses. A seamstress would come in to measure me, and then make the clothes my mother designed. I remember one outfit especially well. Over a white organza blouse with puffed sleeves, I wore a sleeveless dress with a black bodice on which the outline of a red heart was embroidered. The full skirt, gathered at the waist, was sprinkled with little pink printed flowers on a black background.

My mother used to take me to the cinema to see the films of the famous child actress Shirley Temple. I loved the way she danced, and admired her clothes. Seeing them ignited my dream of becoming a designer of similarly beautiful dresses.

I had a rag doll, Berba, who was as tall as I was. I used to dress her in my own clothes.

I also had a smaller, very beautiful doll named Charlotte with eyes that opened and closed. I used to push her around in her little pram. Berba couldn't fit into it; she was far too big.

Every birthday I woke to find myself in a snowstorm. Little white cotton balls would be suspended on strings from the ceiling, just like the snowflakes falling outside. The covers on my doll's pram had been washed and ironed, and Charlotte would be lying right next to my bed, with Berba sitting there too. This was a delightful tradition my mother established.

At our Kraków apartment, Janek once fell out of the high chair where he ate meals and was hurried off to the hospital to have stitches inserted in his tongue. Another time, when he was about three, he was riding his tricycle with us in the Planty Gardens near our home when suddenly we turned to find that he had disappeared. Our hearts seemed to stop—but fortunately he was soon found.

The Planty Gardens were like our playground. They were lush and green, with benches on either side of the grassy path. We often met our cousins Ada and Olga there, since their nanny, Marta, was our nanny's sister.

On the other side of our bedroom wall lived Mrs Szafranowa. Marcel and I would knock on the wall and call to her: *Pani Szafranowa, Pani Szafranowa*—and she even seemed to like it!

Every morning a milkman arrived at our door and ladled fresh milk from his big metal container into a dish, a litre at a time. My parents, Franka and Samek, would eat breakfast before us, so that my father could leave on time for work. They would enjoy delicious freshly baked bread rolls, bought every day by Kasia, and my father always ate a soft-boiled egg left in the shell. He would leave some of the white for me.

Every Friday night Mother lit the candles and Father recited the prayers. We had a full traditional Shabbat dinner. Afterwards, my brothers would go straight to bed since they were still too young to stay awake into the late evening. The rest of us went for a walk, usually to my maternal grandparents' home. Since I was the oldest, I often walked proudly with my parents to their apartment. Other Feuer family members would be there, and I loved being with them. I adored my uncles, aunties and cousins and felt such closeness to them as I saw the tremendous affection my parents had for their siblings and families. In the middle of a large table covered with a plain white tablecloth, a big bowl of tasty, hot chickpeas, called *arbes* in Yiddish, had been placed so that everyone could help themselves. I think the *arbes* were boiled, and salt and pepper added later. I clearly remember their smell and taste.

Twice a year our parents took us on fabulous holidays. We travelled in style in trains with sleeping compartments. My mother was with us the whole time and our father joined us at weekends. Although Mother was raised in a strict Orthodox home, she was sporty and out-going, and an excellent skier. In Poland daughters were rarely encouraged to play sports, but she taught me to ski and skate beside her. Our winter holidays were spent in the mountains at Zakopane approximately 110 kilometres south of Kraków at the base of the Tatra Mountains bordering Slovakia, and our summers in Sopot on the Baltic Sea, or sometimes in Krynica or Rabka. Even in winter, our afternoon naps from 2-4pm were outside on the veranda, to take advantage of the fresh air. Marcel and I would scramble into specially-made soft, warm, sheepskin-lined sleeping bags, using eye masks to block out the light. Today if I want to have a nap in the afternoon, I still use an eye mask.

Once my summer holiday was disrupted when I was hurried back from Krynica to Kraków with scarlet fever. Unfortunately, we discovered that our gorgeous tropical fish in the tank in our apartment had died. I was upset, since I thought it was my fever that caused them to die.

When I was four years old, I started going to a secular kindergarten on the ground floor of a big house around the corner from where we lived. I wore an apron with a seal (the sea mammal) embroidered on it, and this same motif was used on the shelves I was given for my clothes. Twice a week, in the same building, I attended ballet class.

At six I started school at the Hebrew Gymnasium at 5 Brzozowa Street. I would call at my Uncle and Auntie's house around the corner at 7 Bonerowska Street and my cousin Bubek Susskind, three years older, would accompany me to school through the Planty Gardens. I carried my books in a light-coloured leather backpack. Our walk took us about 20 minutes. At school we studied Polish as well as Hebrew, Mathematics, Geography and History. Mrs Haber taught us most subjects, and Mr Kwitner was our Hebrew teacher.

Our uniform was a navy button-through dress with a white collar and a colourful bow at the neck. Our classroom was on the first floor and we sat on pale wooden benches, aligned in three rows with desks, three children to each desk. Right in front of me sat my best friend, Anka Laub.

Most days, my mother picked me up in the afternoons. Sometimes I went to school on my thick-tyred, royal blue scooter with a hand-brake on the handle. I would arrange with my father to meet him in front of his business so that he could escort me across busy Stradomska Street.

My father imported and exported furs with his own father, Juda (in Hebrew: Yehuda) Baral. Theirs was the fifth largest fur business in Poland. His office was at 27 Stradomska Street, in the heart of the business district. I loved going there and admiring and stroking the soft, lustrous furs and breathing in their special scent.

Father travelled often to other places, mostly England and the Scandinavian countries, to buy furs offered at auction. He used to buy them in tremendous quantities, since there was a huge market for furs in Poland because of the freezing winters. He also exported them to other European countries. When he returned home, he brought us beautiful toys. I was proud that he travelled to different countries, since few people travelled like he did in those days.

Occasionally my great-grandfather Josef Schullehrer visited us. He was very old: 102! He would come into our bedroom, settle himself in a chair and pull from his pocket a white handkerchief. He could fold it in any number of amusing ways. I remember he could make it look uncannily like a little mouse.

In our parents' bedroom, in pride of place, hung an enlarged photo of his daughter, our Grandmother Antonieta. I never met her, since she died before I was born, but Auntie Ela would later tell me that I had inherited many of her characteristics, such as good business sense, the ability to make quick decisions on the spot, and a willingness to try new ideas. We were both very disciplined, she told me.

As the 1930s came to an end, it was clear that the free, easy, happy and affluent life we children had enjoyed was threatened. Wild rumours circulated, especially after Hitler's *Lebensraum* ('living space') speech, justifying the occupation of lands bordering Germany. This ignited panic in Kraków; people feared that war was imminent. There were ominous signs everywhere. For example in 1938, when we were holidaying at Sopot on the Baltic Sea, a sign over a shop where we hoped to buy ice cream said in big, bold letters: *Juden Eintritt Verboten* (meaning Jews are forbidden to enter). I was mystified. Even worse, in Kraków I saw graffiti on walls everywhere, saying in big letters and in Polish: *Jews to Palestine*. There were also terrible caricatures of Jews plastered on kiosk walls.

Our last summer holiday in Rabka was cut short. We returned in a hurry to Kraków a few days before World War II started on 1 September 1939.

As Poland was invaded by Nazi forces, my father's last shipment of furs was bombed in the port of Gdansk. He returned to Kraków from England to be with us. He did not close his English bank account—but only a tiny fraction of the insurance money for the furs was ever transferred to it.

My childhood ceased from that moment. A tragic new chapter of my life was about to begin.

Aneta as a baby, Kraków, Poland, 1931.

Top: Franka and Samuel Baral, Kraków, 24 March 1928.
Bottom: Franka's siblings, Kraków, Poland, 1916.
From left: Back row: Jacob, Franka, Bala and Hela.
Front row: Motek, Ignac, Mina, Emil and Tosia.

Aneta and Marcel, Kraków, 1934.

On holidays in Zakopane, Poland, 30 July 1936.
Franka, Samek, Aneta and Marcel.

3

THE WAR BEGINS

◈

At the outbreak of World War II, we were a large, happy and closely-knit family. I was lucky that I knew both sets of grandparents. My father's father, Juda, lived with his second wife, Rachela Baral. As a little girl I would visit them often at 2 Paulińska Street, and I liked to play with rag dolls in their large, sunny sitting room. Their home was in a prime location opposite the River Wisła (in English: Vistula River), not far from Wawel Castle where the kings of Poland used to live. The castle dates back to Medieval times and is the most important historical building in the city.

My other grandparents, the Feuers, were more Orthodox than my father's family. When they married, they had each lost partners, and they brought children from those relationships to the new union. Grandfather brought Jacob Feuer and Grandmother Motek Matzner. Then they had seven children together—two sons and five daughters. My mother was the third.

I had many cousins, since every one of the nine married and had children themselves, except Motek Matzner, who was married but childless. All our families lived quite close to one another, so we could see them often. My mother's sister, the Susskind family, lived just around the corner. Only Jacob Feuer and his family—my cousins Gisele (Tova), Aki (Yechiel) and Charlotte (Yafa)—lived elsewhere. They came to visit us in 1935 from Kiel, Germany, before migrating to what was then Palestine.

The Thursday before War was declared, my father returned home from a trip to London. The next day I, my parents and my two brothers left Kraków for Zgłobień near Rzeszów in the Polish countryside, to stay with my Uncle Ignac Feuer and his fiancée, Toduś Wilner. We travelled in a taxi, taking only essential clothes in small suitcases, as my parents thought we would return after a short time.

But in fact, we would never again live in our Kraków apartment. I had to leave everything—including my beloved dolls. I was almost ten years old and in the third grade at school.

The Wilners lived in a big, comfortable house on their own farm, so for a while we were safe there. In late 1939, the Nazis introduced laws against the Jewish population. These included bans on moving, the compulsory declaration of valuable possessions and bank accounts and curfews. Schools, bookshops and libraries were shut and books were burned. Homes were plundered and synagogues vandalised. Jews could be forced by the German invaders to work for nothing.

Before the bombing raids started on Kraków and the surrounding areas, my family decided to move even further away than Zgłobień. We travelled by horse-drawn cart, heading towards Lwów. Along the road were many others like us, escaping, running away to find shelter. We were relentlessly bombarded by the low-flying planes of the Luftwaffe. I could see that they were targeting people like us, those trying desperately to get away.

We were forced to travel by night and sleep during the day. This was difficult because it was hard to see where we were going in the dark, and to travel across the fields. Once, the cart hit a bump in a field and overturned on to the ground, spilling us all out. The horse was not hurt, but my mother broke her ribs and I fractured my collarbone. There was nothing we could do. We had to wait until we arrived to get proper medical treatment.

In Lwów, my parents found a small apartment at 34 Tarnowskiego Street, and I even started going to school again. Soon the invading forces of the Soviet Union's Red Army arrived. The students in my class and I started to learn Russian, which became a school subject.

My mother was very unhappy in Lwów. She missed the support of her family—her parents, sisters, brothers and their families—and resented the Soviet-style registrations and restrictions. She was often so lonely that she told us she couldn't stand to be parted from her family any longer. But how could we return to the unknown and to uncertainty about our safety?

My mother went to the Nazi authorities and told them we were Volksdeutsche, the term used from the early twentieth century to describe people of German descent who were not citizens, but lived outside Germany's borders. She thought that this would provide a better opportunity to be granted the papers we needed to return to Kraków—and she spoke perfect German. My mother and we children obtained ours, but my father didn't even attempt this. He looked too Jewish. My father had brown, wavy hair, whereas most Polish people had straight blond hair. He was of medium stature and wore fine wire-rimmed glasses. He was trim, as he played soccer—at the outside right position in jersey number 7 for Maccabi in Kraków. He had 'Semitic' features and was a quiet, serious, noble man.

My mother took my brothers and me back to Kraków. On the way, the train stopped at a station where Nazi troops boarded. I was petrified. Suppose they discovered we were Jewish? They examined our papers and were especially fascinated that we children could speak German.

'What's your name?' they asked Marcel, who was eight at the time. 'Moishele,' he innocently replied. Fortunately my mother was able quickly to add that the little boy had got it wrong. This was the name of one of the neighbour's children, not his own, she assured the soldiers. She spoke so convincingly in German that they didn't question whether she was telling the truth. I knew never to contradict nor question my mother. I understood what was happening: that the world was becoming dangerous and complicated.

Back in Kraków four or five months later, we couldn't return to our own apartment because it was occupied by Germans. The Gestapo and their families were given priority to occupy Jewish apartments. I realised that we had no roof over our heads. We went to the Ehrlichs and stayed with Hela and Motek, our mother's sister and her husband and their two daughters, our cousins Ada and Olga, at 28 Starowiślna Street. We were lucky to have a room to ourselves.

It seemed that the number of prohibitions handed down by the Nazis about what we as Jews could and couldn't do increased every day. We could not be on the streets except during daylight; we couldn't go to school; businesses needed special permits that were unlikely to be granted; we couldn't assemble together and—worst of all—we couldn't go to synagogues to pray, since they were shut. People probably gathered secretly in apartments to pray.

Meanwhile my father was making his way back to us in Kraków from Lwów. I'm not sure how he travelled, since it would have been dangerous to apply for a travel permit which would have identified him as Jewish. He travelled illegally with no papers. It's possible he used smugglers. To our relief, he was finally able to join us.

In April 1940, my Baral grandparents, Juda and Rachela, obtained Polish passports, and were able to leave for Palestine. My Feuer grandparents remained for a while in their own apartment. The Barals travelled via Trieste, Casablanca and Madrid, an epic journey lasting two years. In 1938, my step-grandmother Rachela had travelled to Palestine, where she had bought a small orange orchard (*pardes* in Hebrew). In 1942 they were able to sell it and buy a little house in Kfar-Saba.

Why didn't we accompany them? I think it was because my parents wanted to stay near their extended family members, and also to protect the assets everyone had worked so hard to acquire.

In my Baral grandparents' four-storey house at 2 Paulińska Street was a second-floor apartment, into which we then moved. But the German soldiers had a list of wealthy Jews, and my grandparents were on it. One day while we were there, some soldiers arrived in a lorry with a list of what they were going to take. In an orderly and quiet manner, they removed the furniture from the dining and sitting rooms, beautiful pieces imported from Vienna. We had no idea how they had found out what my grandparents owned. I distinctly remember standing in the dining room, watching them in disbelief. I couldn't understand why they were doing this to us. We stood silently since there was nothing we could do. There was no explanation needed from my parents; we simply understood that this was the way it was going to be. It was a fact of this new life.

There followed a time of anxiety and very little activity. My father's business had been confiscated, like others owned by Jewish families. We children couldn't go to school, because our schools had been shut, and we were not allowed to go to the public ones. We spent long idle hours wondering what would happen next.

From the window I watched Nazi soldiers kicking and beating a bearded Jewish man. I was appalled and terrified at the sight. They tore at his beard and I could not fathom why a man simply walking down the street would be attacked in this way.

Early in 1941 a decree with two options was announced: that all Jews in Kraków were to move either into the Ghetto, separated from the main city by the River Wisła (Vistula), or to relocate to the outlying areas of the country. The Ghetto area, created in Podgórze, was a poor neighbourhood in which Jewish people did not usually live. Up until then, most of us had homes in the Kazimierz district. Only the Barals, the Ehrlichs, the Hirschs, the Bleichers and the Künstlers moved to the Ghetto, around which a tall wall was being built. In some parts, where the tram lines ran, it was sectioned off with barbed wire. The fine apartments we left were allocated to Germans, Polish citizens and other nationalities.

My Feuer grandparents, the Susskinds, Tosia Ber and her son Milus, and the Matzners, Ethel and Motek, escaped to Bochnia, where there was as yet no Ghetto—even though one would soon be set up. So the family was split in half. Being separated from them was unbearable for everyone. I missed my grandparents so much that I later travelled on the train by myself to see them. Looking back, I can now scarcely believe that at the age of eleven I found the courage, and that my parents let me go. Our tearful reunion would be the last time I saw them.

For a few months, postcards from my Feuer grandparents, my mother's sisters and their families were sent, first to Ignac Feuer in Romania, and then forwarded to Jacob Feuer in Palestine. My parents never saw these postcards. Years later, after the War, I saw them when Jacob Feuer's son, Yehiel, emailed copies of them to me.

In turn, my mother, Marcel and I also sent postcards to Ignac Feuer to keep him informed about us. My mother's postcards were not sent from inside the Ghetto, but from outside, when she went to work. I have no idea how she managed this.

In Kraków, my parents, brothers and I found a place in the Small Ghetto, also known as Ghetto B. It was enclosed by a wire fence and high walls and guarded by Polish and Nazi police, Ukrainians and other collaborators. To our great shame, there were also Jewish police known as the Ordinungsdienst (OD).

We moved into a house with three other families at 6 Janowa Wola Street. This was extremely lucky as places like this were very difficult to find. My mother's brother-in-law, Motek Ehrlich, had connections with the people who had formerly worked at the *Gazeta Żydowska* *(Jewish Newspaper)* and had arranged for us to live in this building. My parents felt this was a comparatively safe place.

There were about 300 houses in the Ghetto, the tallest two storeys high and crammed together in a continuous line that formed part of the wall built around some areas, while other parts were enclosed either by barbed wire fences or newly constructed stone walls.

The windows of the buildings which were facing the outside street (the non-Ghetto side) were all cemented and bricked up. Most of the houses were tiny, with outside toilets. It was ordered that every room with a window had to be home to at least three people. The adjoining streets were closed to traffic but there was a tram along the street dividing Ghetto B from the larger Ghetto A. Although these trams passed through without stopping, passengers on them could see some of the streets and some of the people confined to the Ghetto.

All four gates were guarded on the inside by Jewish police and on the outside by Polish ones. Anyone who wanted to get out had to have the right documents, called 'special permits'. In October it was decreed that any Jew found outside the Ghetto without permission would be shot—and so would anyone who helped them.

By the autumn of 1941, there were about 16,000 people inside the ghetto. Others—up to 50,000—had already been sent away from the city.

More people crowded into the Kraków Ghetto from smaller villages (*shtetls*), until there were 24,000 people looking for a roof over their heads. In the beginning conditions were not too bad for us—apart from having no freedom of movement. We had sanitary facilities and food. The bedroom was divided by a large wardrobe, and my parents, brothers and I had one side and a father and his two sons the other. In a little room with a separate entrance that comprised the rest of the apartment lived a woman and her adult son. It was crowded but peaceful.

The only schooling we had at that time was a Hebrew lesson for about an hour a week. Our parents paid the teacher. I rarely went outside the room of the apartment, and only sometimes went to the backyard, where I played ball or hopscotch with other children from the building. I also helped tidy and clean our part of the room.

Mother was able to leave each morning for her shop at 16 Floriańska Street in her parents' building. She had at that point a special permit to leave and return to the Ghetto. Such permits were still obtainable, but rare. Before she set out on the 30-minute walk, she removed the white armband with the blue star we all had to wear. Everyone in the Ghetto had to wear this armband of Jewish identity, from the age of 12. It slipped on and off. I also wore an armband, which was white with a blue star, but neither of my brothers wore them, as they were still too young.

Removing her armband was extremely dangerous for my mother, since she would have been shot had she been caught without it. Yet if she did wear it, she would have been tormented by hooligans.

Around this time in the Ghetto, Martin developed a sore

throat and the Polish pharmacist Tadeusz Pankiewicz gave him the medication called Panflavin that he later claimed saved his life.

In her shop, my mother and her friend Franka Schreiber ran the business together. They sold hats to high-ranking Gestapo officers and other German customers. One of them was SS-Hauptsturmführer Wilhelm Kunde. He had the power of determining life or death in the Ghetto. From the money she earned in the store, my mother was able to buy food. She brought it back strapped to her body under her clothing, which again placed her in great peril.

As a result, for a while we weren't hungry. Even though there were small grocery stores in the Ghetto, there was very little food available and everyone was hungry.

Conversing in German with her Nazi customers—who had no idea that she was Jewish—gave my mother the opportunity to learn what plans there were for those who had been confined to the Ghetto.

Meanwhile I felt that my childhood, with its regular schooling and diversions such as ballet, sports and my friends had been stolen from me. Now we lived in continual fear, as if on quicksand. We had no certainty, only the sickening feeling that each day would be worse. We knew that the outlook was grim, with ever-more rules and regulations dominating and destroying our chances of a decent future.

Although a non-aggression document had been signed between Nazi Germany and the Soviet Union, it was just a smokescreen. It wasn't long before Hitler stormed into Russia with a huge armada of planes, panzer divisions and millions of soldiers on armed vehicles. He was sure that he could defeat his enemy before winter set in, with a targeted campaign to create confusion.

The Russians knew that to prolong the bitter fighting for as long as possible would mean the Nazis would have to contend with freezing cold conditions. In 1941, when Nazi troops were laying siege to

Moscow, they needed warmer coats to weather the winter and a decree was handed down that all Jewish people must give up their furs to be sent to the Front. My mother still had two valuable coats which could have been bartered for food.

Around this time, my father had a heart attack in our room, after complaining of chest pain. We had to be quiet and give him privacy. Afterwards, he lay recovering in his bed, and was moved near the stove in the kitchen to give him more space and warmth.

In what I now see was a defiant act, my mother took her two furs and burnt them in that stove. Even though it was a tremendous risk, she was adamant that the Nazis would not get her coats. I still remember the distinctive stench of burning fur.

Emil Feuer, one of my mother's brothers, was one of the few Jews still living outside the Ghetto. He went out wearing his fur coat, not having heard about the decree. He was arrested on the street and thrown into Montelupich Prison, which had a notorious reputation: no one came out alive.

My brave mother went to find him. She didn't care that she might be imprisoned or shot herself. She wanted to save her brother. But when they took her to his cell, she told us that his face was white as chalk and that he wouldn't meet her eyes. He knew that if he did, she would be implicated in his 'crime'.

The following day he was shot—'as an example' we were told—the first member of our family to be murdered. I saw the posters with his name put up on the walls of the Ghetto as a warning, to scare people into giving up their furs. Uncle Emil was only 30 years old and left behind a wife, Mina, and a three-year-old son, Jasiu. I was heartbroken, because I had loved him very much.

We took some satisfaction in hearing the news that furs collected in the Ghetto did not reach the Russian Front. The Red Army knew that trainloads of them were arriving for the Nazi soldiers and they did everything possible to disrupt transport and communications by blocking access to the German forces who were dying in temperatures 20 degrees below freezing. Hitler had learnt nothing from history. His troops outside Moscow were defeated in the same way as Napoleon's.

In June 1942, inside her store on Floriańska Street, my mother heard (or overheard) from one of her Nazi clients that there would soon be an *Aktzia,* or round-up, in the Ghetto. These terrifying operations meant that soldiers surrounded the whole area in a solid, threatening human wall through which no one could escape.

This *Aktzia* happened on 10 June. My mother and father had managed to get the right stamps on their *Kennkarten* (identification cards). The stamps were given inside the Ghetto. Nazi soldiers set up tables, and stamped *Kennkarten,* according to which factories people were assigned to work. But my mother's sister Bala, her husband Salo Hirsch, did not manage to get theirs stamped. They were with their three children who did not have identity documents as they were too young.

My mother ran to the square where people were already being loaded on to trucks. No one knew where they would end up. People were told they were simply being taken to a new workplace, so they would go willingly and not panic. But rumours were already flying around about camps from which no one returned.

My mother spotted her sister's family, took their *Kennkarten* and hurried to the table where officers were sitting and stamping the documents of those who were working in factories.

Kunde was standing nearby. Because she knew him, my mother approached and asked him to stamp the *kennkarten*. Instead, he took out his revolver and said: '*Ich habe nicht gewußt, das sie Jüdisch sind* (I did not know that you are Jewish).'

My mother was desperate to save her sister and her family. In a seemingly suicidal act that she described to us later: 'I touched Kunde's hand in the hope that he would put away his revolver.'

The *Kennkarten* were stamped. But it was too late. Her sister Bala, her husband, Salo Hirsch, and their children Mela, Hesiu, and Menachem had already been loaded on to the trucks. We would not find out where they were taken or how their lives ended. We never saw them again.

Aneta's paternal grandparents, Rachela and Juda Baral,
Kraków, 28 February 1926.

Aneta's maternal grandparents, Matias and Lieba Feuer, on holidays in Krynica, Poland, 1938.

Aneta's maternal grandmother, Lieba Feuer, with her stepson, Jacob Feuer (left) and her son Motek Matzner, Kraków, 1932.

7 Krakowska Street, Kraków where Aneta's grandfather Juda Baral lived on the second floor with his first wife Jenta. It is the middle building, corner house.

Top: The Wilner residence in Zgłobień, Poland, where Franka, Samek, Aneta, Marcel and Janek arrived a day after the War started, 2 September 1939.
Bottom: Engaged couple, Ignac Feuer (Aneta's uncle) and Toduś Wilner in Zgłobień, Poland, 1938.

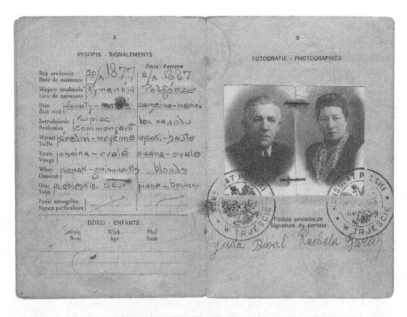

Juda and Rachela Baral's passport when they left Poland to travel to Palestine through Tangiers, Madrid and Casablanca.

Juda Baral's building at 2 Paulińska Street, Kraków, 1994.

Opposite page:
Top: **Building the Kraków Ghetto Wall, 1941.**
Source: Bundesarchiv, Bild 183-L25516. Photo: Koch.
Bottom: **Polish labourers seal off doors and windows of**
buildings on the outer periphery of the Kraków Ghetto, 1941.
Source: United States Holocaust Memorial Museum (USHMM),
Washington, USA, courtesy of Instytut Pamięci Narodowej.

36

Top: View of the entrance to the Kraków Ghetto, 1942-43.
Source: USHMM, Washington, courtesy of Nora Abrahamer.

Bottom: Jewish people being forced to relocate to the Kraków
Ghetto, moving their belongings in carts and horse-drawn
wagons across the bridge over the Vistula River, 1940.
Source: USHMM, courtesy of Archiwum Panstwowe w Krakowie.

[from] S. Baral 2 Paulinska St, Kraków	[posted]: Date illegible Received: 7 June 1940
My dears	
I was very pleased to receive your letter and I'm happy that at least you are doing well. I have received no news from my parents. I implore you to write to general poste restante in Tangier, so they can pass through you some news about the. I beg you for it.	[to] Ignacy Feuer, c/o Mr Antonescu 29 Matei Besarab, Craiova, Romania
Kisses and love, Samek	

Postcard in Polish translated into English from S. Baral (Samek Baral) to Ignacy Feuer (Ignaz or Ignac in different documents) his brother-in-law, sent before Aneta's family went to the Kraków Ghetto. When the Ghetto was being established and the family was split between those who went there and others who moved to outlying areas, postcards like this were how family members tried to keep track of one another through a central person, in this case Ignacy Feuer.

The back of the postcard and its translation (opposite).

My Dear Loved Ones,

As usual, your last letter has given me much pleasure. It is my most pleasurable entertainment. Toduś, you just can't imagine how much just one little letter from you, let alone your writing at length, means to me. I know that you remember us and are doing your best to make it possible for us to visit Janek. We'd love to do that but it seems to us that right now this is just not possible.

Toduś, you have a soothing influence on me. I can call you a blessing to our family, because that's what you are. I'm surprised you haven't written what you think about my work in the millinery business.

The children are well, thank God, which means everything to me. They enormously liked what you added to the letter. Janus says that Tonka is so naughty; she keeps saying she'll come but it sounds like a lie.

I have written to Mum and sisters a few times but did not receive a single reply. I wonder what they are up to. Stay healthy and happy for our sake, as your happiness is ours too.

May God help us happily see each other one day.

Lots of kisses to you,
Franka

My Dear Auntie and Uncle,
I'm very sorry I have not written to you, because Mum didn't tell me when she was writing to you.

Lots of kisses to you,
Aneta

My Dear Auntie and Uncle,
Please write letters to us and send me stamps.

Marcel

I'd like to see you very much.
Love from Aneta and Janek

[from] Ettel Matzner, care of M. Stern, Bochnia	[Posted] 2 September 1940
My dears	
As you can see, we are in Bochnia. With God's help we will meet in Romania.	[to] Ignacy Feuer, c/o Mr Antonescu 29 Matei Besarab, Craiova, Romania
Best wishes, Etka Motek	

Postcard in Polish, translated into English, dated 2 September 1940, from Ettel Matzner, daughter-in-law of Aneta's Feuer grandparents to Ignacy Feuer.

Opposite page: The back of the postcard (translation over page).

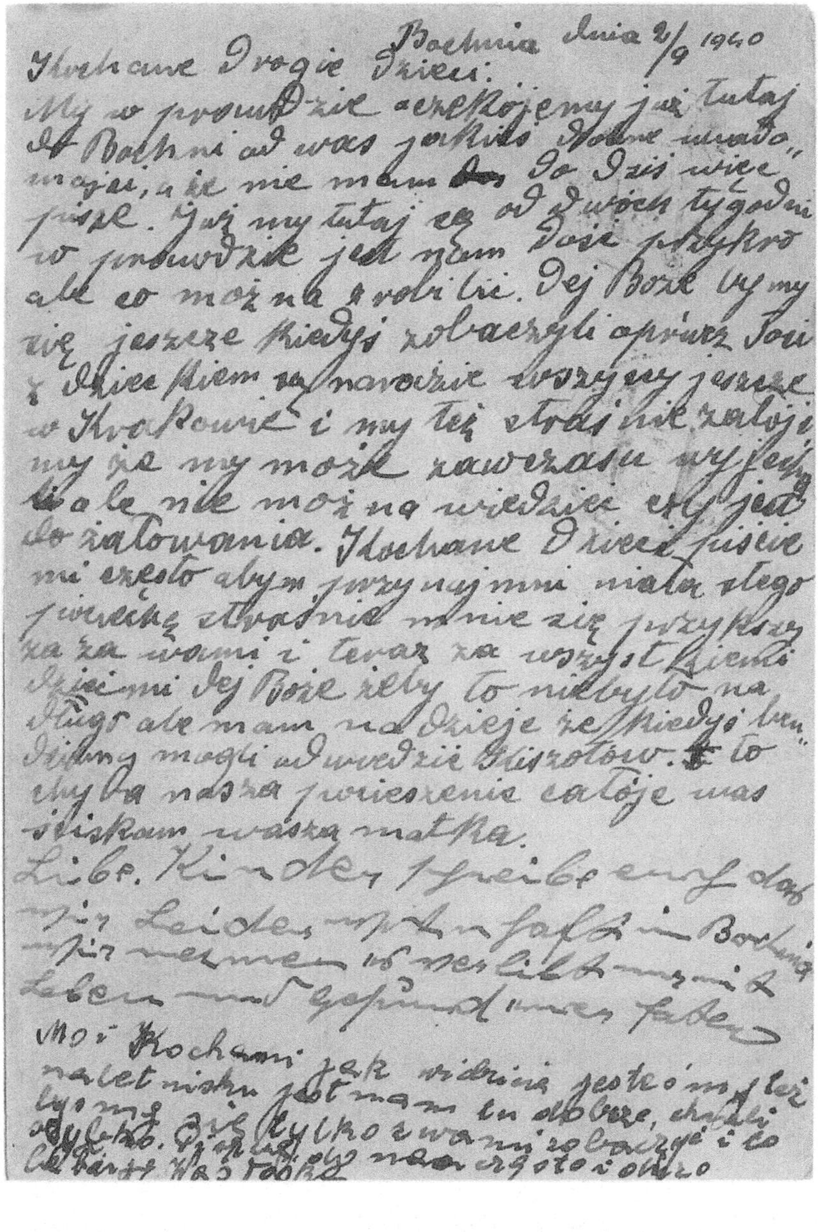

Bochnia dnia 2/9 1940
Kochane Drogie Dzieci:
My w prowincji [illegible] już tutaj
do Bochni od was jakieś słowo [illegible]
[illegible], a że nie mam do dziś więc
piszę. Już my tutaj są od dwóch tygodni
w prowincji jest nam dość przykro
ale co można zrobić. Daj Boże byśmy
się jeszcze kiedyś zobaczyli oprócz Poli
z dziećmi [illegible] wszyscy jeszcze
w Krakowie i my też strasznie żałuje
my że my może zawczasu wyjechali
ale nie można wiedzieć czy jest
do żałowania. Kochane Dzieci piszcie
mi często abym przynajmniej miała z tego
pociechę strasznie mnie się przykrzy
za wami i teraz za wszystkimi
dziećmi daj Boże żeby to niebyło na
długo ale mam nadzieje że kiedyś będziemy mogli odwiedzić [illegible]. A to
chyba nasza pocieszenie całuje was
ściskam wasza matka.
Liebe Kinder, schreibe euch das
wir Leider [illegible] in Bochnia
wir [illegible]
Leben und gesund [illegible] Vater
Moi Kochani
[illegible] jak widzicie jesteśmy [illegible]
[illegible] jest nam tu dobrze, [illegible]
[illegible] tylko z wami zobaczyć i to
[illegible] nam często [illegible]

My Dearly Beloved Children,

We are already here in Bochnia and have been waiting for any scrap of news from you. As I have not received any to this day, I have decided to write myself.
  We have already been here for two weeks. To be honest, we are pretty sad, but what can one do? Please God help us see each other again one day.
  Except Tosia and her child, everyone is still in Kraków. We awfully regret having left perhaps too soon, but it's impossible to know whether one should indeed regret.
  My Beloved Children, write to me often so at least this gives me comfort. I awfully miss you all, my children. Please God don't make it last too long. I hope though, that one day we will be able to visit the Kiszots. I think this is our source of solace.

Kisses and hugs to you.
Your mother

Dear Children,

I'm writing to tell you that unfortunately, we had to go into detention in Bochnia. Remain alive and healthy.

Your father.

My Dears,

As you can see, we are also in this summer resort town. We like it here, but we'd like to see you all very soon.
  Write to us often and a lot.

Kisses to you all from me.
Toska

The back of the postcard translation. The back of the postcard translation. *Your mother* is Lieba Feuer. *Your father* is Matias Feuer.

4

IN HIDING

◈

The first *Aktzia* of 10 June 1942 divided other families as well as ours, and scattered them. Many people we knew simply disappeared.

This created an uneasy atmosphere where everyone was frightened. As rumours spread through the Ghetto that shortly there would be another *Aktzia*, it was decided that my mother would take my brothers and escape, because otherwise they might not survive. Because of our Jewish looks, my father and I stayed where we were in the Ghetto, hoping and praying that we would be spared.

After my mother and brothers left, I felt terribly lonely and distressed. I missed them so much and had no idea when we would see one another again. When my father saw how worried and anxious I was, on 27 October 1942 he took me from Ghetto B to our friends the Bleichers at 17 Plac Zgody in Ghetto A so that I could spend time with my close friend Pola who was the same age as me. I could confide my fears and hopes to her. This made me feel much better, because we had a lot in common.

My father then went out again to see to a few necessary matters.

He told me he would be gone for no more than an hour and a half, and he asked Zvi (Henek) Bleicher to take me back to Ghetto B. However, when Zvi and I came to the gates between Ghetto B and Ghetto A, we found to our horror that no movement was allowed between the two.

This confirmed our suspicions that an *Aktzia* was imminent. Movement in the Ghetto was always limited when one was going to take place. We felt trapped and terrified.

Zvi and I returned to the Bleichers and shortly afterwards, to my great relief, my father also reappeared.

The Bleichers were kind, but much as they would have liked to put the two of us up for the night, physically it was impossible. There was simply no room. Luckily, Auntie Ela lived nearby and we spent the night at her place, sleeping in our clothes on chairs pushed together: three for me and three for my father.

The Bleichers had agreed with their friends the Schulkinds that they would all hide together if necessary in a large loft in the latter's house. I was given the opportunity to join them, and my father left me there at 5am while he went out again to get a stamp on his *kennkarte*.

The specially-prepared ceiling of the kitchen contained a board that had been hinged to allow entrance to the space above, then the hole was painted over to disguise the opening. It was a good big hiding place: 16 feet wide and 65 feet long, above four or five rooms. At night you could even remove a couple of tiles and stand upright in the space between the floor and the tiled roof and breathe some fresh air.

A good few weeks before the *Aktzia*, the loft had been used for another vital purpose. We knew that if we could obtain Hungarian identity documents such as birth and marriage certificates or letters from official bodies, we could approach the Hungarian Consulate, make an 'advance arrangement' (pay a bribe) and acquire Hungarian citizenship. Then we could legally cross the border to safety. If the head of a family could get the correct documents, they also covered his wife and children. Our false papers would not be in our own name, Baral, but changed to Schullehrer, the maiden name of my Grandmother Jenta.

But how did one obtain these precious documents? In the Ghetto were two professional lithographers, brothers, who could easily forge them if they had the right tools and equipment. In August, after being paid a substantial sum of money by a group of family and friends, to which my father made the most substantial contribution, the lithographers climbed into the loft and began their work. The loft was furnished with chairs, mattresses and a locked cupboard—and the Schulkinds had even connected an electricity supply. Boys in the family delivered food to the men every morning and evening.

At 17 Plac Zgody, discussion had been going on about the best time for everyone to go up to the loft to hide. It was suggested that the children should do it right away, taking some food with them. They climbed up the evening before the *Aktzia*. Anyone working at a job, they decided, should stay in his own place for the time being. Then if soldiers searched the rooms, they would not be empty and it would not be suspected that people were hiding.

The adults made bundles of clothing for each person in case they were discovered and deported. Each contained a spare pair of shoes, water, some bread, potatoes boiled in their jackets and freshly-prepared pancakes.

My father went out again almost immediately, still hoping to get the stamp he needed on his *kennkarte* to allow him to stay in the Ghetto. Just before the trapdoor was shut, I climbed up to join those already there. I sat trembling in the dark with Pola, Henek, their parents and also Schulkind's wife, their three children and some

47

of their friends, and the Meibruch parents and their two children. Several of the children were little: five years old and under. There were also two babies. We hoped they would stay quiet and that none of them would sneeze in the dusty air.

We were told not to talk among ourselves or call out to anyone below. Two adults stood on guard there. At a pre-arranged signal, a low whistle, we would open the trapdoor.

Then came the dreaded *Aktzia*. By the evening the area was surrounded by armed and jack-booted soldiers wearing steel helmets. From the window and the entrance to the building OD men could be seen rushing about with lists in their hands, herding whole families from their houses, pushing them into the square and dividing them into groups.

I was distraught and completely desperate, since I had no idea where my father was or whether or not he would be able to get his *kennkarte* stamped. How would he know what was happening to me? And what if we were both taken separately from the Ghetto? How would we ever find one another again?

Up above, we stayed as silent as we could, listening to the shouting, screaming, shooting and the sounds of weeping.

According to Zvi Bleicher, the watchers for the building told him they could see people were carrying bundles like the ones we had made up, with sacks and suitcases and children too small to walk. Even though our building was the closest to the assembly point, no one had yet tried to enter.

Zvi told us he had sorted out tools: pliers, screwdrivers, pincers and metal shears, and wrapped them in rags, intending to take them up to the loft. He had broken two hacksaw blades in half and put two halves in each shoe. He thought they might be useful to escape from any closed space with a metal grid between him and freedom, as a friend of his had already done. These tools would still be in his shoes months later.

At last Mrs Meibruch, still in the kitchen below, could take the endless waiting no longer. She asked who would look after the children if the adults were forced out of the house and taken away. 'We can't desert them like this,' she appealed.

The others agreed: it was now time to act. The lights were turned out and the electricity disconnected. Zvi was the last up to the loft: he was light and could be pulled up on a rope, after hiding the ladder in the nearby courtyard.

There were 22 people in the loft, including the two babies.

From the square we could still hear shots and bursts of firing. Machine guns. Screams and wailing from the crowd. On and on they went.

It was now past midnight.

Gradually we all sank into restless sleep. We knew it was morning when thin light seeped through cracks in the ceiling. We listened; now perhaps the *Aktzia* was over and we could face another day? But we heard bursts of firing from all around the Ghetto.

People murmured, 'What's going on—are they killing everybody?' 'What's going to happen to us? If no one's left alive in the Ghetto, how can we get out of here and where can we go?' 'What will happen when our food and water run out?' 'At least if we all died we'd be together, and wouldn't have to suffer or listen to others suffer'...

As the light gradually suffused our hiding place, we looked wearily around at the others sitting or lying on the floor. Someone began to nibble on his piece of bread while another chewed a potato. The children were all given food but as we ate, the horrible sounds outside went on and on.

Then we heard footsteps below. Someone with heavy boots was

entering the house. There was knocking at the door and a voice calling to Mr Schulkind. 'Where are you? Have you died of plague?' We stayed silent and finally the person gave up and left.

We knew he had been an OD because he had spoken Polish. Someone murmured: 'Perhaps he wants Schulkind for some electrical repairs at Headquarters.' 'May they all burn in darkness,' responded Mr Schulkind angrily.

We decided the person would conclude that we had all been taken away. We continued to wait.

When the long morning was almost at an end, with dread we heard the sound of vehicles, then heavy boots entering and moving from room to room. We could hear the intruders moving furniture, kicking in doors and throwing things around. '*Wie ein leerer Ort—Alle versteck!*' (Such an empty place—everybody is hiding!) they shouted. When they got to our rooms, one of the soldiers said: 'It's empty—they must be hiding.' What happened next was really chilling—their dogs started to bark, as if they'd picked up our scent.

We knew that if we were discovered, we would be finished. The harsh barking of the dogs scared one of the babies and he started to wail and cry. Quickly, a young man, Maniek, put a feather pillow over his face. The dogs stopped barking. Silence fell again.

The baby's father held the mother tightly and they sat rigid, gazing at their child under the pillow. For a moment Maniek raised it from the baby's face, to allow in a little air. But the baby started crying again. The pillow was quickly replaced and the crying ceased.

To our great relief, we heard the sound of boots recede. The baby's mother snatched up her child and began to rock him in her arms. The child tried desperately to cough and suck in air.

'He's alive! Alive!' she whispered with joy.

Outside, the upheaval continued.

Then the father took his child and rocked him gently. We could all see that there was something wrong. The mother took him again and began to speak to him. 'Nu, nu—it's all over now. Stay with us. Don't leave; don't go away. You see how everyone loves you—nu, nu—look at Mama.'

But we could all see that the baby was not breathing properly.

The father was desperate to climb down with his sick child and hurry to look for a doctor. But outside the firing and the running and the screams and cries continued.

All day long the commotion in the square went on. We were devastated imagining the terror, confusion and panic of the people, our brothers and sisters caught in this *Aktzia*. Then we heard the trucks start up and roar off, and gradually silence fell over the whole Ghetto. It was quiet as a morgue. The last light faded from the cracks in the ceiling. After a while we heard different sounds: weeping and voices speaking in Yiddish.

The Nazis had left with truckloads of people jammed together.

Zvi was the first down to see what was going on. He used the rope to descend and didn't put on the light. From the window he could see corpses strewn around the square, with luggage, bodies, pools of blood and other waste fluids: vomit and excrement.

He told us later that he was about to take some cautious steps into the street when he felt, in the dark, another presence. As he moved towards the entrance of the building he called out to the person to close the door quickly, since someone was coming.

The man began to call out to the Bleichers up in the hidden loft. It was with huge relief that my father's voice was recognised. He and Zvi fell into one another's arms as Father asked tearfully where I was and what had happened.

'Aneta is fine,' answered Zvi. 'She's here with us. We're all here.

You'll see everyone soon.'

When he pointed towards the ceiling, my father understood.

Up in the loft we heard a shout from below: 'Aneta? Aneta, where are you?'

'Tato!' I called back.

You could hear sheer panic in his voice. 'Come down,' he said very loudly. 'I'll only believe it when I see you!'

I was the first one down. We clung to each other and cried. We could scarcely believe that both of us had survived this perilous brush with death.

Then he embraced anyone within reach.

The children were told to stay up in the loft until it was confirmed that the *Aktzia* was really over. The saddest story from those terrible days was the baby's. The father did rush out to try and find a doctor. But he couldn't find one who would agree to come. At last one did— but it was too late. The doctor merely confirmed what we all knew: the baby was dead.

When Father and I returned to Ghetto B to collect some clothes, we were horrified by the mess we found in our room. Furniture and clothing had been scattered around everywhere. We knew we would never live there again.

With the help of the Ehrlichs, we moved on to 3 Józefińska Street, to live with them and the Bleichers. For some privacy in the one room we all shared, we put a big wardrobe down the middle, making a division between the Bleichers and us in the larger part and the Ehrlichs in the back.

Gradually the full story of the October *Aktzia* emerged. The OD men had been ordered to round up all those on the lists given to them; they were all the men who were not working or were about to become redundant. But many refused, wanting to stay with their families. If they refused, the OD men—who also lived in the Ghetto—would take their entire family.

Then the SS had installed machine guns all around the square. On the morning of 28 October, those heading to work outside the Ghetto were assembled and divided into the strong and healthy, who were then released to their jobs, and those who looked weaker, who were taken off to be deported. Most of these people were never seen again.

It was decided that the numbers were still insufficient, so then the SS men went from house to house selecting people to seize. It was whispered among the OD that the entire Ghetto was going to be liquidated. This tactic of the Nazis brought more people out of hiding, and they were taken away with nothing, no extra clothes or food. If they resisted, they were shot.

The toll on that terrible day was 6000 men, women and children, all deported by truck or cattle train. Hundreds were shot inside the Ghetto, in their homes, on the streets, in the courtyards or in cellars and cupboards where they tried to hide.

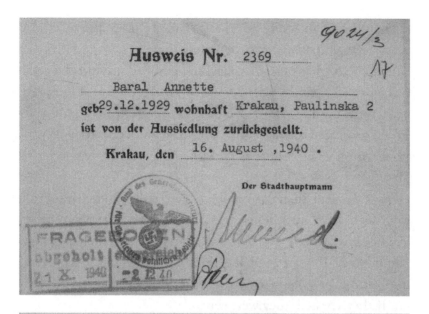

Top: The certificate No. 2369 allowing Aneta (Annette) to stay in the Ghetto rather than being deported. Each member of the family received a similar certificate.

Bottom: Certificates allowing Samuel (No. 2651) to stay in the Ghetto.

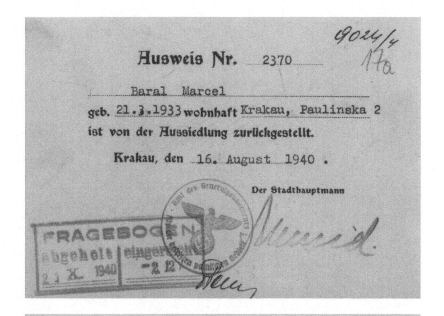

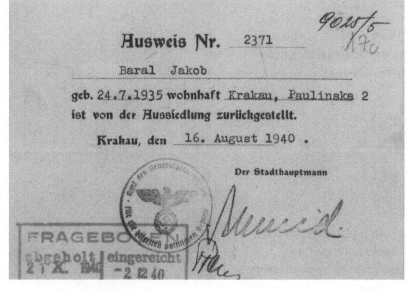

Certificates allowing Marcel (No. 2370) (top) and Jakob (No. 2371) (bottom) to stay in the Ghetto rather than being deported.

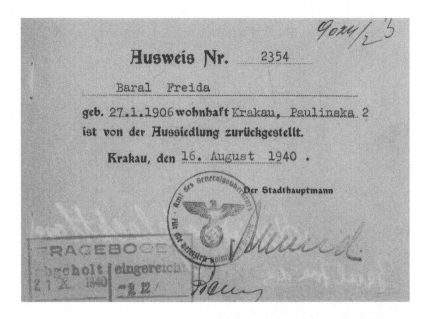

Ausweis Nr. 2354

Baral Freida

geb. 27.1.1906 wohnhaft Krakau, Paulinska 2
ist von der Aussiedlung zurückgestellt.

Krakau, den 16. August 1940 .

Der Stadthauptmann

Certificate allowing Frieda
'Franka' (No. 2354) to stay
in the Ghetto rather than
being deported.

Photo taken in the Kraków
Ghetto to be used for
Hungarian false documents
for Franka, 12 February 1941.

Photographs for Hungarian false documents, February 1941.
Top: (left) Samuel, (right) Aneta. *Bottom:* (left) Marcel. (right) Janek.

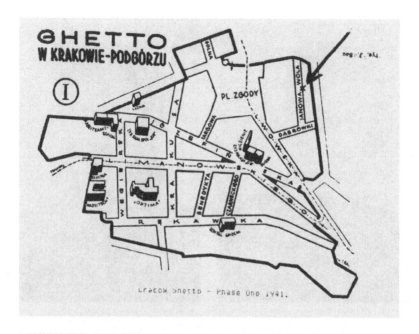

Top: Map of the Kraków Ghetto, Phase One, 1941.

Source: Courtesy of the Joseph Bau Museum, Tel Aviv, Israel, www.josephbau.com

Bottom: Map of the Kraków Ghetto, Phase Two, showing its contraction after the deportations of 28 October 1942. Within the new boundaries, 12,000 people were forced to live.

Source: Courtesy of the Joseph Bau Museum, Tel Aviv.

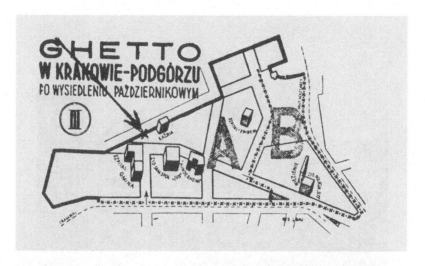

Top: Kraków Ghetto, Phase Three, December 1942. On Saturday, 13 March 1943, the final liquidation occurred.
Source: Courtesy of the Joseph Bau Museum, Tel Aviv.

Bottom: Jewish people's belongings scattered across a major street in Kraków after the liquidation of the Ghetto, March 1943.
Sources: Agency Agreement, USHMM, courtesy of Instytut Pamięci Narodowej, and Yad Vashem Photo and Film Archives.

Top: Aneta was hidden in the loft of the small building at 17 Plac Zgody (centre). The little window on the side (circled) is where people could see what was happening outside. The building has now been demolished.

Bottom: A column of Jewish people march with bundles down a main street in Kraków during the liquidation of the Ghetto overseen by SS guards, March 1943. 'This is exactly how I was walking to Płaszów,' says Aneta.

Source: USHMM, courtesy of Instytut Pamięci Narodowej.

5

PŁASZÓW

◆

After the *Aktzia*, my mother returned to the Ghetto with Marcel and Janek, as it was too dangerous to remain on the outside. However, the situation was getting worse in the Ghetto and again there were rumours that something was going to happen. So a few months later, in March 1943, my mother took my two brothers to the barbed wire fence and lifted the wire so they could go under what separated us from the outside world. She told them to turn right and not look back.

When my brothers escaped from the Kraków Ghetto, Marcel was ten and Janek was seven years old. Marcel said later that getting out was easier than remaining hidden on the outside. The police encouraged anyone who knew where any Jews were hiding—or if they recognised them in the streets—to betray them. They even offered scarce sugar as a reward.

According to Marcel, my brothers slept in large rubbish bins, and stole food from market stalls. They managed to live hand-to-mouth for a few weeks.

Our relatives, the Ehrlichs, knew a lady named Bronka Porwitowa who had worked for Motek Ehrlich in his restaurant before the War. She was a Polish Christian woman willing to help us. We already knew that she was a very accommodating and empathetic person, and during the coming months, she would save our lives.

My mother gave Marcel and Janek Bronka's address. When my brothers knocked on Bronka's door, she crossed herself when she saw who was standing there. Although it was very dangerous for her to help them, she gave them money and showed them where they could catch a train to Bochnia.

Bronka had already risked her life to save Ada and Olga Ehrlich when they had earlier escaped from the Ghetto. She was not able to find a place for Pola to stay, so she was forced to walk the streets of Kraków through the day and stay at a different place each night. Bronka had taken Ada and Olga to their former housekeeper, Hania Lemek, who lived in Brzesko, because their neighbours were growing suspicious. From Brzesko, Hania took them to her brother in Muszyna, where they stayed for a few weeks and pretended to be Catholic.

My brothers managed to find Bochnia Ghetto, which was small, and join the Susskind family.

Then everything became confused and threatening again. By March 1943, transports were taking people off to Płaszów, which we by then knew was a labour camp. Only people who were already working were taken.

A day I will never forget, one of the most terrible of my life, was Saturday 13 March 1943, the day the Kraków Ghetto was finally liquidated. My mother, father and I hid in the basement in one of the buildings on Jósefinska Street, in a tiny space only a couple of metres wide. It was very cramped and uncomfortable and after a few hours, my parents decided, in whispered discussion, that we should see what was going on outside. It was the liquidation and we would have been found anyway. We risked being discovered and shot.

We joined the others in Węgierska Street adjoining Limanowskiego Street where, in 1993, Spielberg was to set part of his film *Schindler's List*.

When we got outside, we saw that people who were working in the different factories, like Madritsch, were already lining up in rows of five. My mother stood beside me on one side, with Hela Ehrlich (Ada's and Olga's mother) on the other side, and Sala Bleicher (Pola's mother) stood next to Hela. This made me harder to see and reach. I was in great danger because the decree was that those under 14 had to go to a 'children's home'. I was short for my age, so my mother had found a long coat with a hood for me, preparing in advance for the possible need for disguise. In it I appeared taller, at least 15, not 13. The soldiers moved up and down the rows, choosing the smaller and younger children. I was so petrified that I was jittery. I watched the Nazis pull out tiny children whose mothers tried to hide them under their coats. Every time a child was taken, there was heart-wrenching crying, wailing and screaming.

I was lucky. I wasn't singled out and managed to stay beside my mother. Then we were ordered to walk to Płaszów, which took an hour and a half to two hours. Płaszów often served as a transport location to send 'prisoners' to Bełżec and Auschwitz-Birkenau concentration camps.

We had no idea what to expect. My father was assigned to the men's barracks, as men were separated from women. Once inside the camp, Mother and I were taken to dark, wooden barracks with very small windows and three tiers of bunks. There was little in these crude huts but the three rows of bunks with straw in hessian (burlap) bags as mattresses. My mother and I found a mattress to share on the third level.

The following day the children who had been picked out of the lines, whose mothers had been forced to hand them over, arrived after being kept back at the Ghetto. They were unloaded from the trucks cold and dead. Their distraught mothers pushed forward to see their beloved children one last time. Slowly, one by one, they came forward to bury their own sons and daughters.

Witnessing this monstrous scene was one of the worst days of my life.

Some of the bereaved mothers would later look at me in a suspicious way, wondering how I had been able to stay alive, separated from the other children.

Płaszów was a place of death. Its streets were paved with gravestones from a Jewish cemetery, once upright. They had been desecrated by being used as paving. They also lined the washrooms, so everywhere we went we were haunted by memorials to our dead.

The camp was set on 80 hectares of land surrounded by two electrified barbed-wire fences separated by a water-filled ditch. From 13 towers men armed with machine guns stood guard. They also patrolled regularly with dogs.

The camp was extensive and well-planned. There were two quarries, latrines and a kitchen, plus a square for parades. We were also to discover that there were three execution sites, including a hill and a ditch. In the administration area stood quarters for the SS and their hospital, the Commandant Amon Goeth's villa and workshops and garages where cars and trucks were serviced.

Relentless bullying went on all day, every day. We could never get away from the routines imposed on us and there was no privacy at all. I particularly hated sharing with so many others the filthy, stinking open latrines, lined up in a row without doors. There were no proper baths or showers, just rows of taps at which we could wash only our faces and hands.

Every day at 5 o'clock in the morning a bugle sounded and we were dragged out of our beds and lined up in front of the barracks to be counted—and recounted. We were usually so exhausted by then that we didn't care what happened. That was just one of the ways the Nazis tried to break our spirits so that we wouldn't want to go on living. Breakfast was a tiny piece of black bread with jam and watery coffee. I had to force myself to eat or drink.

After the liquidation of the Kraków Ghetto, some 10,000 Jews were sent to Płaszów. In mid-1943, 6000 Polish political prisoners were sent there as well.

We were put to work in a factory, Optima, where we sewed German army uniforms. It took two hours to walk there, so by the time we arrived we were already mentally and physically exhausted from this daily routine, whose purpose was wearing us out by stamping on our souls. At the end of the day, having marched back to the camp from Optima, we were given some thin soup before we collapsed on our bunks, exhausted.

We were better off, however, than some who were forced to work from sunrise to dusk in the quarries. Women hauled stones in wheelbarrows to the place where more pavements were being constructed—walkways with nowhere to go.

At this dreadful time, my mother again displayed her enormous mental agility to work out ways to keep us alive. She volunteered us as two of the 300 workers Julius Madritsch wanted for his factory, Optima, in the Tarnów Ghetto. This Austrian industrialist and member of the SS also had a compassionate heart. He was to save more people from death than even the heroic Oscar Schindler, and already employed some 1200 workers there.

But my mother took a big risk volunteering to go to the Tarnów Ghetto. She didn't know much about the work or whether we were being told the truth about it: that we would be sewing buttons on Nazi winter uniforms. She simply knew it was easier to escape from a Ghetto than a camp.

Through the wire fence that separated men from women we were able to tell my father what we were planning. We knew that if we were caught we would be killed. With desperate hearts we farewelled one another.

On the day we left, we joined the other women on trucks. When we arrived in the Ghetto we were put into a room to share with three others. Then each morning we were all marched under armed guard to the factory, returning each evening. This took approximately half an hour.

Very soon after my arrival in the Ghetto I fell ill with a sore throat and a temperature. It was dangerous to be sick at work, so the doctor was called and wrote a note to excuse me. He also gave me a sulphur injection, which made me faint. I have been wary ever since of any medications containing sulphur.

I was soon, however, back at work with the other women. All day long, from eight in the morning until six in the evening, we toiled sewing buttons on to heavy uniforms. Looking back, I scarcely know how we could tolerate working on the hated uniforms in these horrible conditions. I was disgusted to have to handle or even look at them. I can still hardly bear to sew a button on to any piece of clothing.

Every day, kind Polish Christian women (who also saw a business opportunity) came to the factory to sell cheese, wurst and other staples, and since we still had money, my mother was able to buy items from them. I believe my mother's money came from what she had been paid in her millinery store. She carried the food to the camp in a bag with hollow handles specially made for this purpose. The handles could accommodate gold or money or whatever else we wanted to hide, while the bag itself contained our basic food.

One day on our way to the Ghetto we were surrounded by soldiers. They ordered us to put any food we had with us on a big pile. That day we had managed to buy some delicious wurst. As I saw what was going on, I whispered to my mother that I was going to eat it all in one go, before they could get their hands on it—which I did, gobbling it up even though I knew what the consequences could be. My whole body was trembling.

Another woman threw her food behind a nearby fence, clearly hoping to retrieve it later. Unfortunately, she was noticed and shot in the head. Blood poured down her body and she fell dead.

I put the rest of our food on the pile. But I kept the bread in the bag—which was very dangerous. Somehow it was overlooked. This was a miracle, since inside it was hidden some well-camouflaged jewellery.

Bronka Porwitowa was our lifeline to many of our family members during these terrible days. We were exceptionally lucky to know her. She was able discreetly to pass letters from my father to my mother, handed across the chest-high brick wall at Optima. This was, of course, extremely dangerous.

It was incredible that we could even communicate, to have some concrete knowledge that my father was still managing. It really boosted our morale. We called Bronka *our angel from heaven* (in Polish: *Anioł*).

As our hard, monotonous days in the factory passed, my mother was constantly planning ways out. Above all, she wanted to reunite with my brothers. Perhaps she could pose as one of the Polish food sellers? One night she sewed hats for both of us and told me that the next day we would wear them to walk out of our workplace and escape. The hats were a very good idea, because Jewish people in the

Ghetto never wore such headgear.

Bronka engineered our escape from Tarnów. A man was paid to come and meet us at an agreed place at lunchtime, at the building's first ground-floor window. There was a lot of movement and activity at that time of day. People were eating, talking, walking about and no one was taking much notice of who was going where. We put on our hats and coats and headed out. As we approached the gate, we could see Polish policemen, Jewish policemen and Nazi soldiers between us and the outside world.

'Smile,' whispered my mother, 'Show your teeth.' This was one of the hardest things I ever had to do. Then she marched forward murmuring *'Przepraszam, przepraszam'* (Excuse me, excuse me), passed through all the guards, and walked out of the gate. My heart was pounding so much that I thought it would leap out of my chest.

The man Bronka had contacted met us, then took us to the station, bought tickets and boarded the train to Bochnia with us. This gave the impression that we were a family.

In Bochnia, Bronka had rented a little cottage for us, and we were able to bring my brothers there from the Ghetto. Of course, we were overjoyed. But we were deeply sad, too, because we knew that when anyone escaped, reprisals were taken on those left behind in the Tarnów Ghetto.

It was clear to my mother that there was no future for us in Poland. She made contact, through Bronka, with smugglers who would take us across the border into Czechoslovakia.

Before we left, Bronka visited and picked up a postcard from us for my father, reassuring him that we were fine. Sadly, he was still labouring in Płaszów. My mother wrote that we were safe and that he shouldn't worry about us. His correspondence back to us was always signed 'Staszek', a Polish name, since Samek was recognised as Jewish.

The idea was that if Bronka had the misfortune to be caught, there was a small window of safety for her.

We travelled in a hired lorry, also arranged by Bronka, lying down and covered in tarpaulins, to Piwniczna, near the border. Just before we arrived, the lorry got a flat tyre. In the countryside if a vehicle stopped, everybody gathered around. Since we had no idea what was happening, we spent anxious moments waiting to find out what would come next, lying low and keeping as quiet as possible.

Fortunately they were able to repair the tyre, so we could continue on our way. We were taken to a barn where a number of other Jewish people had also gathered, waiting to cross the border, and slept there until nightfall, which was the safest time to escape. We set out around 1am, and we were 20 people in all, men and women. My brothers and I were the youngest.

Each of us had a little bundle of clothes. Our guide led us through water and over hills. It was hard for us as children. At dawn, we heard the sound of shooting from the border police and some people panicked. The bullets zinged past us, one very close to my head, another by my leg. Our guides took off, leaving us to fend for ourselves.

Those shooting the guns were the Slovakian border police. They stole almost everything we had—although my mother managed to hang on to the hollow-handled bag—and took us off to prison. We were left with only our clothes. For more than three weeks we were locked up in a filthy room. The little cell had a small barred window through which, during the night, the guards shone torches.

When we complained that we were cold, we were thrown a dirty blanket crawling with lice.

The Jewish Underground somehow heard that a mother and her children were being imprisoned. They bribed the guards and we were freed. Our rescuers kindly took us to their homes and after a few days, during which we could rest, new guides were engaged to smuggle us across the border into Hungary. I have always wondered how the Jewish Underground knew about us.

After walking for hours over fields and shallow streams and up and down hills, we crossed a river and climbed hills on the other side, leading to a dense forest. The trees grew so thickly that we could barely see the others in front of us and the branches scratched us every time we moved. We became separated from our mother and were left with a strange man who seemed very agitated. He was sitting on the ground, crying and murmuring to himself. 'What will we do?' he wailed. Sadly, I knew we couldn't help him. I took command. 'You look after yourself and we'll look after ourselves,' I told him.

We knew we were lost, and sat down to work out which direction we should take.

When daylight came we emerged from the forest—and we were instantly arrested by the Czech police. We remained at their station and they treated us well, giving us food and water.

After searching for us for hours, my mother made her way out of the forest. She went into the first Czech police station she could find and told them that she had lost her three children. The policemen in both stations contacted one another and, miraculously, we were reunited. That was astonishing. To describe our emotions at that moment when we saw our mother again, knowing that she had found us, is impossible. Equally astonishing: we were travelling again and it seemed that we had reached Hungary.

Bronka (Bronisława) Porwitowa.

Commandant Amon Goeth rides his white horse in the Płaszów concentration camp, March 1943-September 1944. 'I saw him on his horse. It was chilling,' says Aneta.
Source: USHMM, courtesy of Leopold Page.
Photographic Collection: Raimund Titsch.

Opposite page:

Top: **Płaszów concentration camp.** Source: USHMM.

Bottom: **Jewish tombstones paved the roads in Płaszów and were also used in the toilets.**
Source: The Archive of the Central Commission for the Investigation of German Crimes in Poland.
Courtesy: Ghetto Fighters' House Museum/The Photo Archive, Western Galilee, Israel.

Franka's famous hollow-handled macramé bag, produced by Salo Hirsch's factory, Fabryka Pasmanterii, at 18 Zielna Street, Kraków. Money in American dollars and jewellery (gold chains) were placed inside the handles. Usually the basket carried bread, but Franka hid more jewellery in a hole in the bread.
Source: Samuel and Franka Baral Collection, USHMM, on loan from the family. Photo: courtesy USHMM.

Ada and Olga Ehrlich with a German soldier, 1941, probably
on the outskirts of Kraków. If the soldier had known that
Ada and Olga were Jewish, they would have been killed. After
living with Bronka Porwitowa, they were taken to stay with
Hania Lemek (the Ehrlich housekeeper) in the countryside,
where it was safer for them.

[from] Bronislawa Porwit 9 Dekerta St, Kraków, Poland	Posted: [Date illegible] Received: 7 June 1940
Bronia is not leaving us and is helping us a lot. May God watch over you all.	[to] F. Baral,
Kisses to you all, Staszek	c/o Club Pension, 34 Terez Körut, Budapest, Hungary

Postcard written by Samek Baral at the Optima factory, 16 November 1943, given to Bronka Porwitowa to mail to Franka in Hungary at the pension in Budapest. He signs his name 'Staszek' so as not to invite suspicion with a Jewish-sounding name. He writes about Bronka and comments twice on Aneta, once as 'Anula' and then as 'Anna'. English translation below.

Opposite page: The back of the postcard.

[illegible date]

My most precious treasures,

The letter from our dearest Anula has brought us great joy, but unfortunately something worries me a lot. We haven't had any news from Frania for a whole month now. Frania has absolutely no reason to worry about us; we have all we need, and God is watching over us.

Write to us a lot. Any news from you is like music to us.

Why isn't Olga living with Jasio and Anna yet?

6

LIVING IN HUNGARY

◆

The Jewish Underground helped us get a train to Budapest. Our clothes were ragged, we were sick and even though we didn't express these feelings to each other, we all felt the hopelessness that comes from not knowing what the next second would bring nor our next move.

In the city, we were left out on the streets with no roof over our heads. My mother, ever-resourceful and always thinking about the future as she planned and devised the next steps for me, Marcel and Janek, went into a Club Pension, a type of boarding house, at 34 Teréz körút, that the Jewish Underground had suggested to her. They took us in—out of pity, I think. We were able to stay there in luxury for a few days. To us the clean rooms, freshly washed sheets and good food seemed like paradise on earth.

After a couple of days, we found out from my brothers that there was a price on our heads and that the Gestapo were looking for us. I definitely recall this, even though I don't know how my brothers found out. Again we had to wander the streets with no idea from day to day where we would sleep at night. It was clearly too risky to stay together, so my mother found a different place for each of us every evening. The following morning she picked us up and gave us each a piece of bread. Sometimes we were lucky enough to share a bowl of soup—but we were always cold and hungry. We followed this pattern for a few weeks.

My mother discovered there was a Polish Christian community with a school in Dunamocs, a little village not far from Budapest. Because she thought it wiser to leave the city, and also because she wanted us to receive some education, we moved there, to a little hut with a mud floor where we stayed for a few months. To sweep it clean we first had to sprinkle the floor with water. We slept on mattresses filled with straw and were often sick. All of us became very thin.

It was a country place and there were live pigs for us to feed. I enjoyed throwing food to them while calling *Puca na na na*.

The owner of the hut was a man named Bachor bácsi. He didn't like Jews and admired Hitler and the Hungarian leader, Horthy. When he visited us, we had to march around the room with him, singing songs in Hungarian: *Long live Hitler and death to the Jews*. He indicated how he would cut 'their' throats.

In the meantime, Pola Bleicher was forced by circumstances to go back to Kraków. She was also living day-to-day on the streets. She had been in Bochnia with her Uncle Godek Bleicher, when they tried to escape by train. She had been traumatised after seeing her uncle randomly pulled off the train and shot. Now she was barely surviving in a room facing a cemetery. She could only use it at night and during the days was forced to wander aimlessly—and dangerously—through the city.

Ada and Olga Ehrlich were in the country with Hania Lemek's brother. With help from the Jewish Underground, my mother worked on the idea of bringing all three girls to join us. She also wanted to send for her brother Emil's son, Jasiu, who was still in Bochnia—but he was only three, and the risk of crying while the group was crossing borders or needed to hide was too great.

Again Bronka was our saviour. She took it upon herself to contact a smuggler and organise a place and time to meet with Pola, Ada, and Olga with payment from both sets of parents. Money was hidden by sewing it into clothing.

Pola had to be persuaded to try and escape all over again—and finally she agreed. She was able briefly to visit the Optima factory, together with Ada and Olga, to see their parents and say good-bye before the journey. How they managed to do this is unclear. Then all three girls set out with Bronka. This is the last time Ada and Olga saw their mother.

First the girls crossed the border to Czechoslovakia and were taken into an orphanage in Košice. As far as I can recall, my mother went there and made up a story to get them out, working with a well-connected woman who helped her negotiate their release.

Mother was now responsible for six children: me, my brothers, Ada, Olga and Pola.

Two weeks later we were able to send word to Bronka to let my father, as well as Ada, Olga, Pola's parents and Zvi Bleicher know that the girls had arrived safely and were with us. 'A heavy stone rolled off our hearts,' Zvi commented.

We were so pleased to see the girls. They became like sisters to us. Once a month my mother travelled to Budapest to pick up the money that supported us, which came from the JDC, the American Jewish Joint Distribution Committee, known as the Joint.

When the girls joined us in Dunamocs, we all had to pretend to the village people, most of them Poles, that we were not Jewish. We told them we were Roman Catholics. All six of us were able to attend school under assumed names. Mine was Anna Baral. Pola was known as Apolonia Róg and Ada and Olga's last name was Pydych.

My school certificate from that time states in the 'religion column' that I was Roman Catholic. I wore my locket containing a picture of Saint Francis of Assisi, my good-luck gift from Bronka. We, along with another brother and sister, Henya and Romek Stiglitz (they did not take an assumed last name), were the only Jewish children in the school.

One of the subjects we studied was the Roman Catholic religion. I was asked for the name of my previous Religious Studies teacher and answered that it was Katecheta, not realising that this was the word for a preacher or religion instructor. I was so scared when I realised my mistake. Would this Polish teacher now know all six of us were Jewish?

Every morning there were prayers before we started school, and we had to cross ourselves. I remember that in December 1943 we gathered around a Christmas tree to sing carols in Polish. I still recall all the words and tunes of those carols today, and over the years my Polish friends and my own family have been surprised that I still know how to sing them.

On that Christmas evening some hooligans arrived and knocked loudly at the door and on the windows. We were petrified—especially as our mother was away in Budapest for her monthly trip to pick up funds from the JDC.

These same hooligans would wait for us when we walked to school, throwing things at us and shouting insults. I would shout back 'I'll tell the Judge!' That seemed to discourage them.

One day Pola went to get her shoes repaired, cutting through a forest to get there. But on the way back she became lost. She heard, then saw some people in the distance—and called out to them in

Hungarian: *'Hej, várjatok! Van itt egy kislány, aki nem tudja hogy kell hazamenni,'* (which meant 'Hello, wait! Here's a little girl who doesn't know her way home.')

Pola finally arrived back with these gypsies and my mother rewarded them with some money. After that, we teased Pola all the time. We made up a song, singing the exact words she had used to let the gypsies know she was lost.

My mother grew concerned that the Director of our school, Mr Palamarczyk, was beginning to suspect that we were Jewish. It was an intuition. She thought our lives would be more and more under threat and that when the Nazis invaded Hungary, we would be exposed.

After a few months, we escaped again. Early one morning, when it was still dark, we boarded a fishing boat and crossed the River Danube to arrive near a station where we could take a train to Budapest.

Again we were homeless, out on the streets of Budapest, terrified. My mother saw this as a fight for our lives. Our most immediate problem, however, was still where we would sleep each night.

In the city my mother instructed us not to walk together, since it was dangerous for us to be seen in a group. Janek, who was by then nine years old, was one day walking the streets, crying: 'I'm hungry. *I'm hungry.* I'm cold.' He appeared to be on his own.

A woman, a complete stranger, came up to him and asked: 'Where is your family?' My mother, who was nearby, approached her and said that Janek was her son. The woman, Ilonka Nemes, would become our second angel. She swept all of us up and took us to her apartment at 17 Pongrácz Street. There she took care of us and fed us. She let us stay for a few weeks and even bought clothes for Janek. We didn't go outside once. She was very, very kind. She took a tremendous risk in helping us. We didn't tell her we were Jewish—although she certainly knew.

Ilonka's husband was away fighting on the Russian Front with the Hungarian forces. As the Nazis moved closer to Budapest, she suggested that we would be safer at her parents' place, the Vaskó family home in the countryside close to Nyíregyháza. Before we left, Marcel and Janek underwent an ordeal. They had a very painful operation to reverse the circumcision that 'proved' they were Jewish. This was the safeguard that had to be taken to save their lives if ever they were caught and 'tested'.

The operations were done at Ilonka's apartment, and both my brothers recuperated there. For weeks they were in pain and very subdued. Worse, in the end it didn't work.

There was a railway line just outside Ilonka's apartment. She took each child either singly or in twos, to Nyíregyháza, to a village called Rozsrétszőlő which was two hours away from Budapest. My mother was the last to arrive. Of course, this was a further enormous risk for Ilonka.

Her parents welcomed us with open arms to their peaceful farm. We told them that we were Polish Catholic children. They were so kind to us that we called them Nagymama and Nagypapa, meaning 'Grandmother' and 'Grandfather' in Hungarian. The countryside also gave us the chance to relax for the first time in months. We worked beside them on the farm, doing chores. They saw I wanted to help, and showed me how to feed the geese with kernels of corn, water, oil and salt to fatten them up. During the War people loved to eat fat to supplement their meagre rations. I would sit on the steps of the house with a goose between my legs, holding its beak open and stuffing in the mixture so that the bird would become big and fat. I kept pushing the food down their throats until there was no room left. The geese would then be placed in a tiny cage so they couldn't move around and lose weight.

Every Sunday we walked five kilometres to Nyíregyháza, to a

Roman Catholic church called Magyarok Nagyasszonya (Our Lady of Hungary). We walked barefoot through the fields, as our only shoes were clogs which hurt our feet if we had to walk in them. At the church we sat in the same seats in the same row each week, towards the front of the church on the right. During the service, we never knelt or crossed ourselves. But no one ever bothered us. We felt safe there.

We shared the house with Ilonka's parents, their granddaughter Jutka (or Jucika) who was about 17, and a small baby, Ancika (also known as Anna), their great-granddaughter. They were very hospitable. They would put on the table a communal bowl of delicious macaroni sprinkled with poppy-seeds and sugar, for everyone to eat. Another dish they served was called *paprikás krumpli*.

Ilonka had a brother, Jancsi, who was fighting with the Hungarian Army against the Soviet Union. The 'grandparents' liked me so much that their wish was that when I was older, say 18, he might marry me. They even produced a big wooden chest and began to gather together sheets and feathers for eiderdowns, as a dowry.

One day Jancsi came home on leave, to the great delight of his parents, since he was their favourite son. He was a handsome young man. After a couple of days he returned to Nyíregyháza—and never came back. This was a typical tragic disappearance. The Red Army was moving through Hungary, and if they caught young men like Jancsi, they were transported to Siberia after a cursory interrogation. The Russians would have been able to tell immediately that he was against them.

After the War, Ilonka wrote us a letter that I still have. It revealed, sadly, that after 1944 the family never saw Jancsi again.

While we were hiding on the farm, we heard from the villagers that cattle trains filled with people were passing through Debrecen, Hungary's second largest city. People could be heard wailing and screaming. These were our people, Jewish Hungarians, on their way to the death camps.

One day when I was feeding the geese, a group of Nazi soldiers arrived. I froze with fear. But once again, my mother showed how resourceful she could be. She welcomed them, invited them in by using hand actions and gave them tea. They went into a room with a large table and spread out maps. My mother pretended she didn't speak their language, but listened in on their conversation. She saw them indicate on the maps the recent course of the War. They were worried. It was clear that Nazis forces were being defeated on all fronts.

When the Red Army broke through and reached the village of Rozsrétszőlő, they fought the Nazis door to door, with tremendous force. These soldiers were after revenge—and everyone panicked. Women were raped by Russian soldiers and there were thefts and violence. Girls disguised themselves as old ladies with scarves and loose clothing, to try and escape notice.

The young Russian soldiers loved watches. My mother was able to keep hers for some time, but one day she was leaning on the farmhouse fence when a soldier approached her and asked her what time it was. When my mother told him, he said 'Give me your watch.' She had to hand it over.

Marcel remembered the terrible atmosphere of those times when drunken Russian soldiers physically threatened and harassed women. My brother believed that my mother was in danger, probably because there had been an incident that sparked this worry. She went to a high-ranking Russian officer to report her fear, and he realised that she was Jewish. He told her not to worry; he was Jewish too. He found us another place back in Nyíregyháza for a few weeks, a villa in which the Mayor had been living, formerly a Jewish house.

We said goodbye to Ilonka's incredibly generous family with heavy hearts and moved into this spacious place. To our surprise, children had abandoned toys in one of the rooms and we could play with them. We hadn't seen a toy for years. The Russian officer even visited, bringing wonderful food.

In 1944 we headed back to Budapest. Mother's plan was to move to Bucharest, Romania. She decided that, for the moment, Ada, Olga and Pola would be safer with Ilonka, and could follow us later. Crossing illegally through a border with six children would be hazardous, and she did not want to take that risk.

We were caught crossing the border by Romanian police and thrown into gaol. We were set free only after agreeing to go back to Hungary to never again enter Romania.

We were released into a thick forest with a group of other people. My mother, brothers and I became separated from them. My mother kept us together until we emerged from the forest, then led us out into a field. There, according to Janek, Marcel lay on the ground and refused to move. He wanted to go in a different direction than the one my mother indicated. This would have been fatal.

It was the middle of the night. We heard dogs barking so we knew people must be living nearby. Since I spoke Hungarian, my mother sent me into the first house we reached to ask if we could sleep there. I knocked on the door and said: 'My mother and two brothers are here with me. Would you kindly let us sleep the night?'

Miraculously, they agreed. There were only two beds, but we fell into them. We were so exhausted that we slept until the following afternoon. Awoken by noises, we rose to find that the border patrol had arrived.

My quick-thinking mother didn't speak Hungarian so she told me in Polish what to say to them in Hungarian. 'I am delighted to see you. I was looking for you last night. We've come to the village to look for work—and these nice people let us sleep here,' she explained.

She always seemed to be able to come up with the right story in even the most perilous situations.

The border patrol took us with them to their barracks and fed us. Then they went to the nearest train station and bought us tickets to Bucharest. This was so lucky. The occupants of the house in which we had slept, not knowing what to do with us, had called the border control to betray us. No doubt our hosts were afraid.

Our wanderings and border crossings during the War had taken us from Kraków to Tarnów, Bochnia to Czechoslovakia, then on to Hungary and Romania. Every time we were about to cross another border at night, I would look up at the white scatter of stars, which I later found out were called the Milky Way. At these moments, I felt a great sense of hope and that we would be saved. If the Milky Way was not visible, I began to fear the worst.

We were in Bucharest when it was officially declared on 5 May 1945 that the War had ended. I remember the big screen in the city square, like an outdoor cinema, beaming the words THE WAR IS OVER in Romanian. Everyone was singing and dancing with joy.

My mother then arranged, through Ilonka, for Ada, Olga and Pola to join us in Bucharest. I remember our four-month stay there, supported by Jewish relief organisations.

'Everyone knew about the woman who had escaped from Poland and saved six children,' Zvi Bleicher comments in his account of his own experiences, published in 1980, *Would God It Were Night*: 'We saw in Frania a real heroine. This noble-minded woman, already burdened with the care of her own three children, had asked us to send her both Ada and Olga, her sister's two daughters, and my sister Pola as well, who was not really a relation of hers at all. We felt that this super-generous offer was an attempt to repay us for having saved

Aneta, when we took her with us up into the loft in Plac Zgody, in the October *Aktzia* in Kraków.'

After the War my mother never mentioned what she had done. She simply wrote a two-page description for herself, remembering the constant fear as we wandered 'without bread, ragged and sick… bullets flying over our heads'. By the end of that time 'we all looked like living corpses'. She had worried that there was no way for her to ensure our healthy development, or obtain even the most primitive education. 'The children were constantly sick and feverish. To cool off they sat on stone blocks or the steps of houses, since they had no home of their own, only a temporary place to sleep that they had to leave each morning.'

She never again spoke or wrote a single word about those years.

In Bucharest, she was able to rent a tiny place for us to live at 6 Craciun Street—but it was too small to accommodate six growing children. Luckily two kind Jewish families we had met, the Rosenbergs and the Wincigsters, took Olga and Janek into their homes and looked after them because they were the youngest. I stayed with my mother but had to sleep on top of a dining room table. I would laugh and tell Pola that it felt like flying in a plane.

As the months passed, we still didn't know whether our father had survived the War. Then one day my mother and Marcel were on a bus, talking to one another in Polish. A young man sitting next to them, who introduced himself as Abraham Horowitz, nickname Pepi, suddenly joined their conversation. My mother asked if by chance he knew what had happened at the end of the War to the prisoners in Płaszów concentration camp.

Pepi told us that in October 1944, if our father had not been at the final liquidation of Płaszów, he might well still be alive. Those who had worked for Schindler only returned each night to the camp, and at the liquidation had been transferred to other factories in Gross-Rosen, Lower Silesia and Brunnitz.

We desperately wanted to believe that our beloved father had survived.

Like so many others, we were later to discover, he had returned to Kraków after the War ended and registered there with the Red Cross. While we were looking for him, he was looking for us. The Red Cross told him that we had all survived and were in Bucharest. They even gave him our address.

My mother, brothers and I never forgot the day we were reunited. We had no idea our father was coming to see us; he simply appeared before our eyes. He arrived at the room where we were staying, opened the unlocked door and there he was. It is impossible to describe the emotion of that reunion. I remember the moment we first saw him and how shocked we were. He was horribly thin and grey, like a skeleton. He had survived a heart attack, thrombosis and injuries to the spine, and weighed only 46 kilos, half his original body weight.

I hardly recognised him and was frozen in disbelief. It was so distressing to see him in this condition. This was the person who had been a vibrant, successful, and sophisticated international business-man who had worn clothes like those of a perfect Englishman. Now he was a broken man who had aged far beyond his 41 years.

He had been through Hell. But nothing mattered more than that he was with us, alive.

We were overjoyed when our good fortune extended to others. Ada and Olga's father and Pola's mother and brother Zvi were also reunited with them.

Janek, Aneta and Marcel enjoying a few months of comparative safety in Dunamocs, 1943.

Opposite page: The Polish school under Red Cross control for Polish Catholic refugee children, Dunamocs, Hungary, end of 1943 to early 1944. The Jewish children in our class are: (1) Romek Stiglitz (Stieglitz or Sztiglic in Polish), (2) Janek, (3) Aneta, (4) Marcel and (5) Henia Stiglitz.

ŚWIADECTWO SZKOŁY POWSZECHNEJ

Baral Anna

(nazwisko i imie)

urodzon*a* dnia *24 grudnia* 19*29* r. w *Krakowie*

powiatu *krakowskiego*, religii (wyznania) *rzym-katol.*,

uczeszczał*a* do klasy *piątej* i otrzymał*a*

za rok szkolny 19*43/44* oceny następujace:

sprawowanie	*bardzo dobry*
religia	
jezyk polski	*dobry*
jezyk *węgierski*	*dobry*
historia	*bardzo dobry*
geografia	*bardzo dobry*
nauka o przyrodzie	*bardzo dobry*
arytmetyka z geometria	*dobry*
rysunki	*dobry*
zajecia praktyczne	*bardzo dobry*
śpiew	*dobry*
ćwiczenia cielesne	*dobry*

Opuścił*a* dni szkolnych *12*, w tym nie usprawiedliwiono —

Na tej podstawie *przechodzi do klasy szóstej*

Publiczna Szkoła Powszechna stopnia *III*

OŚRODKA MŁODZIEZOWEGO

Obozu Uchodzców Polskich na Wegrzech

w. *Dunamocs* dnia *23 kwietnia* 194*4* r.

Nr. *1*

pieczęc

Opiekun klasy   DUNAMOCS (WĘGRY)   Kierowni*k* Szkoły

Skala ocen : bardzo dobry, dobry, dostateczny, niedostateczny.

Helikon-nyomda, Keszthely. 2192.

Aneta's primary school certificate, and its translation (opposite), from the Polish Catholic refugee camp in Dunamocs, 23 April 1944. Aneta gave her name as Anna, since it sounded less Jewish.

PRIMARY SCHOOL CERTIFICATE

Anna Baral

born on 24 December 1929 in Kraków, district of Kraków [Poland],
being of Roman-Catholic faith, has attended Year Five and has received
the following marks for the school year 1943/1944:

Conduct:	Very Good
Religious Instruction:	---------
Polish Language:	Good
Hungarian Language:	Good
History:	Very Good
Geography:	Very Good
Nature Study:	Very Good
Arithmetic and Geometry:	Good
Drawing:	Good
Handiwork:	Very Good
Singing:	Good
Technology:	Good
Physical Education:	Good

Has missed 12 school days, including unexcused absences: -----

She has therefore been promoted to **Year Six.**

Level 3 Public Primary School
ATTACHED TO THE YOUTH CENTRE
of the Polish Refugee Camp in Hungary

Issued in Dunamocs, Hungary, on 23 April 1944.

No.1

Class Supervisor
[Illegible name and signature]

School Principal
[Illegible name and signature]

[Round seal with the words:
POLISH PRIMARY SCHOOL IN DUNAMOCS, HUNGARY

Scale of marks: Very Good, Good, Satisfactory, Fail.

Ilonka Nemes, 1943.

Ilonka's parents, the Vaskós, whom we called Nagymama (grandmother) and Nagypapa (grandfather), Nyíregyháza, Hungary, 1939.

95

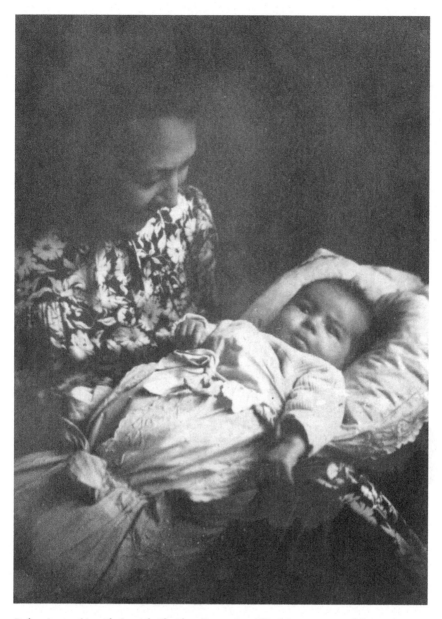

Baby Anna (Ancika) with Ilonka, Rozsrétszőlő, Hungary, 1944.

The back of the house, 1944. Back row, from left: Jutka (also known as Jucika, Ilonka's youngest sister), Franka, Ilonka, Aneta and Ada. Front row: József Muri, Erzsébet Margaret Muri and Olga.

Samuel Baral before the War, probably in England, 1937-38.

Samuel Baral (right) soon after the War, with Motek Ehrlich, 1945.

7

TO ISRAEL

◆

In 1945, except for my father, we had no idea which family members and friends were still alive. At the beginning of the War there had been 60,000 Jews in Kraków. In April 1940, approximately 35,000 Jews were forced out of the city after the Germans gave them orders to leave their homes, for the Ghetto or for country villages. By December 1942, after the two *Aktzias* of June and October, there were only 15,000 people left in the Ghetto. Between 8000-10,000 people were moved to the camp at Płaszów and the rest were either killed or sent to Auschwitz. At the end of the War there were only 2000 Jewish survivors. Others who had been scattered, like us, now wanted to start new lives.

We carried on with our daily living, but we were wounded, suffering a depth of sadness that was so pervasive and unfathomable that we couldn't talk about it. Always in our hearts were those who had perished during the War. The following names are of my closest family members who were murdered:

My Feuer grandparents, Lieba and Matias

My mother's brother Emil Feuer, his wife Mina and their son Jasiu

My mother's four sisters, Mina, Bala, Hela and Tosia, step-brother Motek Matzner and his wife Ethel

Mina Susskind's husband Chaskiel and their daughter Tusia

Bala Hirsch's husband Salomon and their three children, Mela, Hesiu and Menachem

My mother's nephew, Milus, who was her sister Tosia Ber's son

My Auntie Ela's husband, Moniek Künstler

All of my school friends were gone except one, Anka Laub

My uncle Motek Ehrlich survived the camps, as did his children Ada and Olga.

Our friend Zvi Bleicher survived, as did his sister Pola and their mother, Sala. My cousin Bubek Susskind, at 18 years old, was the sole survivor of his family. We were the lucky ones. We remained intact as a family of five people.

I still have those precious postcards from the War years, communications between many of those who died. They were sent, as already noted, to my mother's brother, Uncle Ignac Feuer, in Romania and India, and he in turn sent them on to his older brother, Uncle Jacob Feuer, in Palestine.

In 1934, you will remember, he visited from Kiel in Germany with his wife Toni and their children to say good-bye to our family as they left Europe. After he passed away in Kfar-Saba, Israel, his son Yechiel found and took the postcards with him to the United States. He later forwarded them to me. They were clearly farewells from these lost family members who did not expect to survive. These postcards were the only way they could try to find out about each other's circumstances—and to learn as much as possible about what was happening to their loved ones. At the same time, they let them know, however covertly, where they were and how they were faring.

Of course, there were never any replies.

A few months after the War ended, in recognition of my mother's extraordinary bravery in saving me, my two brothers, two cousins and Pola, she was given Visa No. 1 by the British authorities to transit through to what was then Palestine, on the way to India.

Uncle Ignac and Auntie Toduś in Bombay, India greatly assisted us in our efforts to begin a new life. They were able to send us the additional documents we needed to travel from Bucharest to Bombay, with all of us listed under the name Baral.

Very excited, we travelled from Bucharest to Bulgaria, to Greece, to Istanbul in Turkey and then on to Lebanon. But my mother had no intention of ending up in India. From Lebanon we went by bus to Israel. As soon as we crossed the border, we sang *Shalom Aleichem*. This was one of the happiest moments of my life. Finally, I knew I was free.

We arrived in the Biblical land known as Eretz Yisrael in 1945 when I was 15 years old—my real age after all the disguises I had been forced to assume during the War. Emotionally and physically, the six of us were no longer children. We had to re-learn how to become human once again, how to build up our strength and live without fear.

We arrived worn out, hungry and completely disorientated. However, I was also full of joy. I had survived the War and so had my beloved family: my heroic mother, my father and both my brothers. It was announced on the radio station Kol Yisrael, that the mother who had saved six children had just arrived on Israeli soil. The story ended with a triumphant: *The people of Israel are alive!* (Am Yisrael Chai).

After accompanying us, Ada, Olga and Pola would marry and stay on in Israel. My two brothers would eventually go on to join my Uncle Ignac and Auntie Toduś, by then in Australia.

In those first few days, we felt we were in a completely new place where we had a chance to start a normal life again and breathe the fresh air of freedom. I was so happy to have survived that my feeling every day was one of tremendous happiness and gratitude. I was determined always to be positive and never give up. At 15, I realised with mature eyes what my mother had done for all of us. She had been completely fearless, taking risks even if there had only been a small chance of success—and she did this over and over again. That is why my favourite saying to my children since they were young has been: 'Whatever the mind can conceive and believe can be achieved.'

A bus took us to Atlit. We were puzzled that we were accompanied by a British soldier with a machine-gun—but Palestine was still then a British Protectorate. As we drove, I looked out and was mesmerised by the cloudless blue sky. We sang Hebrew songs all the way, especially *Hevenu Shalom Aleichem* (*Peace be upon you*), the traditional song of Jews returning from the synagogue and welcoming angels to the Shabbat.

We arrived in Atlit on 9 September 1945. This was a shock. It was a camp, fenced with barbed wire and protected by armed guards in high towers. We felt as if we were entering another concentration camp. For two days we slept in dormitories, one bed beside the next, and ate in a canteen. Then Uncle Jacob arrived with Yechiel and with permission from the Atlit authorities, they took us out. I have the papers which my mother filled in. One of the questions was: *Who do you know in Palestine?* We knew Jacob Feuer and my grandfather Juda Baral. We presume that the authorities had contacted my uncle.

The Feuers picked us up in their truck. My mother sat in the front with her brother, the driver, and we six children stood in the open back with Yechiel. I was astounded by the green fields and the orange orchards with their laden trees, sprinklers spinning among them. I was so impressed seeing my people turning the desert into Paradise.

We travelled this way to our uncle's home in Kfar-Saba, where we met Auntie Toni and our other cousins, Tova and Yaffa. Tova lived next door with her new baby, Kuti, only two weeks old. It was wonderful to see this new little member of our family and also to see our Grandfather, Juda Baral, and his second wife Rachel (now known as Rosa), who also lived in Kfar-Saba. We ran to them, light with happiness, and hugged and kissed.

We survivors were ravenous from the War. We ate everything that was put before us on the table. We were insatiable: we couldn't believe the amount and diversity of food Auntie Toni had prepared and offered us so generously. We hadn't seen such a feast for years. After breakfast we sat in our uncle and aunt's garden under the orange and mandarin trees with their heady aroma. We could pick and eat as much fruit as we wanted. We could simply reach up and pick it off the tree—and we did. It was so delicious!

This simple action symbolised for me the reality of being in Eretz Yisrael. At that first breakfast, my aunt went back to the kitchen to fetch more rolls and found my brothers standing there with their shirts bulging. 'Boys—you don't need to hide the bread rolls,' she said, wiping away a tear. 'Let me assure you that never again will you be hungry. Israel is our land of milk and honey.'

After that she ran between the kitchen and the table bringing more and more dishes. During our stay she would prepare wonderful meals for six incredibly hungry young people: the finest dairy products, including huge cheeses; salad, fruit and the fabulous fresh bread rolls.

Uncle Jacob gave us a room and we slept on mattresses on the floor, borrowed from a nearby kibbutz. When our cousin Bubek Susskind arrived, he shared sleeping space on the veranda with Yechiel.

I wanted to do everything at once: go to school, explore the land and its history, attend concerts and the cinema, make new friends.

Now we could learn whatever we pleased. I looked forward to becoming a proud Israeli. In my new country I took a new name, Yaffa, after my cousin, with whom I was very impressed. In Hebrew it means 'beautiful'.

Since we had missed years of education, my Uncle Jacob recommended that I, my brothers, Ada, Olga and Pola should go to a religious school to learn more about Judaism and catch up on our lessons. Uncle Jacob was a religious man. He knew many people in Europe had been saved (as we were) by righteous Christians, and that we had pretended to be Christian ourselves in order to survive, and so he understood the urgency of finding us the best schools to help us reclaim our Jewish identity.

Because we spent all our time together during the War, the six of us were like one bonded family. I had become very close to my brothers. We could communicate through the slightest signs, merely by making eye contact, for instance. We knew then that our fates were bound together and did everything we could to help one another.

The three of us were sent to different places. I went with Ada and Pola to Beit Zeirot Mizrachi in Jerusalem, a girls' school, where I moved quickly through several classes. But I did this eagerly; I wanted to learn what would be useful for my future life. We were treated well, like human beings, with good, clean accommodation and nourishing food. We were taught to clean, iron our clothes and cook, and I grew marigolds in my patch of garden. I loved being close to nature in my new surroundings. Because of the friendliness of the teachers, I learned Hebrew very quickly. Today I remember my time at this boarding school very fondly.

Olga went to the same school as Martin, an Orthodox boarding school, until she transferred to be with her sister Ada, attending the

Kfar Hanoar Hadati school near Haifa. At 14, Martin performed his Bar Mitzvah in front of the school and our whole family. My little brother Janek went to another Orthodox boarding school in Petach Tikvah. These schools were to prove vital in returning us to our Jewish roots and slowly coaxing back a feeling of love for our religion.

I remember vividly that early on Friday evenings, when the first stars appeared in the sky, we would hear the sound of the ancient horn, the *shofar*, signalling the beginning of the Shabbat. I would put on my most beautiful dress and go with my classmates to the synagogue. Everyone from our school went. At the beginning this felt strange, and I would even hide in the wardrobe to avoid going, but after a while I relaxed and began to enjoy the ritual. I particularly enjoyed the cantor's melodious voice. He would sing:

The children of Israel shall keep the Shabbat, observing it throughout the generations as an everlasting covenant. It is a sign between God and the children of Israel forever that in six days the Lord made the heavens and the earth, and on the seventh day He rested.

Therefore the Lord blessed the Shabbat day and hallowed it.

וְשָׁמְרוּ בְנֵי יִשְׂרָאֵל אֶת הַשַׁבָּת, לַעֲשׂוֹת אֶת הַשַׁבָּת לְדֹרֹתָם בְּרִית עוֹלָם. בֵּינִי וּבֵין בְּנֵי יִשְׂרָאֵל אוֹת הִיא לְעוֹלָם, כִּי שֵׁשֶׁת יָמִים עָשָׂה ה' אֶת הַשָׁמַיִם וְאֶת הָאָרֶץ וּבַיוֹם הַשְׁבִיעִי שָׁבַת וַיִנָפַש

עַל כֵּן בֵּרַךְ ה' אֶת יוֹם הַשַׁבָּת וַיְקַדְשֵׁהוּ

Every Friday night a celebratory dinner was provided. Shabbat mornings were exceptional, peaceful and serene. The shops closed, there was no traffic and it was lovely to see families walking to the synagogue with their children in a leisurely manner. After the service, the festive lunch was always a happy occasion, with my friends and

I singing all through the meal, just as my husband does now on Shabbat. Then we would all have a siesta. As my teachers told me, more than we Jews keeping Shabbat, Shabbat kept us Jewish.

After my father arrived from Romania, he and my mother lived for a few weeks with my Baral grandparents in Kfar-Saba. But my parents desperately wanted to be independent. After a short time they moved to Tel Aviv and rented a little room in a small, cheap hotel on the corner of Allenby Street and Shuk Ha'Carmel Market. Despite the noise and bustle all around them, they were happy. After those long years apart, at last they were together again.

After a year at boarding school, I joined them in the city but was unable to live with them, since their living space was so cramped. I boarded with my step-Grandmother Rachel's niece, Helen, her husband Manes Pfefferbaum and their two children Bibi and Zvika, sharing their bedroom.

'We loved you very much,' Bibi wrote to me when she found out I was researching this book. 'You were our big sister over those months you were sharing our room.'

There was nowhere quiet I could do my homework—except the toilet. One day I was in there with my books when someone knocked on the door. I quickly stacked the books on top of the cistern and pulled the chain. To my horror, they were dislodged and fell down— fortunately not into the toilet pan.

I remember little Zvika calling to me: *Aneka—pipi*, my signal to run and get his potty.

Uncle Ignac Feuer, by then in Sydney, sent my parents a very generous gift of 400 pounds to use as 'key money' to secure a beautiful new apartment which would be completed in a few weeks on a prestigious street: Apartment 2, 124 Ben Yehuda Street. From there my mother opened a dress-making salon. Their flat had a bedroom, a family room, kitchen, dining room and two balconies.

Since I already spoke Hebrew, I had no problems fitting in at high school. It was a School of Commerce, and I could walk from the Pfefferbaums on 31 Ahad Ha'am Street to my school, Beit Tichon Le'Mizchar, at 30 Geula Street. Almost every morning before classes began there were exercises. Twice a week we had to be at school at 5am and then we ran through the streets of Tel Aviv, still empty of traffic, through Allenby to Ben Yehuda Streets and back to the school. There were also exercises the Army prepared for us, such as a rope being thrown over a stream and attached to the other side. We had to grip the rope with our hands and legs and make it over to the other side. My body was flexible and strong and I was physically fit, so I had no difficulty reaching the other end without falling into the water. My school report noted that I was outstanding at this challenge. I was always determined.

Though I was occupied from morning till night, I missed my brothers and often went to visit them on weekends. After my parents' move, they would come home and spend time with us. It was crowded—but we didn't mind. We loved being together again.

My mother's dress-making salon immediately did well. Mr Pfefferbaum gave my father some work, and a small machine for a lot of the repetitive work. My father punched holes into metal cubes. Mr Pfefferbaum would deliver and pick up the completed work.

After I graduated from school, I applied for a job in the office of the Prime Minister, Polish-born David Ben-Gurion, the Father of Israel. It was such an honour when one day he came into our office to greet us. I worked there happily from June 1949 until March 1950.

My parents were constantly planning our future, and what my brothers and I would do with our lives once the best education they could provide was completed. They conceived the idea of sending my brothers to Australia, to Uncle Ignac and Auntie Toduś in Sydney. They told us they would be happy to look after the boys. Martin was interested in textiles, so he planned to study at a well-known institute in Geelong, Victoria called the Gordon Institute of Technology, from which he would graduate as a textile engineer. From the beginning, Janek was interested only in Medicine, but initially went with Martin to the school in Geelong. He would go on to graduate from Sydney University as a pediatrician, and later as a dermatologist.

In later years I could speak easily with Martin about business matters. But Janek and I could speak heart-to-heart about anything—including, of course, medical matters.

Many friends came every day to visit my parents in their new home. My dear Auntie Ela had tragically lost her husband, Moniek Künstler, the day after Liberation. After a year in Cyprus, she came and stayed with us for a while, then took up a new job as a dietician in a hospital in Haifa. We were very proud of her, and overjoyed when she found a new husband, Moshe Plessner. I became extremely close to her.

Itzhak Stern and his wife Suza were also visitors. They told us many wonderful stories. Years later when we saw the film *Schindler's List*, I was amazed to discover that Stern had been Schindler's chief adviser and accountant at the Emalia factory. He and my father had met there but neither had ever mentioned Schindler or anything at all about what they had gone through.

Who should I meet one day in 1947 on Allenby Street, but my Kraków classmate, Anka Laub. We were so surprised to see one another and I invited her back to our apartment at Ben Yehuda Street. With other friends we spent a truly happy evening together. Although it was wonderful to meet up with my only surviving classmate, everyone was so busy developing their new lives that we unfortunately lost contact.

Some of the friends I made in Israel are, however, still my friends today. Marysia Schenker Maly is one. We have a lot in common: both born in Kraków, of similar background. We are still in contact after 68 years. Another was my life-long friend Pola Bleicher. What we experienced together and what our friendship meant was extraordinary. My beloved Pola passed away on 18 September 2009.

I loved the hustle and bustle of Tel Aviv. It had great energy. Cars in a constant stream were always in a hurry as they negotiated the narrow streets—and their drivers were not known for their politeness. I learned to be careful when I crossed a street, even at the lights—that were often ignored.

The coffee shops and restaurants were always full, and you could hear spoken languages from every corner of the globe. After dinner at home with my parents, I would often go to a nightclub. In those days you could order a soda water or coffee and sit all night with your friends. Bands played the latest romantic songs, the songs of our new country, and we danced. The boys behaved very well, simply ordering a single glass of beer or wine for themselves, so that there were no drunken fights. I made a point of being home before midnight so my parents wouldn't worry about me.

Often on Saturday mornings before it became really hot, I would go to the beach to swim. Lying on a lounge which I rented and listening to music from loud-speakers was absolute bliss. I would wander along the promenade looking at the little shops and restaurants. They smelled fresh and wonderful. I bought freshly-squeezed juice made from delicious oranges, mixed with grapefruit, carrots and celery. You could buy Israeli, Polish, Russian and Hungarian food in Tel Aviv.

As soon as it became too hot, I would return home for a siesta. When I got up to go out again, the whole city would be bustling around us. I would go with my friends to my favourite coffee shops (Roval or Pinati, both on Dizengoff Street) and from the tables outside on the pavement, observe the passing parade. I watched 18-year-old boys and girls with their Uzis slung over their shoulders with great pride. They made me feel safe and proud too. No one could threaten us now.

I was lucky to be in Tel Aviv when Israel was officially born. With thousands of other people, I stood on Allenby Street at the corner of Carmel Market, while the countries of the United Nations were voting on whether or not Israel could join them. When the United States voted *yes*, there was a great shout of joy. People were laughing, crying, hugging one another and dancing, even with complete strangers.

I was engulfed by groups chanting *Am Israel Chai!* (Israel is alive!). We were united. We knew no enemy could defeat us now.

When Prime Minister Ben-Gurion came out on a balcony to address us, there was pandemonium. This was the birth of our own State.

Young people who arrived from overseas and Israelis who were 18 years and older were drafted into the Army of the new State. I was soon the right age to join the Israeli Defence Forces.

We trained for six solid weeks in a camp outside the city, learning to shoot and use arms—which was very traumatic for me. I could barely stand the sound of guns firing. We were taught to use Israeli-made Uzis and hand-grenades, and had to practise using them. We also had to complete exercises: running, jumping and crawling, and sliding by rope from the second floor of a building to the ground. Another exercise involved moving hand-over-hand along a rope strung between two points. We were taken one night to a field and shown how to crawl along the ground without being detected by the enemy.

I am not good at taking orders from those of higher rank. I would rather give orders. After a while the Army elevated my status to sergeant. In later years, the man who would become my husband was surprised by this.

'How is it that a petite and feminine girl like you became a sergeant? They're usually big, rude, loud men,' he said.

My answer was: 'I was in charge not with my muscles, but with my brain.'

This saying in Hebrew is:

לֹא בְּכֹחַ רַק בְּמֹחַ

'Now I understand your perspective,' he said.

My six weeks of Army training prepared me for life, reinforcing my beliefs: keep fit, think positively and never give up. I felt powerful being able to defend myself.

Pictures from that time show me bursting with happiness. When it was time to be placed in an Army job, I told them that I had previously been selected to work in the office of Prime Minister Ben-Gurion, and that my job had been to operate the large IBM computer.

I was immediately posted to an Army office in Yafo to work in a similar capacity. I was lucky not to have to live in barracks, instead going home every night—a big plus for me. After two years I was chosen to attend an officers' course—but I had other ideas about what I wanted to do with my life.

In 1952, I obtained a job as a typist with the prestigious Shell Oil Company of Palestine, working with the new IBM machines that would become computers. I liked this job very much and had my probationary time renewed. I was with the company from September 1952 to February 1953.

But I was ready to be even more adventurous. The first flight of my life on a plane was in 1953, to Bombay, India on the way to Australia to visit my two brothers. I stayed in the luxurious Taj Mahal Palace Hotel. However, since it was my first time in India, I was cautious and made sure that my room was securely locked. I even climbed on top of the wardrobe to close a small open window above it, facing a hallway.

In Bombay I boarded a huge P&O ocean liner, the SS *Himalaya*. After the voyage, as I stepped off the ship on 27 March 1953, a Friday, I was warmly welcomed not only by Uncle Ignac, Auntie Toduś and my brothers, but also by a reporter from *The Sunday Herald*, who interviewed me.

My brothers were lucky enough to be renting an apartment at 322 Edgecliff Road, Woollahra, a comfortable suburb of Sydney. After the War, such apartments had been scarce.

Everything in Australia at first seemed strange to me. I had just arrived from Israel, where I was very happy. It had become my post-War homeland, my place of renewal, and my eight years there were some of the best of my life. When I came to Australia I knew only a tiny bit of English.

The day after I arrived, Uncle Ignac and Auntie Toduś, now known as Toni, took me into the city to show me what it was like. I wore a smart custom-made coat and a cheeky hat made by my mother. But in the car on the way, my aunt and uncle made a passing comment about how sports' clothes were worn on the weekend in Australia. I was so hurt that I burst into tears. They meant well, not realising that the combination of being in a new country and missing my parents brought all of my emotions to the fore.

Auntie and Uncle were such kind people that I'm sure they were surprised. They took me out for a delicious lunch. When they returned me by car to Edgecliff Road, I was walking up the stairs to my brothers' apartment when I met a presentable young man heading down. I was conscious of how he looked me up and down, from the top of my hat down to my fashionable shoes—and smiled. I remember I was embarrassed that my eyes were still red from crying. At least I was wearing sunglasses. I certainly didn't look happy.

That young man was Joseph Weinreich. The following Monday morning, Auntie Toni's sister, Dorcia Faust, rang him at the factory where he was working, to excitedly tell him that a beautiful girl had just arrived from Israel. Would he like to meet her?

Joseph burst out laughing. He was able to tell Dorcia that he had already met me. He invited her, her husband and me to his flat at Artarmon for tea the following Saturday.

Some of Aneta's cousins, Kraków, 1935.
From left: Bubek Susskind (survived Auschwitz), Tusia Susskind (killed in the Holocaust), Mela Hirsch (killed in the Holocaust) and Gizela Tova Feuer (emigrated to Palestine in 1935).

The wedding of Emil and Mina Feuer, who perished in the Holocaust, 15 November 1936.

Opposite page: Jasiu Feuer, born 27 July 1939, only son of Emil and Mina Feuer, who was too young to accompany Ada, Olga and Pola to safety, and so perished.

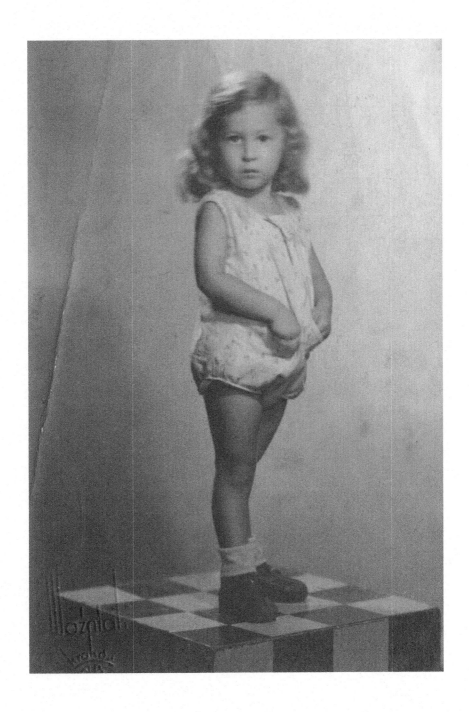

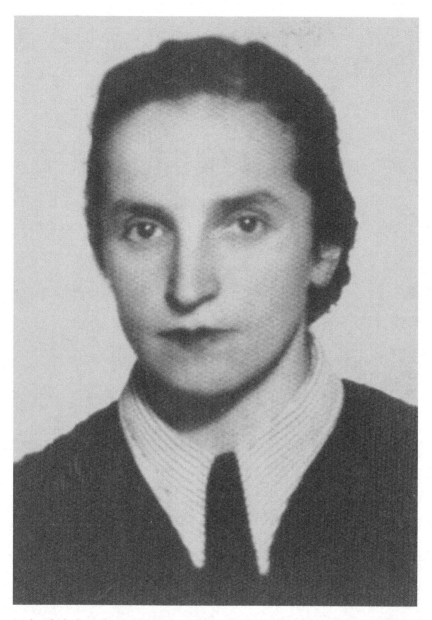

Hela Ehrlich, Ada and Olga's mother, who died in the Holocaust.

Motek (Marcus) Ehrlich, Ada and Olga's father, survived.

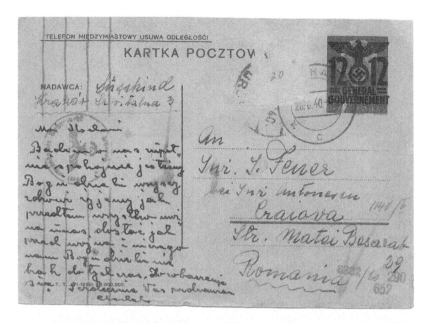

Postcard from Chaskiel, Mina and Tuska (Tusia, also known as Esther Susskind) to Ignacy Feuer, 25 June 1940, with its translation, opposite.

[from] Susskind
3 Szpitalna St, Kraków

My Dears,

Don't worry about us at all. We are all well, thank God. One can again get everything here, just like before the war. So far, thank God, we have all we need. See you again.

Lots of love to you all.
Chaskel

[dated] 25.6.1940

(to) I. Feuer, Eng.
c/o Mr Antonescu, Eng.
29 Matei Besarab
Craiova Romania

Posted on 25.6.1940

My loved ones!

Your letter has really pleased us. I honestly had the impression that you were angry with us. Granted, we don't write often because it's hard to get round to it.

Everyone here is well, thank God. We see the parents every day. We all live close to each other anyway, just like before. The parents, especially Dear Mum, look forward to letters from you.

The children are already grown up. You wouldn't recognise Tuska; she is already as big as you Dear Iciu and has become an-all grown-up young lady. Bubek is a rascal, but they say he is very handsome, although I don't see it that far. Tuska keeps learning her trade and is well advanced in it. She makes very pretty things. She is really talented.

I have to finish here as I want to leave some space for Chaskel.

Lots of love and kisses to you.
Mina.

Lots of love and kisses from
Tuska.

PS. We are not sending any of Bubek's and my photos for now, as we don't have any good ones.

Postcard from Toska (Tosia) and Bala and Salo Hirsch to Ignacy Feuer in Romania. According to this, Toska made it to Bochnia and Bala, Salo and their three children were taken away, never reaching Bochnia. Franka tried to save them from boarding the transport, but they did and never returned.

[from] Bala Hirsch
18 Zielna St, Kraków

My Dears,

As Bala has already written to you, we are setting off to Bochnia tomorrow and we will be staying there for the time being.

And how are you? How are you doing? We will be staying at Sztern's so his place will now be our address. Write to us often, because any letter from you makes us very happy.

Lots of kisses to you from me.

Toska

Posted:
24.08.1940
Received:
September [Full date illegible]

[to] Flor Antonescu, Eng.
29 Matei Besarab, Craiova, Romania

My Dears,

Today we have received your greetings through Bulaj. He showed us your postcard. Also today, Dad and Mum have gone to Bochnia and they will be living there. Their belongings had been sent there two weeks ago.

Toska and Milus are going there tomorrow. As for the rest of us, we don't yet know who is staying in Kraków. We will all know in a few days' time. We are very happy to hear that you are doing well. Do you want to go to see Lopek? And can you write to my brother-in-law to let him know that everything is fine with us? And how are they?

Lots of kisses to you. Write frequently and a lot.
Bala

My Dears,

We hope we will be allowed to stay here, we will only know next week. Otherwise, everything is the same. We met dear Todsu and like her a lot. Write directly to us what is happening with you.

Warm kisses
Salo

[from] Bronisława Porwit 9A Dekerta St, Kraków, Poland I wonder if you have any news about Rózia [two illegible words here]. Write a lot and don't worry, because I can see that God is with you all. Kisses to you all, Stasek	Posted: 11.12.1943 Received: September [Full date illegible] [to] Marceli c/o Club Pension, 34 Terez Körut, Budapest, Hungary

Postcard dated 11 December 1943 from Bronka to Marcel (Marceli), actually written by Samek as Stasek, from the Optima factory. It was collected by Bronka to mail to Franka in Hungary. Samek writes that Ela (his sister) and Hela (Franka's sister) 'are staying with me', meaning that they were all in Płaszów.

Opposite page: The back of the postcard.

124

My Dearest ones,

The letters we receive from you are like music to us. We are doing relatively well. We don't need anything. Ela and Hela are staying with me. And Bronia is an angel; a mother wouldn't be able to do what she can. If you started getting news from us less frequently, don't worry about us at all; God is with us.

I haven't received your nameday present.

Bronia went to [illegible word here, possibly town name] but couldn't sort things out; they know nothing there.

Top: Mina and Chaskiel Susskind, whose daughter Esther (Tusia) perished, while their son, Bubek, survived.

Bottom: Bala and Salomon Hirsch, whose three children, Mela, Hesiu and Menachem, perished.

Opposite page: Emergency Certificate, Visa No. 1 (page 1), from the British Mission in Romania, showing the family's passage from Bucharest, Romania to India. Franka always intended to go to Palestine, where the group arrived on 31 August 1945. Permission to remain was refused on 12 September 1945. See the stamp bottom right of third page.

Source: Samuel and Franka Baral Collection. USHMM, on loan from the family. Photo: courtesy USHMM.

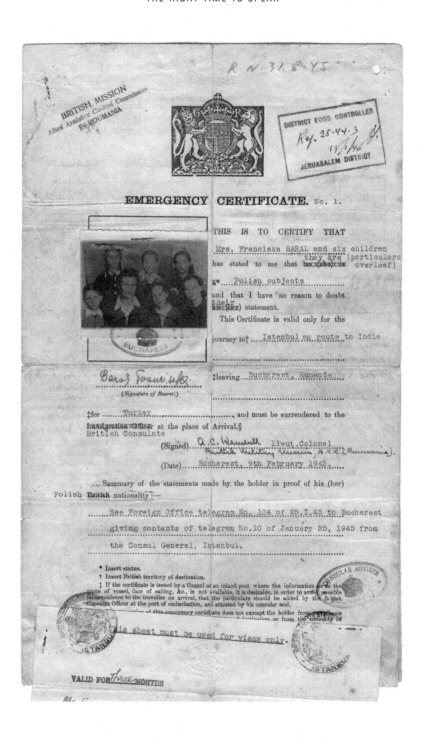

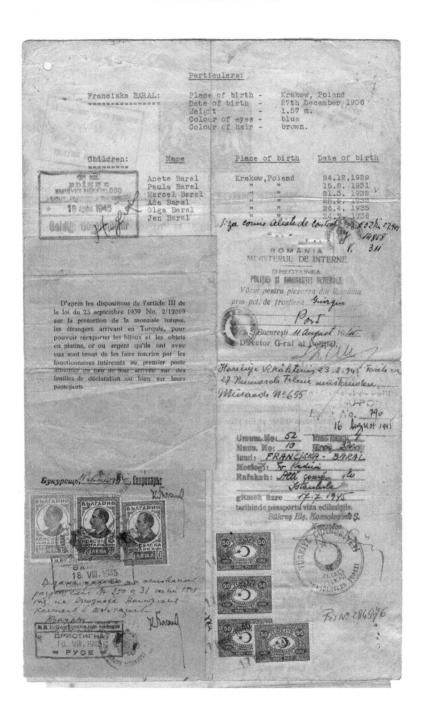

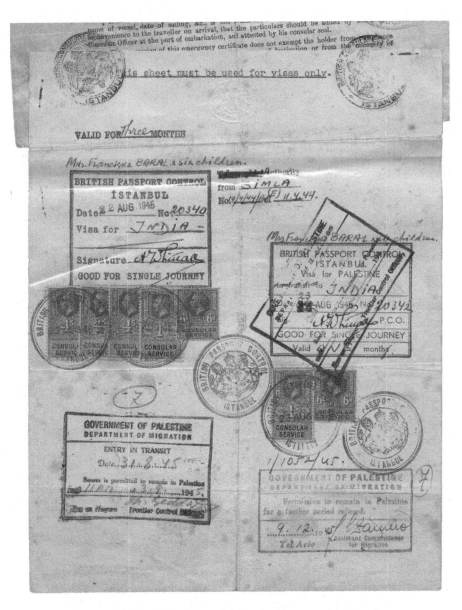

**Emergency Certificate, Visa No. 1 (page 2), opposite page, and
Emergency Certificate, Visa No. 1 (page 3) above.**
Source: Samuel and Franka Baral Collection. USHMM, on loan from the family.
Photo: courtesy USHMM.

Top: Mock-up of a bus like the one in which Franka and the children crossed the border from Lebanon to Palestine; note the armed British soldier, since the Atlit Detainee Camp was then under British rule.
Source: Atlit Detainee Camp Museum.

Bottom: Aneta revisited her boarding school, Beit Tzirot Mizrahi, Jerusalem in 1966. Back row, from left: Hila (Ada's daughter), Aneta and Joseph. Front row, from left: Henry, Ada and Ronen (Ada's son).

Top: In front of the apartment at 124 Ben Yehuda Street, Tel Aviv, 1947. From left: Marcel, Aneta, Janek.

Bottom: The family reunited, 12 December 1949. From left: Aneta, Franka, Janek, Samek and Marcel.

Aneta with her best girlfriend, Marysia Shenker Maly,
at the Sheraton Hotel, Tel Aviv, 1999.

Opposite page:

Top: Class photo at Beit Tichon Le'Mizchar. All the students
were Israeli except me (second row, fifth from left) and the
boy with the raised fist sitting next to me, 17 June 1947.

Bottom: Family Pfefferbaum, Tel Aviv, 1946.
Left to right: Manes, Zvika, Heli and Bibi.

133

Franka (left) with her seamstresses at Ben Yehuda Street,
making dresses for her customers, 1947.

Opposite page:
Top: Franka and Samek on their balcony,
124 Ben Yehuda Street, Tel Aviv, 1948.
Bottom: Franka's business card, Tel Aviv.

פרנקה ברל
סלון לתפירה
תל־אביב רח' בן־יהודה 124
קומה א' דירה מס'פ 2

FRANKA BARAL
Dressmaking Salon
124 Ben-Jehuda Street
First Floor room 2
Tel-Aviv

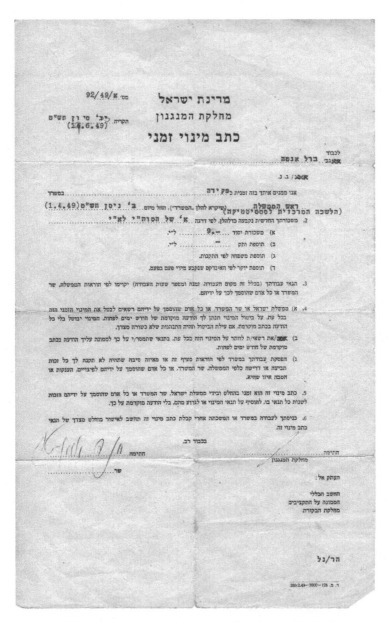

Letter of employment in Hebrew, translated into English
(opposite), from the Office of Prime Minister Ben Gurion,
4 January 1949, showing the terms of Aneta's employment.

THE STATE OF ISRAEL   No. A/49/92

DEPARTMENT OF HUMAN RESOURCES   The Kiriyah   22nd   Sivan 5709

LETTER OF TEMPORARY APPOINTMENT

To

Miss BARAL ANETA,

Dear Madam,

We hereby temporarily appoint you as a clerk in the Office of the Prime Minister, (The Central Bureau of Statistics) (henceforth to be called 'The Office'), commencing 2 Nisan 5709 (1.4.49)

2. Your monthly salary has been fixed as follows, in accordance with grade A of the Jewish Agency for the Land of Israel

       a) Base salary   9 Israeli liras

       b) Seniority supplement   -- Israeli liras

       c) Family supplement in accordance with regulations.

       d) Cost of living supplement in accordance with the index which is fixed from time to time.

3. The conditions of your employment (including place of work, time of commencement, and number of hours of work) will be kept in accordance with Government instructions, the Minister or anyone authorized to do so by them.

4. a) The Government of Israel or the Minister of the Department, or anyone who has been authorized by them, are entitled to cancel this temporary appointment at any time. At least a month's notice will be given to you if the appointment is cancelled. The appointment will be canceled without any prior notice, if the reason for the cancellation will be improper behaviour on your part.

   b) You are entitled to relinquish this appointment at any time, on condition that you will notify your supervisor in writing at least one month in advance.

   c) Termination of your work in The Office in accordance with instructions of this paragraph or because of another reason will not give you the right to claim or demand against the Government, the Minister of the Department, or anyone who has been authorized by them for compensation, gratuities or any bonus whatsoever.

5. This letter of appointment is entirely of a temporary nature and it is the right of the Government of Israel, the Minister of the Department or anyone authorized by them, to change any conditions in it, to add or deduct from them, without prior notice of such.

6. Your commencement of work in The Office or continuing in it after receiving this letter of appointment will be considered as an absolute confirmation on your part of the conditions of employment.

Very respectfully,

Signature.........(*Signed*)...(illegible)...........   Signature.........(*Signed*)...(illegible)..............
Department of Human resources   Minister

Copy to:

Accountant-General

In Charge of Budgets   (Blank)

Auditing Department

HR/NL

Document Number 126 – 7000 – 280/2.49

Top: Janek (by then Jim) at the Gordon Institute of Technology textile school, Geelong, Victoria, 1951.

Bottom: Marcel (by then Martin) at the Gordon Institute of Technology textile school, Geelong, 1951.

Aneta (centre of photo) celebrating Independence Day on the second anniversary of the State of Israel, Tel Aviv, 23 April 1950.

Aneta in her Israeli Army summer uniform, October 1950.

Sergeant Aneta in her Israeli Army winter uniform, 1951.

Aneta, left, enjoying fresh corn with her Army friends after work,
Jaffa, Tel Aviv, October 1950.

Top: Aneta going for a drive with her cousin Bubek (seated left) and a friend, Zygmunt (standing), Tel Aviv, 1950.

Bottom: Aneta, standing, giving instructions about how to work the IBM machine, Israeli Army, Jaffa, Tel Aviv, October 1950.

143

Happy Aneta, Tel Aviv, January 1950.

Form 2004 טופס

חברת "של" לארץ ישראל בע"מ
(רשומה באנגליה)

THE SHELL COMPANY OF PALESTINE·LTD.
(Incorporated in England)

שק נעול, Locked Bag Service,
ת ל-אביב Tel-Aviv

Miss A.Baral,
Tel Aviv.

תאריך Date 1st Sept.1952.

ENGAGEMENT ON PROBATION - REGIONAL STAFF.
קבלה לעבודה בנסיון - פקידים אזרריים.

Dear Sir, Madam,   א.נ.,

With reference to your application
for employment dated 31st.August.1952...
this letter confirms our offer and your acceptance of employment on probation from the
date of this letter for a period of three
months (extendable at our option to six months).

בהסתמך על בקשתך
להתקבל לעבודה, מכתב זה
מאשר את הצעתנו ואת הסכמתך
לעבוד אצלנו לנסיון, החל
מתאריך מכתב זה, לתקופה של
שלשה חדשים (אשר בידינו
להאריכה לשש חדשים).

The probationary employment may be
terminated by the Company or by yourself by
giving two days' notice in writing without
assigning any reason for the termination.

תקופת הנסיון תוכל
להסתיים ע"י החברה או על ידך
ע"י מתן הודעה מוקדמת בכתב
של יומיים, מבלי לנמק את סיבת
הסיום.

The position for which you are being engaged under the Company's Job Classi-
fication - Regional Staff - is as follows:

התפקיד אשר עבורו אתה
עומד להתקבל לפי מכנית השיבוץ
של החברה - פקידים אזוריים -
הוא כדלקמן:

Grade: X   דרגה:

Job: Copy Typist   תפקיד:

Basic monthly salary: משכרת יסודית
IL.73.-   לחדש

As a condition of employment you
agree to be bound by the Company's Employment
Regulations for Regional Staff now in force
and as they may be amended by the Company
from time to time.

כתנאי להעסקתך הנך
מסכים להידלת כפוף לתקנון
העבודה של החברה לפקידים
אזוריים, אשר הנו בתקף כעת
וכפי שהוא עלול להיות מתוקן
מזמן לזמן ע"י החברה.

Please sign and return to us the
duplicate copy of this letter in acceptance
of the above terms of employment.

נא לחתום ולהחזיר אלינו
את העתק מכתב זה, לאות הס-
כמתך לתנאי העבודה הנ"ל.

FOR THE SHELL CO. OF PALESTINE LTD.
בשם: חברת "של" לא"י בע"מ.

Signed in acceptance of the
above terms and conditions

נחתם לאות הסכמה
לתנאים הנ"ל.

Signature: Anita Barel חתימה   Date: 1st September תאריך
                                      1952.

Above and following 3 pages: Aneta's employment papers for the Shell
Company of Palestine: Engagement of Probation—Regional Staff.
Accepted Application for Employment, dated 1 September 1952.

Tel. Address: SHELL TEL-AVIV
Telephone: 80201-2-3
PRIVATE BRANCH EXCHANGE
Address: 1, JAFFA-TEL-AVIV ROAD

כתבת למברקים: שלל תל־אביב
80201-2-3 :טלפון
מרכזיה פרטית
כתובת: דרך יפו־תל־אביב 1.

חברת „של" לארץ־ישראל בע"מ
THE SHELL COMPANY OF PALESTINE LTD.
(Incorporated in England)   (רשומה באנגליה)

Head Office: HAIFA
Branches: Tel-Aviv, Jerusalem
Agents throughout Israel

<u>Form 2006</u>

המשרד הראשי: חיפה
סניפים: תל־אביב, ירושלים
סוכנים בכל רחבי הארץ

Dept. STAFF .... מחלקה

Ref. No. 3007 .... מס׳

TEL-AVIV, 24th November 1952. תל־אביב,

Miss A. Baral,
TEL AVIV.

EXTENSION OF EMPLOYMENT ON PROBATION

Dear Madam,

   With reference to our letter of the 1st September 1952, we hereby notify you that we have decided to extend the period of your probation to six months terminating on the 28th February 1953, the other terms and conditions remaining unchanged.

      Yours faithfully,

    FOR THE SHELL COMPANY OF PALESTINE LTD.

I have received this notice
and confirm my acceptance.

Date........................   Signature:........................

Extension of Employment on Probation, 24 November 1952.

Tel. Address: SHELL TEL-AVIV
Telephone: 80201-2-3
PRIVATE BRANCH EXCHANGE
Address: I, JAFFA-TEL-AVIV ROAD

הכתובת למברקים: "שלי תל־אביב
טלפון: 80201-2-3
מרכזיה פרטית
הכתובת: דרך יפו־תל־אביב I

חברת "של" לארץ־ישראל בע"מ
THE SHELL COMPANY OF PALESTINE LTD.
(Incorporated in England)   (רשומה באנגליה)

Head Office: HAIFA
Branches: Tel-Aviv, Jerusalem
Agents throughout Israel

FORM 2019

המשרד הראשי: חיפה
סניפים: תל־אביב ירושלים
סוכנים בכל רחבי הארץ

Dept. .... מחלקה
Ref. No. 3007 .... מס׳

TEL-AVIV, 20th February 1953. תל־אביב,

Miss A. Baral,
TEL AVIV.

Dear Madam,

ACCEPTANCE OF RESIGNATION
We acknowledge receipt of your letter of even date
and hereby confirm acceptance of your resignation from the Company's
employment with effect after 28th February 1953.

Yours faithfully,
FOR THE SHELL COMPANY OF PALESTINE LTD.

Acceptance of Resignation letter, 20 February 1953

147

8198 — 7.52 — 500

Form No. 2021

חברת "של" לארץ ישראל בע"מ
(רשומה באנגליה)

THE SHELL COMPANY OF PALESTINE LTD.
(INCORPORATED IN ENGLAND)

CERTIFICATE OF SERVICE – תעודת־שרות

Mr.- Miss Anetta Baral   ח'

תאריך חחילת השרות: Date of Commencement:	התפקיד בתחילת השרות: Work at Commencement:	משכורת בתחילת השרות: Salary at Commencement:
1st September 1952	Copy Typist Grade X	Basic Salary IL.73.---- H.C.L.A. * 41.610 T.E.A. ** 8.---- IL.122.610
תאריך גמר השרות: Date of leaving:	התפקיד בגמר השרות: Work at time of leaving:	משכורת בגמר השרות: Salary at time of leaving:
28th February 1953	Copy Typist Grade X	Basic Salary IL.73.---- HCLA 54.750 T.E.A. 8.---- IL.135.750

* High Cost of Living Allowance
** Temporary Emergency Allowance

בשם חברת "של" לארץ ישראל בע"מ
For THE SHELL COMPANY OF PALESTINE Ltd.

Place of Issue: Tel Aviv   : הוצא ב

Date of Issue: 25. 2. 53.   : תאריך

FURTHER PARTICULARS WILL BE FURNISHED
ON REQUEST BY ANY PROSPECTIVE EMPLOYER.

פרטים נוספים ינתנו למי
בקשת נותן העבודה בעתיד.

Certificate of Service, 25 February 1953.

148

Israeli Women Conscripted For Military Service

WOMEN conscripted for military service in Israel spend their first three weeks—from 5 a.m. until the night—learning to throw grenades and to shoot, said 22-year-old Miss Annetta Baral, who comes from Tel Aviv.

She arrived by the Himalaya yesterday to join her brothers, Messrs. J. and M. Baral, at Woollahra.

Miss Baral, was a sergeant in the Israeli women's army. She said "We wear skirts, battle-dress jackets and berets. And, after we learn to shoot — with rifles — we're drafted to which ever section of the Army we can be most use."

She was a clerk in the Government's war department.

Every girl over 18 must do two years army service—the boys 2½ years.

"But we're not really conscripted," she said, "because every girl likes to do military service." They are fed and clothed—and paid £5 a month pocket money.

Married women, instead of the two years continuous service are called into camps for one week every year, Miss Baral said.

All Israeli Girls Must Join Army

Every Israeli girl is conscripted for two years' military service when she reaches the age of 18 years.

She spends her first three weeks of service—from 5 a.m. to nightfall—learning how to throw grenades.

This was said by 22-year-old Miss Annetta Baral, of Tel Aviv, when she arrived in Sydney recently.

Miss Baral was a sergeant in the Israeli Women's Army.

"We wear skirts, battledress jackets and berets," she said.

"After we have learnt to shoot with rifles, we are drafted to the section of the army in which we can be of most use."

During their service in the army, the girls are fed and clothed, and paid £5 a month.

Married women are called into camps for one week every year.

Top & right: 'Israeli Women Conscripted for Military Service', *The Sunday Herald*, 29 March 1953, Full page and actual article.
Source: Trove. National Library of Australia https://trove.nla.gov.au/newspaper/article/18503742

Left: 'All Israeli Girls Must Join Army', *The West Australian*, Perth, 7 May 1953.
Source: Trove. National Library of Australia https://trove.nla.gov.au/newspaperarticle/55801775

8

JOSEPH

◈

In the apartment building where Joseph lived, at 23 Hampden Road, Artarmon, there were four flats. He lived in one with his mother and on the same floor opposite his place lived his aunt, Mina Blumenfrucht and her two sons, Maurice and Jan. Auntie Mina was a happy, jolly soul and he was able to talk to her very frankly. When he knocked at her door and announced 'Mina, I have just met my wife,' she laughed. When he explained further, she laughed again.

'Are you crazy? You saw this girl for one minute—and now you want to marry her? Get out of here!' Then she laughed even more, and said 'Come in and tell me all about it.' Joseph insisted it had been love at first sight.

He had invited me to his place for afternoon tea on Saturday at 3pm, only a week after I had met him. Joseph's mother was also there. During the War, she had lost everyone in her family except her son. He told her about me just ten minutes before I arrived because he was worried about her reaction. She was terrified that if Joseph married, she would be left alone with no one to look after her.

Joseph had told his mother that I was from Kraków, and from a very good and well-known family, related to Ignac and Toduś Feuer. This, he told me later, reassured her.

I arrived with Dorcia Faust, my Aunty Toduś' sister, and her husband. Joseph introduced us all and I talked with his mother for a while, feeling very comfortable. He left us together and went across the hall to fetch Auntie Mina. He reappeared with her holding a cake he had asked her to bake.

She had been anxious to meet me, and we talked together for some time. After we had spent more time chatting with everyone, Joseph asked if I wanted to stay on or go with him to a movie in the city, followed by dinner. I chose to go with him to the city, and so began our long romance.

Joseph told me that he had already met my two brothers in Katoomba, which he explained was a holiday resort in the mountains two hours from Sydney, where many young people would go to get away from the city. They met during the Christmas holidays of December 1952, when my brothers told him I was finishing service in the Israeli Defence Force. After I finished I would visit them, and need a mattress to sleep on.

Knowing that Joseph was part-owner of the Everlastic Mattress Company, they ordered one from him. They had very little room in their apartment and needed a non-standard mattress. Joseph had called Martin and said they usually didn't make mattresses to order— but he would certainly make an exception for a young woman who had just been through the War and was now serving in the Israeli Army. Three months later, on Saturday 28 March 1953, we had met. Joseph had just delivered the mattress to my brothers' apartment.

At this exciting time, I was in constant touch by mail with my parents in Tel Aviv. When I told them I would not be returning, since I had found the person with whom I wanted to spend the rest of my life, they immediately began to ask questions. Who was this young man? Where did he come from? Who were his parents and grandparents? What business was he in?

As soon as I told them about Joseph and his background, they were elated. My father and my grandfather had done business with Chaim, Joseph's father and with Abraham, his grandfather, buying sheepskins from them to make waistcoats. What a remarkable coincidence! My father gave his permission for me to go out with Joseph. He said Joseph's family was honest and decent, and had been good customers.

Our growing relationship had another good result: since my parents' three children were all in Australia, they decided to move and make their home here so the family could be together. They sold everything to set out on this new venture.

The Monday after my tea with Joseph and his family, my brother Martin rang to ask him if he knew of a firm where I could use my skills on the IBM computer. Joseph helped me get a job in the tax office in the city, through a friend who set up an interview for me. The other young women there were extremely nice to me, even though I was the only foreigner. On the first day they gave me tea, but asked if I could bring my own cup and tea after that. When they saw how I made it, they burst out laughing. I put loose tea leaves into the cup first and then poured the boiling water on top of them, so they floated in the cup. It was impossible to drink this way. Kindly, they taught me to make a proper cup of Aussie tea by heating the pot with hot water first, pouring it out and then placing the tea leaves in the pot with a strainer. I still follow their instructions.

One day in November my workmates asked me for 20 pence to bet on the horses. Of course, I had no idea what the Melbourne Cup was. I can still remember the name of the first horse on which I ever placed money: Friendly Feeling. He was not so friendly to me, because he didn't win. But years later I still bet money on the Melbourne Cup. I love that feeling of competition and a winner.

Adjusting to my life in a new country wasn't always easy. When you arrive to live in a new place you leave your whole life behind. It's a real struggle at the beginning to find connections and identify with a new environment and its culture. I was so lucky to have Joseph to help me. We started to see one another regularly, and though I knew from the beginning he was in love with me, I wanted to make sure I had the same feeling for him. We soon agreed that we had found *a zyvok min Hashamayim,* a union made in Heaven.

On Friday 3 October 1953 he picked me up to meet my parents who were arriving by ship at Circular Quay. We headed up the gangway (which you could in those days) and almost immediately spotted them. The moment when I introduced Joseph to my parents was so joyful—unforgettable.

He dealt with the luggage and took it back to 322 Edgecliff Road.

The Sunday after my parents arrived, Joseph rang me to enquire if they were at home. We had already picked out a beautiful diamond engagement ring through his friend Eric Schlanger, a diamond merchant. As is the Jewish tradition, when the groom wants to propose, he goes first to the father of the bride, to ask permission. Joseph arrived carrying the ring in a dainty box, and asked to speak in private with my father. It wasn't long before they re-emerged from the closed room, both smiling, and my father announced that his beloved daughter was officially engaged. Joseph helped me put the ring on my finger while my mother looked on, delighted.

Joseph never actually proposed to me. We had been forced into adulthood while still children, so we were older, more mature and more focused on what we wanted in our lives than our actual years.

We simply treated our forthcoming marriage as something very natural and inevitable.

After I put on the ring, my brother Martin announced that he was going to call Uncle Ignac. Joseph stopped him, saying the first person to tell should be his mother in Artarmon. When we entered her apartment together, he said simply: 'Mother, meet my fiancée.'

My future mother-in-law called out: 'Josele, what have you done to me?' I was so shocked that I wanted to hide under the table. My parents didn't witness this scene—but they heard what was said. Joseph assured me that his mother was crying tears of joy.

In future years she would live near us on Hampden Road and we would see each other on a daily basis. We also greatly appreciated the help she gave us when our first child was born. After our engagement, we discussed her fears about how she would finance her future. She had originally been from Chrzanów, Poland, but she and Joseph were taken to Russian labour camps in the Urals. After the War ended, they landed in France, and took a boat to Australia. Since arriving in June of 1947, Joseph had worked hard and saved a considerable amount of money. I suggested he invest this in his mother's name. We were young—I was 24 years old—and we could work together to save for ourselves and build a new future.

Years later, when Joseph's mother went to Israel and remarried, our lawyer continued to send her the returns from the investment. My husband has told me how much he appreciated my good advice and the generosity of my heart.

After meeting Joseph's mother, we rang Uncle Ignac, Auntie Toduś and Auntie Mina to tell them about our engagement, and everyone arrived in Artarmon to celebrate. Joseph's mother soon settled down and we all toasted our coming marriage.

In the weeks that followed, everyone supported us. Before we became engaged, Joseph had rung his Auntie Helena Schreiber to let her know the good news: he didn't need to travel to Israel to find a wife because one had come to him. She immediately invited us to afternoon tea in her mansion in Killara.

After we were comfortably seated, Auntie Helena rang a small golden bell and a woman in a black dress, white apron and white cap entered with a tray of tea and beautiful cakes.

I was shocked. This sort of thing would never have happened in Israel. '*Ma ze*,' I whispered to Joseph in Hebrew ('What is this?' in English). Auntie Helena and I went on to develop great rapport with one another. Later she called Joseph and said she wanted to throw an engagement party for us in her lovely home. When we asked how many people we could invite, she said: 'As many as you like. Just let me know the number.'

She and Uncle Lester were very generous and magnanimous. We enjoyed an elegant engagement party in a beautiful setting. On the day I arrived with my parents, Auntie Helena graciously welcomed us at the front door. My mother walked in and said to her: 'Good-bye Mrs Schreiber,' to which Auntie Helena tactfully replied, without missing a beat: 'Good-bye Mrs Baral. Now please come inside.'

For Joseph and me, it was much more than a mere party. During the War my brothers and I had never celebrated anything. Joseph had been born into a Hasidic family and celebrations like birthdays were not the custom. This party had special significance. It opened the door to the greatest event of our lives: our marriage. For our family and friends it was a great joy, a *simcha*. We were the first in our family to wed after the Holocaust.

We decided to marry on 15 November of that year, when Joseph had his annual leave. But there was so much to organise in six short weeks! I needed a wedding dress. We had to find a hall for the reception.

I wanted beautiful flowers, and we needed a rabbi to officiate.

Joseph's family were members of the prestigious Great Synagogue, a place with which he was very impressed. His uncle introduced him to Rabbi Dr Israel Porush, with whom he was equally impressed. Joseph had already explained to me why he wanted us to be married by Rabbi Porush in the Great Synagogue. The rabbi was obviously a scholar, and even more important was the tremendous empathy he had for those who had arrived in Australia after the War.

We were invited to meet him at his home on Macleay Street, Potts Point, since it was usual for an officiating rabbi to find out more about a young couple before he agreed to marry them. He welcomed us with respect. One of the questions he asked Joseph was why he wanted to marry. Joseph answered: 'The Bible says a man should marry when he is 18—and I am already 25!'

The rabbi then asked about Joseph's family, saying: 'I know you and your family because you are members of the Synagogue. Now I'm interested to hear about your fiancée. Where was she during the War? What does she know about being Jewish?'

I gave a short summary of my life, including the fact that during the War I had hidden my Jewish identity in order to survive, and adding that after I arrived in Israel, my uncle had arranged for me to attend a religious school in Jerusalem. Then Rabbi Porush asked me about the story of Moses and the burning bush—and was astonished when I could recite that passage from the Bible in Hebrew:

וַיֵּרָא מַלְאַךְ יְהֹוָה אֵלָיו בְּלַבַּת־אֵשׁ מִתּוֹךְ הַסְּנֶה וַיַּרְא וְהִנֵּה הַסְּנֶה בֹּעֵר בָּאֵשׁ וְהַסְּנֶה אֵינֶנּוּ אֻכָּל

An angel of the Lord appeared to him in a flame of fire from within the thorn bush, and behold, the thorn bush was burning with fire, but the thorn bush was not being consumed.

Then he shook Joseph's hand and said he would be honoured to officiate at our wedding.

We had a lot to arrange. For my dress, I wanted something classically simple and elegant. The fashion of the time was for long dresses with puffed sleeves and a long train. I wanted something unique. I went with my mother to choose some lovely guipure lace, and together we designed a short-sleeved dress with a slim-fitting bodice and ankle-length full skirt. My mother sewed it on a Singer machine which I still have.

Joseph told me later that when he saw me in the dress walking on my father's arm down the aisle of the Great Synagogue, through the hushed crowd, he fell in love with me all over again. When I joined him under the *chuppah*, he opened his eyes wide and smiled at me.

We honoured both families with our attendants. My bridesmaids were Joseph's cousins Jacqui and Mildred Schreiber, and my cousins Marie and Lillie Feuer were flower girls. Rabbi Porush gave the blessings and the celebrated cantor of the Great Synagogue, Isador Gluck, sang to us. The melody was so beautiful that we still sing it together. It is called *Boi, Boi Kalah*:

בּוֹאִי בְשָׁלוֹם עֲטֶרֶת בַּעְלָה   גַּם בְּשִׂמְחָה וּבְצָהֳלָה
תּוֹךְ אֱמוּנֵי עַם סְגֻלָּה   בּוֹאִי כַלָּה בּוֹאִי כַלָּה

Come in peace, crown of her husband
Both in happiness and in jubilation
Amidst the faithful of the treasured nation
Come O Bride! Come O Bride!

We took the same hire car to our reception at 80 Oxford Street in Bondi Junction that had brought my father and me to the Great Synagogue. Waiting for us were 120 guests. It was such a happy occasion. We also hired a band and opened the dancing with a waltz that went: *Oh how we danced on the night we were wed.* Soon our guests joined in.

Rabbi Porush gave a most memorable speech. He was deeply moved by my story and embraced everything we had told him. Then my new husband spoke. I was surprised that he didn't have a prepared speech. He spoke powerfully from his heart, addressing me directly. 'You'll be the Queen of my realm,' he promised. And he has kept his word.

Joseph's two uncles also gave short speeches. He had asked them to keep these brief, as the reception needed to finish by 6pm. Since my father felt his English was not good enough, he didn't feel comfortable speaking. But I could see how overjoyed he was for us.

A few days before the wedding, Auntie Helena had asked Joseph where we were going on our honeymoon. He had told me that he did not want to disclose the destination. Before we were married, others had also asked where we would spend it. Joseph kept them guessing by asking if they could keep a secret.

'Don't tell anyone—but we're going overseas.'

'Where?' they would ask.

'Overseas to Manly,' he would joke.

He liked Auntie Helena so much that he told her the truth: he would take me to a magnificent resort hotel, called the Hydro Majestic in Medlow Bath in the Blue Mountains.

'Have you got a car?' enquired Auntie Helena.

'Yes,' he said. 'Our truck.'

She laughed. 'You're cuckoo. A truck with your logo, Everlastic Mattress Co., for your honeymoon!'

Then they both laughed. 'I've just bought a new car [it was a Vauxhall],' she continued. 'I'll lend it to you. My son Spencer will give you the keys. On the way, drop him off at his boarding school.'

Spencer attended The King's School, a prestigious school in North Parramatta. When we picked him up after the wedding, he was wearing the uniform of the school cadets. So we set off on our honeymoon with an Army escort.

The Hydro Majestic had extensive views that ranged across the valley to the next mountain. We stayed in the luxurious wedding suite called The Belgravia.

Joseph and I spent our honeymoon walking in the picturesque surroundings of the blue-hued mountains and green valleys, out in the fresh, cool, clean air. We swam in the hotel pool. We also drove down to the Megalong Valley, about three kilometres from the hotel, to enjoy a proper Aussie afternoon tea with home-made scones, jam and whipped cream. Every night after dinner we danced the night away. We could not believe how lucky we were to be able to enjoy the first days of our new life together in a free country.

Joseph Weinreich, Sydney, 1950.

Aneta, Tel Aviv, 1950—the photo Joseph has carried in his wallet since then.

Aneta and Joseph at 322 Edgecliff Road, Woollahra, 1953:
a happy beginning.

Martin, Aneta, Joseph and Jim at 322 Edgecliff Road, Woollahra, 1953.

Aneta and Joseph on their wedding day, 15 November 1953.

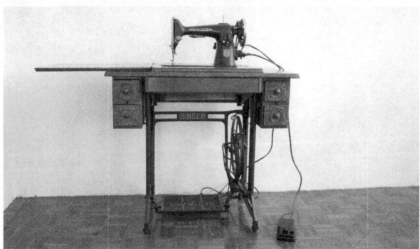

Top: Lillie and Marie Feuer (flowergirls), Aneta, Mildred Schreiber and Jacqui Schreiber (bridesmaids) at the wedding.

Bottom: The Singer sewing machine Franka used to make Aneta's wedding dress.

Family wedding photo. From left, first row: Spencer (son of Lester and Helena Schreiber), Samuel, Lillie Feuer, Jim and Martin (kneeling), Marie Feuer, Jacqui Schreiber and Mildred Schreiber. Second row: Helena Schreiber, Toduś Feuer, Frania Weinreich (Aneta's mother-in-law), Franka, Aneta, Joseph, Mina Blumenfrucht (in Australia known as Mina Bloom) and Jan Bloom (Mina's son). Third row: Lester Schreiber and Ignacy Feuer.

Opposite: page
Great Synagogue, Sydney, on the wedding day checking the *Ketubah* (Jewish prenuptial agreement)
From left: Samuel, Aneta and Rabbi Dr Porush.

167

Top: Leaving the wedding to go on their honeymoon. From left: Leonie Whitmont (future sister-in-law), Aneta, Joseph and Henry Brodaty, who would later become critical to Franka's care.

Bottom: Honeymoon at the Hydro Majestic Hotel, Medlow Bath, Blue Mountains.

9

MIGRATION

◈

In May 1946, Joseph had arrived in Kraków from Kzyl-Orda (now Kyzylorda), Kazakhstan. He, his mother Freidl (Fanny), his Auntie Mina, and his cousins Maurice and Jan, sent a letter to his Uncle Lester and Auntie Helena, then living in Killara in Sydney, to ask for sponsorship for migration. His uncle was somewhat reluctant to take on his two sisters and three teenage boys. Both Uncle Lester and Auntie Helena were wealthy, each in their own right, and it was Auntie Helena who wanted to take on this huge responsibility for two families—and she did. Joseph's Uncle John was also by then living in Sydney.

Migration was a very complicated process. First visas were needed for them to cross Germany, which was then divided into four zones administered by Britain, the United States, France and the Soviet Union. Then they had to enter France on a three-month visa in order to leave by ship or plane. These crossings and travel had to be paid for in advance; Joseph's uncle arranged for payment.

Joseph travelled by train from Kraków to Warsaw ten times over nine months to visit the consulates that issued the precious visas. He says he will never forget the epic journeys which took place on those trips. The trains were in poor condition with their windows broken, exposing passengers to the freezing outside air, and without lights. In the narrow compartments, four people sat opposite four more.

On his last trip, Joseph sat facing a couple and whispered to them the word *Amchu?*, which is the universal code word meaning 'our people' that only Jewish people would understand. They nodded and whispered just one word, *Melbourne,* meaning they were on their way to Melbourne, Australia. Joseph was not immediately recognisable as Jewish, since he had fair hair and was wearing a Polish Army cap and a German overcoat—with a blood-stained hole in the back. His mother purposely bought this for him in a market to make him look like a regular Polish man.

Suddenly everyone froze. Men were moving along the corridors with torches, flinging open doors. Two rough-looking men entered their compartment and looked menacingly around. Their gaze settled on the couple. 'Finally, we've got the Jews,' they said.

Nobody knew that these hooligans had bribed the driver to stop the train so that they could rob Jews before it reached Warsaw. They grabbed the couple and marched them down the corridor and off the train. They stood just outside the window where Joseph was sitting. He was horrified to witness their shooting in cold blood.

This tragedy still weighs on his mind.

Europe was still a dangerous and unpredictable place. Joseph, his mother, Auntie Mina and the two cousins were relieved when they finally left Poland, crossed Germany and arrived in Paris. There they waited for three months before boarding the ship *Ville d'Amiens*. After a six-week voyage they finally reached the promised land, Australia.

It was June 1947.

When they arrived in Sydney, Auntie Helena was waiting to greet them. Joseph says that at first he couldn't understand anything people were saying. The only English word he knew was *Darling*. How did he know that word? Uncle Lester and his new bride, Helena, had visited Joseph's family in Chrzanów on their honeymoon, and asked to play tennis. That there was no court didn't seem to deter them. Ever-resourceful, Joseph and his friends had made one for them in a large field behind the house, chasing away the cows and stringing a thin rope between two poles to use as a net.

Uncle Lester, dressed in white trousers, shirt and shoes and Auntie Helena, all in white as if for Wimbledon (including a cap), strolled out on the improvised tennis court. Half the population of Chrzanów had gathered to see this spectacle.

While Joseph ran around picking up balls for them, he heard his uncle address his aunt as *Darling*. So this was my husband's English greeting to his aunt when he arrived in Australia 15 years later. She immediately burst out laughing. 'My name is Helena, not *Darling*— and after 15 years, even my husband no longer calls me *Darling* any more.'

'Our home in Australia was not Buckingham Palace,' continues Joseph. They shared one room in Kings Cross with Auntie Mina and her two sons. But his two goals were clear: to find a job so that he could become independent, and learn to be fluent in English.

Before he arrived, he had told Uncle John, Lester's brother, that he was interested in textiles. His uncle told him: 'You can learn the trade and get a job in a minute. There's a factory on Ann Street, in Surry Hills, that makes knitted fabric, and then produces singlets and men's underwear from it.'

Joseph arrived on a Friday morning. By the following Monday

he was working in the knitting factory suggested by Uncle John. His workplace was the room where the fabric was dyed in huge vats of hot water. It was always fiery hot. Joseph found the heat unbearable because he was used to chilly northern Europe temperatures—but he persevered for a few weeks.

His second job was at Burlington Mills, where a whole floor was set up with knitting machines. He quickly picked up the skills needed to use them, and soon was working with four looms to earn more money.

He liked this job. His Australian co-workers were kind and helpful. The only drawback was that it took an hour-and-a-half by tram to reach his workplace and a similar amount of time to return home. Three hours travelling added up to a long day's work.

He rose at 5am to travel across the city to Newtown, down the road from the University of Sydney. 'Every day as I passed it, I prayed to God that when I found a wife, my children would go to this university,' he said. In later years, they did—and graduated with honours.

Four nights a week, Joseph went to government-sponsored English classes in Chalmers Street, Surry Hills, from 7-9pm. Mr Savage, his teacher, who knew German and French but taught only in English, was 'the kindest and finest fellow you could come across'. At the beginning of the first lesson he wrote the lines from Hamlet: *To be or not to be ...* up on the blackboard. 'If you learn English, you will *be*,' said Mr Savage. 'If you don't, you'll end up sweeping the streets of Sydney.'

Sitting next to Joseph in class were two Hungarian brothers, John and Emil. Joseph asked them in Yiddish: 'Who is Shakespeare?' The two brothers answered back in Yiddish that they had no clue. The two brothers never had time to do their homework but they tried very hard, even though they worked day and night. They never learned to speak or understand English well. But within a very short time, they would become one of the biggest manufacturers in Sydney, the Hilton brothers.

After a year at Burlington, Joseph became restless. He was more confident, since his English had improved greatly and he knew there was no future working there. His Uncle Lester, a 50 per cent owner with business partner Paul Berr of a factory in Newtown called Sleepmakers, produced mattresses, and offered to teach him the business. Joseph began working there and, two years later, when he was 22, went into business with his Uncle John and Cousin Maurice, opening a mattress factory, first in Kogarah and then overlooking the Harbour in Balmain.

'Half the Jewish population of Sydney were conceived on Everlastic Mattresses,' says Joseph. He ran the factory with 60 people. 'My uncle was the businessman in the beautiful suit, beautiful shirt, beautiful tie, and Maurice was the salesman. I wore khaki shorts and shirts to show my equality with the workers. I was on the production floor with them. We produced lots and lots of mattresses.' Joseph enjoyed the production process.

'We had more orders than we could fill—and in that time of full employment, it was hard to find workers to do dirty or grimy jobs like filling mattresses with kapok. The dust got everywhere! So I went to Long Bay Gaol and spoke to the governor. 'When one of the prisoners has served their sentence, send them to me,' I told him. 'Just so long as they're not murderers or rapists.'

'We helped them find somewhere to live, too. And the women sewing the mattress cases? I went up to Kings Cross and found some "ladies of the night" who had finished with the profession. None of these people gave us any trouble for the whole five years I was in the mattress industry. Working with them humanised them for me. They always tried to do the right thing.'

Joseph and I started married life in 1953 with 100 pounds, since most of his savings went to his mother. He had a 20 per cent stake in the very profitable Everlastic business, so we knew he could go on to make a good living. The company had two other stakeholders besides Joseph: his Uncle John, who owned 60 per cent and Cousin Maurice Bloom who, like my husband, had a 20 per cent share.

After our honeymoon we returned to Sydney to our fully-furnished apartment at 29 Hampden Road, Artarmon, looking forward to our new life together. We both went off to work with enthusiasm the next Monday morning. Joseph told me that a pile of orders needed his attention, since it was just before Christmas.

That morning, Uncle John called Joseph into his office and told him he had some good news. Maurice was engaged to a very rich girl named Roslyn. Her Aunt Dora Feinberg, also very rich, wanted to buy out Joseph's share of the business so that 'Roslyn can live in the manner to which she is accustomed.'

Worse was to come. The deal had already been struck between John, Lester and Maurice. Joseph was at first astonished, then angry and outraged. He had worked hard for years to build up the business and now he had to provide for his own new wife and the family we wanted. How dare his uncle accept this proposal which could well leave him without the means of making a living? He had put in so much hard work building up the factory and had been the first to join it. Surely the rule was first in, last out?

He told Uncle John that he thought Maurice was greedy and ungrateful. Hadn't his own father been nursed by Joseph in Kzyl-Orda when he had typhus, and died in his arms? My husband said he would not accept the proposal: 'It will happen over my dead body. I'd rather burn down the factory and go to gaol for it.'

John then told him that Aunt Dora would invest a considerable sum of money in the business, enabling the factory to manufacture furniture as well as mattresses. Lester, a keen gambler, was interested in Roslyn's family business, as her uncle was a bookmaker. He knew he could look forward to unlimited credit.

Joseph was incensed. He stormed out.

He came to see me immediately at my workplace, the tax office. I knew at once something dreadful had happened; I had never seen him so upset. He was pale and shaking. I took time out from work and went with him to the Botanical Gardens, where we sat overlooking the Harbour. I knew I could help my husband calm down in this beautiful spot.

When he told me the full story, I reassured him that we would get through this disaster. 'There is nothing so bad that good can't come out of it,' I said.

Two days later, Uncle John increased the premiums for the factory's fire insurance.

Joseph continued to go into Everlastic. He told me that he had a responsibility to deliver orders to his customers. After all, he had done good business with them for many years. For a few days there was an armed truce—or at least 'peace on the Western front'.

This did not last long. Uncle Lester asked to meet Joseph and Uncle John to discuss the situation. It was clear that things could not continue as they were, with such a poisonous atmosphere in which John, Maurice and Joseph didn't speak to one another. Uncle Lester said there were two options: Joseph could sell his share or they could close down the factory. He encouraged his nephew by pointing out that he was a proven, highly professional manufacturer and so could easily get another job in a similar factory.

But Joseph refused to be bought out. He explained to his Uncle Lester that although he had enabled him to come to Australia to start a new life, 'now you are killing me.' Their proposal would deprive him of his livelihood, he pointed out. He supported closing the business.

Joseph told his uncles that he was disgusted. He did not give them an immediate answer about his choice. He told me that Lester and John were very close, and looked after one another. My husband could not understand how members of his own family, whom he had always respected and loved, could treat him so unfairly. He felt betrayed. He was steeped in the values of his beloved city of Chrzanów, where family loyalty was paramount, where the love and affection they had for each other was never to be betrayed. It was holy. He told me he would never forgive them.

The factory did close and its building was sold. For the following three months Joseph went in to work, but only to fulfil existing orders.

Now a difficult time began for us. My new husband sank into a deep depression. For two years he was unable to work. Although he tried and tried, a vigorous young man, usually full of laughter and in the prime of life in his late twenties, he could not find the right place for himself. He suggested ideas such as buying a taxi or becoming a truck-driver on the Sydney-Brisbane-Melbourne-Adelaide runs.

I talked him out of these jobs, as I knew Joseph's abilities were far greater, and that taking his time would provide an opportunity to think clearly and find a better path.

Our first baby, Lilian, had just been born.

On the ship *Ville d'Amiens* from Marseilles, France to Sydney,
Australia, June 1947.

Joseph with his mother Frania, before boarding
the ship to Australia, 1 April 1947.

Joseph, Coogee Beach, 1947.

10

LILIAN

❖

I went every day to help my parents in their boutique where they were selling ladies winter jumpers (sweaters) in Kings Cross. As my pregnancy progressed, it became harder to make the journey from Artarmon by train, with a change-over at Town Hall by bus—a long haul of more than an hour.

I gave birth at the Roslyn Private Hospital in Lindfield. No words can describe the elation we felt when our first baby was born. Both families joyfully celebrated her birth. She was the first grandchild of my parents and my mother-in-law, and the first niece of my brothers Martin and Jim. Since she was the first child born after the Holocaust, she gave meaning to our survival and our lives, and ensured the continuity of our family line. From the beginning she showed us her intelligence and independence, and was absolutely beautiful.

Joseph says he will never forget entering the room at the hospital to see me cuddling my daughter. The Sisters at the Catholic hospital asked me what her name was, and I explained to them that, according to Jewish tradition, the name would be announced in the Synagogue on the following Saturday.

Joseph, as is customary, would be called in front of the congregation to give the baby's name and receive a blessing.

Lilian's Jewish name is Lieba, after my maternal grandmother. Her middle name in Hebrew is Chaja, after Joseph's grandmother. Her English name is Lilian Helen. Later on she would acquire a nickname: Number One. Lilian loves this title of distinction.

She had the unique privilege of all our children of being able to meet her grandfather, my father, Tato Samek (Samuel). She has always remembered his last words to her: 'Be good to your parents.'

According to Jewish tradition, no clothes are purchased until the baby is born. After Lilian's birth, my mother and mother-in-law went on a shopping spree, driven by Joseph. He told me that the department store David Jones did very good business that day.

He brought a suitcase of baby clothes to me at the hospital. I was so happy to see nighties, jackets, booties and lots and lots of nappies.

When the day arrived for us to bring Lilian home, Joseph was so excited that he wanted to get us there as quickly as possible. When we arrived, the baby was crying, so I asked my husband for a nappy. To his surprise, he realised that in the bustle of getting everyone into the car, he had left the suitcase on the street.

He rushed out again. It wasn't long, however, before he returned carrying the case.

'Aneta, this is the most honest country in the world,' he said, with a big smile. 'Nobody stole the suitcase or even moved it. We're so lucky to live in Australia.'

My mother-in-law helped us look after Lilian. When our daughter reached the right age she took her to kindergarten each day. Lilian was very spoiled by her grandmothers and grandfather, and she was adored and revered as the first grandchild. She insisted on being carried rather than riding in her stroller. Joseph discovered this when he encountered them on their way home one day.

In a jovial conversation in Yiddish, Joseph said to his mother 'What are you doing? Why are you carrying Lilian, and pushing her stroller?'

'The child wants me to carry her a little,' replied his mother in Yiddish, laughing.

From the moment her sister Michelle was born three years later, you could see and feel the love and affection between them. Lilian adored her little sister and tried to do everything for her: dressing and bathing her, giving her rides in her stroller, and placing her in a doll's pram and walking around proudly. I allowed her the freedom to do this, while keeping a close watch.

Not far from where we lived in Artarmon, in Lane Cove, there was a beautiful park and playground where we had picnics in summer. As they grew up, Lilian and Michelle could run around and play on the swings and slippery-dips. Lilian was always very energetic, independent, and wilful.

Once after a glorious day I was steering Michelle in her stroller. Lilian also wanted to push by herself and I let her, as I walked alongside. Then as we were crossing a little bridge, which had no handrail, Lilian started to run, thinking this was a game. I quickly ran after her, but she suddenly jumped from the bridge into the water because she saw a rowing boat going under the bridge and she wanted to jump into it and stop me from catching her.

I just caught the stroller in time, rushing forward to grab its handle. Then I was paralysed with shock. Joseph was the one who acted, immediately jumping into the water after Lilian. To my great relief, I saw him pull our daughter out by her hair.

A crowd of people gathered and we were given every assistance, including towels to dry Lilian and Joseph. They were so helpful to us.

Later, when he calmed down, Joseph told me that the water had been cold and murky. He knew he had only seconds to rescue his daughter.

We look at this incident as a metaphor for Lilian's adventures in her life. She has always jumped without fear on to different paths—but with a definite plan. Her focus was always on her studies, whether she was pursuing her academic interests or her immeasurable artistic talent. Lilian has extraordinary flair. Her creativity is unique, and was evident from a very young age. Our house is filled with her paintings. She earned a Bachelor of Architecture with Distinction from RMIT, Melbourne and a Bachelor of Arts with a double major in Fine Arts from the University of Sydney, placing second out of all the students in her final year.

When Lilian reached the age of 12, it was time for her Bat Mitzvah, a milestone for our family. Joseph approached Mr Harold Nagley, the Headmaster of Moriah College, as they were on very friendly terms. Lilian's class was the first high school class in the history of the school. Joseph said to Mr Nagley, 'Usually a Bat Mitzvah is done in a synagogue but I would very much like to have Lilian's Bat Mitzvah in our school.' Mr Nagley immediately agreed, provided we included other girls. We approached the parents of eight of Lilian's classmates and all were happy to take part.

On the day of the Bat Mitzvah the hall was packed. Each girl had made her preparations so that she could recite her part both in English and Hebrew. Mr Nagley was the Master of Ceremonies and Rabbi Dr A. Fabian presented the girls with certificates.

Lilian recited:

I am but a rose of Sharon, even an ever-fresh rose of the valleys …
And God said to Israel:
Like the rose maintaining its beauty among the thorns,
so are my faithful beloved among the nations.

We were so grateful to have both my mother and Joseph's mother at the Bat Mitzvah to witness this rite of passage for Jewish girls. Joseph and I, as well as our son Henry and Michelle, were so thrilled to see Lilian confident and looking beautiful in a blue dress, her hair coiled into a chignon. Lilian presented her Bat Mitzvah speech with such grace, care, elegance and knowledge. It was an unforgettable afternoon, and we are proud that our daughter was a pioneer of the Bat Mitzvahs at Moriah, beginning the tradition. Everyone talked about this first one.

Lilian has always been driven by the pursuit of perfection. She approaches life seriously and studiously. We often had to beg her to simply go outside and play. When Michelle and Henry needed to study, it was Lilian who set the pace and gave them the discipline to sit at their desks and concentrate.

I must mention the unique and deep relationship Lilian had with my mother. From a young age, she went to study at my mother's apartment on weekends. Finally she moved there and lived with her grandmother from the age of 16. My mother understood that Lilian needed quiet to study, and relished having her granddaughter with her. This is where the title 'Number One' originated. Franka understood Lilian's temperament, and her driven desire to work hard to attain excellent results; she had also experienced this intensity with my brother Jim when he arrived to Sydney and was studying to be a doctor. When Lilian was studying, my mother and I would have whispered conversations. When she left early in the morning to go to work, my mother literally tip-toed out of the apartment so as not to 'disturb' Lilian, who was known to be awake from 4am. Even today Lilian continues the habit of waking well before dawn to meet her professional deadlines.

Whether it is because of her unique position as the first child, grandchild and niece, or the stories she absorbed from us, we think she has the heart of Chrzanów, where my husband was born, and the business sense of Kraków, where I was born. She is steeped in Jewish tradition, and her kindness and caring are well known.

When she arrived in New York and had to compete in one of the toughest environments in the world, she was determined to give herself the best chance. She had to get re-licensed, this time according to the American requirements, in order to practise architecture in New York.

To our delight, Lilian met her wonderful husband, cardiologist Dr Michael Ezekowitz, and they married in New York City in May 2013. Michael's strength, intelligence, solidity and gravitas as a person, as well as his willingness to happily climb mountains of study and education with our daughter, fills our hearts with great satisfaction. Dr Mike takes an active role in Lilian's professional life, so much so that when her clients initially meet Dr Mike, they mistakenly think they are a husband-and-wife architectural team, until they learn he is a world-renowned cardiologist named in Thomas Reuters as being among the top 1 per cent of scientific minds in the world. Lilian is overjoyed with her husband.

Lilian's niece and nephew—twins Zoe and Max, now eight years old, and Michelle and Peter's children—are the other centre of her universe and love. We know she speaks to Michelle every day, and without fail every conversation begins with 'Give me a twinnie story!' She teaches them about architecture, learning and drawing, and enhances their love of Judaism and our traditions. She relishes their every word and action, and loves them with her heart and soul.

Lilian has succeeded in all aspects of her life. What we are most proud to witness every day are two results for which, with children, there is never a guarantee. Firstly, the bond that Lilian has with Michelle and Henry is one of our greatest achievements. She is like a lioness protecting them. Secondly, we are proud of her constant love and respect for Joseph and me. We have always valued our children's understanding of us and what we have been through, as a means to gain power from our histories. We tried very hard not to burden them; however, it was impossible. They know everything, and Lilian was the first to receive the feeling that our lives were different.

Happy grandparents Franka and Samuel with their most beloved
first grandchild, Lilian, 1955. Lilian is the only grandchild
privileged to have a photo with her grandfather.

Top: Lilian, three years old and Michelle, six months old, Artarmon, 1957.
Bottom: Aneta's first trip to Israel with the girls, Michelle (left) and Lilian in a captain's hat, December 1964, Tiberias, Israel.

188

Lilian's fourth birthday party at Anthony Hordens, Sydney city.

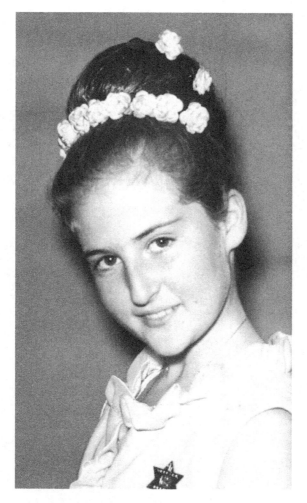

Lilian at her Bat Mitzvah, Moriah College,
4 December 1966.

Opposite page:

Top: Lilian's graduation from the University of Sydney,
5 May 1979. From left: Aneta, Joseph, Lilian and Franka.

Bottom: Lilian with her beloved art teacher, Professor
Maximilian Feuerring at Eliza's Restaurant in Double Bay,
21 August 1974, with Aneta in foreground.

Lilian, architect extraordinaire, in New York City with one of her jobs.
Source: *Wealth and Finance International Magazine*, November 2016. Photo: Steve Freihon.

Wealth & Finance International | November 2016

Wealth
& finance
international

CPD MEMBER
The CPD Certification Service

The New Modern in New York City

Led by Lilian Weinreich, AIA, RAIA, LEED AP BD+C, NCARB, we find out how Lilian H Weinreich Architects aims to transform ordinary spaces into spectacular and unique environments in the most straightforward, practical, precise and functional way.
PAGE 10

The Benefits of Investing in Renewable Energy Assets

James von Claer from Notz Stucki (London) Limited and Mortimer Menzel of Augusta & Co Limited talk to us about the approach to excellence that has led to the selection of Augusta & Co, a leading adviser in the renewable energy industry.
PAGE 26

Leading the FinTech Challenge

We speak to Rich Wagner, CEO of APS financial (APS) about the company and his own CEO of the Year - UK accolade.
PAGE 44

TYLER TIPS®
21st Century Edition by Richard Tyler

Your Essential Guide to Building a Profitable, Sustainable Business in Today's Marketplace.
PAGE 38

Lilian on the cover of *Wealth and Finance International* magazine, November 2016.
Photo: Andy Marcus/Fred Marcus Photography.

Lilian on the cover of *Lux* magazine, February 2017.
Photo: Andy Marcus/Fred Marcus Photography.

An example of Lilian's work, Noho, New York.
Photo: Francis Dzikowski.

Top: Lilian marries Dr Mike Ezekowitz, 19 May 2013. Aneta and Joseph in Australia and Ida Ezekowitz (Mike's mother) and Carol Ezekowitz (Mike's sister) in South Africa, participated in the ceremony via Skype. Photo: Andrea Fischman Photography.

Bottom: Lilian and Mike after the ceremony on their wedding day, Park East Synagogue, New York City.
Photo: Andrea Fischman Photography.

11

SETTLING IN AUSTRALIA

◆

Our Artarmon flat at 29 Hampden Road had a living room, two small bedrooms, a dining room and a kitchenette. The rent was controlled, which meant that our landlord, Mr Webb, who owned the block, couldn't charge us more than 2 pounds 10 shillings a month.

It wasn't long after we moved in that I knew I was expecting Lilian. Mr Webb wasn't happy with the idea of babies being in the building since he didn't like them. He used various means to make our lives unbearable. Our building was erected on a hilly slope, and I was really frightened one day when a bucket of water came crashing down directly in front of me from the first floor.

One evening, just as we were getting into bed, I saw a face at the window. Joseph thought it was an intruder and rushed to repel him. In fact, it was just Mr Webb standing on a ladder, snooping. My husband's reaction could have extended to pushing him off—but he didn't. Thank God he didn't; there could have been a tragic accident.

One day, Joseph met our landlord in the foyer. Politely, he offered to pay increased rent to leave us in peace: 3 pounds 10 shillings a month. Mr Webb dismissed the idea at once. 'No! Just leave. I don't want you and your baby in these flats.'

When my husband told him we weren't going anywhere, Mr Webb challenged him to a fight. He was an ex-policeman, tall and in good physical condition. They laid into one another, and Joseph managed to punch him on the nose with such force that it started bleeding.

Mr Webb covered his nose with his coat and retreated. A few days later, Joseph was summoned to appear in court in North Sydney.

Mr Webb told his version of the altercation and presented the stained coat as evidence. Then Joseph told the story from his point of view, just as I have. When the magistrate gave his verdict, he stared hard at Mr Webb, and told him to stop harassing his tenants, the Weinreichs. He added that the next time Webb appeared before him, he would impose a prison sentence. After this incident, we enjoyed some peace and quiet for a while. We agreed that at the first sign of trouble with Mr Webb, we would go to the police.

When Lilian was born we were left in peace.

Two years later, Mr Webb noticed that I was expecting again. The harassment started anew.

In fact, all our children, Lilian, Michelle and Henry, were born while we were living in Artarmon. The girls shared one bedroom, and Henry was with us in our bedroom.

During those years in Artarmon, we were also suffering the financial effects of the Everlastic closure. Many family members and friends completely abandoned us. We realised that they thought we would ask to borrow money, since Joseph did not have work and was not earning a living. They did not understand our character, our strong wills, and our pride. In fact, this misfortune provided an even greater incentive to succeed. We never give up. But we knew we wanted to be rid of Mr Webb and his harassment so that we could provide our children with the best that Australia has to offer.

My parents and brothers, my mother-in-law and Joseph's second cousin, Iziu Goldberger, stood by us. My husband cut off all ties with Maurice. Uncle John became very religious, and went to live in Jerusalem. Ten years passed before he sent us a Yom Kippur card wishing us all the best. He knew that a truly observant man must go to the people to whom he has knowingly done wrong, and ask for forgiveness before Kol Nidre service on Yom Kippur, so that he can 'present' himself to God without blemish.

Joseph tore up the card. The following year, however, I was in Tel Aviv for a visit and Uncle John came to my hotel and cried his eyes out, asking for forgiveness. When my mother-in-law was dying, she had asked me to promise to make peace between my husband and his uncle—so I did, before she died in 1971.

As for Uncle Lester, he liked to bet on the horses. One Saturday, many years later, he lost at the races and, desperate for money, rang Joseph and asked to borrow 500 pounds for a few days. 'Sweet revenge,' said my husband—who, without hesitation, lent him the money. Uncle Lester kept his word and paid it back promptly.

My father was often sick. His lungs suffered from breathing in the chemicals used to make matches at the concentration camp factory during the War. This affected his health very badly. Also, he smoked heavily when he lived in Israel and then Australia. Sydney doctors could no longer do anything for him, and neither could my brother Jim, who was studying Medicine.

Our family always looks for a way through difficulties. We were desperate to find a solution, so it was decided that Jim would take our father to Mount Sinai Hospital in New York, regarded as the finest in the world for cancer care. Sadly, they could do nothing more for my father. For the long overseas flight, he was made comfortable on a special mattress, allowing him to lie down in the plane. After the return journey to Sydney, Joseph was permitted to go on to the plane to assist in carrying him down to the waiting ambulance that would take him home.

All the passengers were cleared off the plane first, then everyone, even the air hostess, tried to help get my father off. In this commotion of getting him off the plane, they left the special mattress behind. It had been specially crafted to support the back and help prevent bed sores. It was made of foam without metal springs, and my father used it at home, where he wanted to die.

My family didn't let me near my father, as I was nearing the end of my pregnancy with Michelle, and they didn't want me to be upset. They didn't tell me how sick he was, but simply that he had travelled to the mountains for fresh air. It was Joseph who understood the importance of the mattress.

Joseph ran back to get it, but was told it had already been unloaded on to a rubbish truck and taken to the dump. He discovered the route the garbage truck had taken and sped to catch up with it, from Mascot through O'Riordan Street in Alexandria. Miraculously, he located it, tooted his horn, and ran in front of them. They stopped and asked 'What's wrong, mate?' Fortunately, they remembered loading the mattress and when Joseph explained how important it was to his sick father-in-law, they threw all the bags of rubbish on to the road to uncover the mattress at the back of the truck. Joseph says this story demonstrates the humanity, kindness, and strength of the Australian people. I agree—and also think it illustrates much about my husband's own qualities.

Joseph and Lilian at the entrance to 29 Hampden Road,
Artarmon, 5 May 1955.

Uncle John and Aneta making peace, Tel Aviv, 1983.

12

MICHELLE

◈

Michelle's birth at 1pm on 18 February 1957 was relatively easy. I was in labour for only four hours. King George V Memorial Hospital in Camperdown is one of Australia's best for mothers and babies, and Dr Cunningham, who looked after me, was highly respected. As he handed over my new daughter, he said: 'Mrs Weinreich, you've given birth to a most beautiful baby girl—and both of you are fine.' He also told Joseph, impatiently pacing the corridor outside with another expectant father, that both mother and new daughter were well.

My husband was so nervous that he at first thought the doctor was talking to the other man. 'Congratulations, Mr Weinreich,' the doctor said. 'She is certainly your baby; *you* are the lucky father.'

My own beloved father hung on until Michelle was born. I prayed all the way through my labour that he would be able to hold her in his arms. When Michelle was three-and-a-half weeks old we took her to see him, and I was shocked to discover how sick he was; he couldn't even speak any more. They gave him ice to suck and he kissed Michelle's right hand. A couple of days later the family called me to come quickly. I was feeding Michelle and continued to feed her in the car while Joseph drove me, together with Lilian. By the time I got there it was too late. He was still worrying about us, not himself, when he passed away on the day before Purim, 16 March 1957, at the age of 52.

To go between this tragedy of losing my father and the birth of Michelle was unfathomable.

It's hard to describe the love I felt for my gorgeous daughter. I always had one word to describe each child when they were born. My first thought was that Michelle would be 'a lady'.

The Saturday after the birth, the first Shabbat, Joseph went to the Great Synagogue in Elizabeth Street, the site of our marriage, and named the baby Malka-Rachel, Malka after Joseph's grandmother and Rachel (Rachela) after my step-grandmother. In Hebrew, Malka means 'queen'. This is appropriate, since she has grown into a commanding, elegant and regal person. Our daughter's English name is Michelle Rachel.

Rabbi Dr Israel Porush presided at the naming. Since he had also married us, we were honoured. I didn't feel strong enough to attend and Joseph then took charge of this important ceremony.

When we were taking the baby home, the nurse went to hand her to me as I sat in the back of the car. Then Lilian stretched out her arms, calling: 'This is my baby: I want to hold her.' I nodded to the nurse to indicate she could give Michelle to my elder daughter to hold—even though I could see Joseph was petrified that she would drop her.

I could see immediately the love and affection Lilian felt for her sister, and how gently she cuddled her. Later she closely observed how I changed her sister's nappies, bathed, powdered and dressed her—and soon offered to help.

From that first meeting, their connection and love has grown to become the most unique, solid bond. We are overjoyed. Joseph and I believe the warmth and love of a close family is one of the most important aspects of life.

It was a great joy for us to have two girls at home. From the beginning, Michelle had a calm and lovely nature, not demanding a lot and seldom crying. She often had a beautiful smile on her face and such intelligent and wise eyes. This is her character. She sees everything and acts with calm, measured steps.

However, at this time life was not easy for us. Since our landlord didn't want babies in his four flats, ensuring that we could only hang out nappies and other washing to dry two days a week was a way of harassing us. If it rained on either of those days, we had real problems.

We saved enough money to buy a Bendix washing machine, which we installed in the bathroom. This gave us a few blissful weeks of help with the laundry. But our landlord found out what we'd done when he heard it operating, and told us we had to dismantle it.

In their younger years, Michelle and Lilian attended Artarmon Public School. Lilian held Michelle's hand when she arrived for her first day of school. They encountered a group of curious children and Lilian said to them: 'This is my sister. Don't you touch her.' Michelle has always felt Lilian's protective arm around her in every aspect of her life.

When it came time for our daughter's Bat Mitzvah in November 1969, in the auditorium at Moriah College, Michelle excelled. She and her friends made a significant impact on the community, opening parents' eyes to the value of the excellent Jewish education offered at the school. We all sat at long tables with our families and friends, proudly listening to her speech. Then she sang, in both English and Yiddish, the famous song *My Yiddishe Mama*:

In vasser in fayer volt zi gelofn far ihr kind
nisht halten ihr tayer, dos iz gevis di gresten zind
Oy, vi gliklekh un raykh iz der mentsh vos hot
Aza Shayne matuneh geshenkt foon G-t
Nor ayn altichke Yiddishe Mame
Oy, Mame Mayn!

In water, through fire, she would have run for her child
Not to hold her dear is surely the greatest sin
How lucky and rich is the one who has
Such a beautiful gift presented from God
Like the old Yiddishe Mama
My Yiddishe Mama!

When she finished her performance of the song, there were tears in our eyes. Everyone rose to their feet and gave her a standing ovation. Michelle's beautiful singing voice was developed in later years at the Conservatorium of Music in Sydney, by her teacher, Elizabeth Todd.

Even though Michelle is a middle child, she has never displayed the so-called middle child traits. She is always thoughtful and adores her family. She had a particular bond with Granny (Freidl) and Mumusiu (Franka), her two beloved grandmothers. While she was living in New York, she sent regular cards to Franka in red envelopes and Franka loved receiving them, waiting eagerly for each one. Franka also sent Michelle written notes, always calling her 'Malka the Beauty'. Michelle learned to understand and speak Polish so as to understand what everyone was saying, especially Franka. We never realised this until one day she commented in English on our Polish conversation.

Joseph's dream was for our children to attend the University of Sydney. Michelle completed her BA with Honours in Political Science there.

There was only one time in Michelle's life that I can remember Joseph and I asking her not to do something. Michelle began taking flying lesson at Teterboro Airport, New Jersey. She was learning to fly on Cessna and Piper single-engine planes. One year when we arrived for a visit to New York, she took us up to show us what she had learned. When we arrived back to Sydney, we asked her to please take no more lessons. We were truly worried for her safety. Michelle listened to us and we never had to ask again.

Michelle has a unique ability to calm and soothe, and has never given us one second of worry. She is talented both in her design work and savvy in business. Michelle had a yearning to go out to the big world, to utilise everything she had learned. She spread her wings when she left Sydney. She arrived in 1986 in New York City and worked for three years at the Australian Consulate at the Rockefeller Centre. From there, she blossomed and continued with her love of bridal dresses, trying to find a way to build a business in New York. She started in a studio apartment, and expanded from there. This was an enormous task that she took upon herself but she was very determined to find her success and we believed in her approach every step of the way. My brother Janek was already established in New York and he really looked after her. He was a superb uncle and we were so pleased that a close family member was there that we could rely upon.

The hallmark of Michelle's character is her kindness and understanding beyond what can be expected or even imagined. When Michelle met her husband Peter Roth, we felt so secure that in Peter she had met the person who would understand her and cherish her. He is a most proper, intelligent and worldly man. His strength of character is evident in everything he does. Peter is measured, thoughtful and humble. His business acumen, honed at the University of Pennsylvania and the Wharton School of Business, and his charity work, particularly at St Mary's Hospital for Children, make us so proud. Michelle and Peter are an incredible team. They have cultivated a beautiful life together in New York with their twin children, our beloved and precious grandchildren.

We miss them, but the ache is replaced by conversations, usually twice a day. We are integrated daily into her family's life as they are in ours: Michelle, our Malka, whose accomplishments were cultivated and grounded in her formative years in Australia, has remembered her heritage and the lessons we tried to impart.

Top: Baby Michelle aged three months, Artarmon, 1957.
Bottom: Michelle's Bat Mitzvah at Moriah College, November 1969.
From left: Lilian, Michelle, Aneta, Joseph and Henry.

Michelle aged three years and three months,
in kindergarten in Chatswood, 1960.

Michelle in New Delhi, India, 1968.

Aneta and Michelle in Hong Kong, 1969.

Opposite page:
Top: Michelle's University of Sydney graduation, May 1979, a very proud moment in our lives. From left: Aneta, Michelle and Joseph.
Bottom: Michelle at Teterboro Airport, January 1991, with the plane she flew behind us. From left: Michelle and her friends Eddie and Arlene Cummins, Joseph and Aneta.

Joseph and Aneta at the factory, 87 Foveaux Street, Surry Hills, 2004, with Henry (top left) and Michelle (far right).
Photo: Photography by Ingrid.

214

Michelle, Spring runway, New York City, 2011.
Photo: Courtesy Dan Lecca.

Visitors to Olola Ave, Sydney, February 2017. Back row, from left: Peter, Michelle, Joseph and Aneta. Front row, from left: Zoe and Max.

Opposite page:
Top: Michelle and Peter Roth's wedding, Penn Club, New York, 18 January 1998. From left: Henry, Lilian, Michelle, Peter, Aneta and Joseph.
Bottom: Happy family, May 2010, New York. Front row: Aneta holding baby Zoe, Lilian, and Joseph holding Max. Back row: Henry and Michelle.

13

RAINBOW BLOUSES

◈

When Joseph lost his job and found it hard to find another that was worthwhile, we decided to start a business in which we could succeed and where we could work together, with me in design and Joseph in sales. I told him I was talented at designing ladies' clothing. In the Optima factory in Kraków under Julius Madritsch during the War, my mother had shown me the basics when we were sewing those hated German uniforms together. I was eager to begin work again, since my head was full of ideas for new designs.

We were enthusiastic and ready to begin. One day we went into the CBD (Sydney Central Business District) for lunch and visited the ground floor of the up-market department store, Farmers, which was displaying a large selection of ladies' blouses, all in white.

'I've got it!' I said to Joseph. I knew then exactly what we could do. At that moment, I decided to make blouses in all the colours of the rainbow. I wanted to make them as chic and elegant as possible, using my own sense of style. I wanted the colours to be more interesting than just plain white.

We went to see my brother Martin, who was running London Textiles with my mother at 127 York Street. He gave us some material: a fantastic new fabric called terylene, which was drip-dry and needed no ironing—just what busy Australian girls would find different and practical.

At home, Joseph took the bedroom door off its hinges and placed it on our bed. Using it as a cutting surface, I made patterns for the blouses. Joseph cut the fabric with scissors he had used at Everlastic. We took six different styles of blouses to Mrs Riha, a skilled Czechoslovakian Jewish seamstress in Crows Nest, to make up into samples, each one in a different colour. We went together to see her, and explained exactly how they should be sewn. A few days later, she had them ready.

Joseph told me that when a salesman goes to see a buyer, the first impression is all-important, even before the samples are produced. There is some small talk, he said, usually about the weather, and only then are the samples shown.

For this important meeting, he bought a double-breasted navy suit and a smart Borsalino hat. He paired these with a white shirt and a conservative tie. He carried the samples in a suitcase on the train, and approached the buyer in Farmers at her little desk in the middle of the floor.

'I have some coloured blouses, beautiful colours in a drip-dry fabric—' he began.

'Wonderful!' she said. 'Finally—some colour.'

She immediately took out her order book and asked for our business name so she could place an order for the blouses. Joseph told her he hadn't registered a name.

'Since your blouses are all the colours of the rainbow, why not Rainbow Blouses?' she suggested.

Joseph went across the street to Nock and Kirby, which was a retail store trading in hardware and household goods. On the third floor was an office that registered business names. He filled in the form: 'Rainbow Blouses' for 20 pence, and when he returned to the buyer at Farmers, she ordered 156 of our blouses.

A few days after the delivery, she called. Joseph answered the phone in a melodious tone: 'Rainbow Blouses.' She asked him to come in and see her. Immediately he was worried that something might be wrong.

'Put on your Borsalino hat and go. Worry later,' I told him.

The buyer said: 'I have hundreds of blouses on the floor but your Rainbow Blouses sold out in a few days.' She ordered 500 more.

Joseph's response was typical. '*Mazel tov!* (Congratulations),' he said about the sales.

He arrived home with a big smile on his face. 'We're in business.'

We rushed to London Textiles and picked out more beautiful terylene fabric in six colours. However, 500 blouses could not be cut on the bedroom door.

From our first business location at our apartment, we moved to my mother-in-law's dining room at 23 Hampden Road to set up part of the business. The room was on the ground floor, so we could put Michelle in her pram just outside, where we could keep an eye on her while we worked and I could feed her every four hours. In between feeding times, she lay quietly in her bassinet, as if she knew her busy parents needed to focus on business. After a few months we employed a wonderful mother's helper, Kasia, and she looked after Michelle at home during the day while we concentrated fully on work outside the home.

By this time, Lilian was going to kindergarten.

Our immediate task was to look for another location. We found a cottage in Artarmon at 108 Reserve Road, close to where we lived and rented a room there where we could install a cutting table. We employed a cutter, Mrs Pemberton, and bought an electric cutting machine.

Our first big order also sold out quickly. Two days after we had delivered it, the buyer called Joseph in again. All the blouses had been sold.

We decided to open our production to more stores. Joseph selected the retailers to whom he would sell our blouses, and chose suburbs where good sales were likely, such as Newtown, Bankstown, Redfern and the North Shore. He never made an appointment to see retailers but simply arrived with the samples. That way, if he arrived after travelling an hour or two for an appointment and the buyer wasn't in, he could easily visit other stores in the area.

When our business was more established, the buyers eventually came to our showroom. Buyers from small stores often went from manufacturer to manufacturer to pick up the goods, as in those days the problem wasn't so much selling the product as producing it, since there was a shortage. There weren't many manufacturers.

Once the buyer got the first orders in their store, and they sold quickly, they would travel to the manufacturer. There was an influx of immigrants to Australia at that time, and they came with very little or no clothing. The first things they needed were mattresses and clothes.

As a result, the volume of work became so great that we needed even larger premises. We found a larger space to rent on the ground floor at 28 Palmer Street in Chatswood. At last, we were able to install a proper long cutting table and employ a first-class cutter, Mrs. Stellard, with skills that ranged beyond a small machine. We also found a highly-qualified book-keeper, Miss Brooks, to handle our invoices and book-keeping.

Kasia was still with us to look after Michelle. My mother-in-law would pick Lilian up after kindergarten and bring her home to Kasia.

I found these new work conditions better for designing, making patterns and marking them on the fabric. Joseph and Mrs Stellard would lay the fabric on the table and then Mrs Stellard would cut it.

The next step was finding a factory to sew our blouses. In Leichhardt there was a place run by a Greek husband-and-wife team, Barbara and Nick. They employed 30 skilled machinists, and we paid per piece. It wasn't long before we took up 100 per cent of their production. Barbara and Nick were so skilled that we preferred to work with them exclusively because they were perfectionists—like us.

Despite the fact that we were producing so many blouses, the profit margin was small. They sold at 21 shillings and sixpence. Since I have never been short of ideas, I knew exactly what we were going to do next. Frocks!

This was a time when women loved to wear smart tailored dresses. What could be more logical than adjusting the pattern to make the blouses a bit longer, adding a belt and producing a shirt-waist dress? We could even use the same patterns. We called the dress *the shirt that grew.* We were able to sell these for 26 shillings and sixpence.

Fashionable young working women loved them. We made them in plain colours, in checks and in all kinds of patterns. The new drip-dry fabrics meant that they only had to wash these dresses and hang them up. No more ironing! We also branched out into uniforms.

My next invention was the slack-suit. It was 1955. We began to buy the finest fabrics from Prestige since a good fabric makes all the difference to the look of a garment. I don't think the buyers had ever seen such attention to detail. The style of the slacks made women want to try them on immediately. 'They're beautifully cut,' the buyers would tell me. We sold them at three pounds and the full suits retailed from five to nine pounds. We continued selling them for years.

We always paid for the fabrics we required within seven days, to get discounts. We changed our name to Rainbow Productions, since by then we had stopped producing blouses.

In the mid-to-late 1950s, the manufacturer was king. Shopkeepers had to find the best sources for the merchandise they sold. The centre of textile manufacturing in Sydney was York Street in the city, where there were factories, offices and showrooms. We could see that it would be advantageous for us to move again, to where all the businesses were concentrated. We found new premises in a suitable building at 38 York Street, on the fourth floor. It had big windows letting in plenty of light. Mrs Stellard and Miss Brooks came with us, and we also employed another cutter, Mr Shields.

York Street brought us luck.

The agent from Prestige came to visit with some fabric samples in which I was very interested. I asked him about the composition of a particular fabric because I wanted to know whether it could be pleated, since I wanted to make pleated skirts in sunray and knife-pleat patterns. After I had selected the fabric, Joseph went to a couple of pleaters and they tested it on the basis of his research in the library as to the correct heat and pressure for pleating. After testing and work by a knowledgeable pleater, the pleats remained sharp after the skirt had been washed. Joseph sold 10,000 of these pleated skirts to Woolworths, in black, navy and bone (ivory). It was the largest order we had so far received.

Then Mrs Stellard left us. Her husband was an officer in the Navy and, since he was sent to work in different places, she wanted to go with him. Mr Shields brought in his daughter, Barbara, and we found she was an excellent cutter. I also took on an apprentice, Diana, a smart and gifted girl, and taught her how to cut fabrics both by hand and machine.

Unfortunately, as soon as she had learnt all the skills I could teach her, Diana gave notice and left immediately to work in the factory of one of our competitors. Today, you would call it head-hunting. I thought she was disloyal and was bitterly disappointed, since I imagined her giving away all our secrets. Even though I am a very stoic person and know the vagaries of life, I had trusted her implicitly to be more loyal and dedicated. Her defection even made me ill; I suffered pains in my chest.

However, Diana's aunt, Mrs. Martin, who occasionally worked for us, began to help me with the marking-in of the patterns, since there was too much work for me to handle alone. She proved to be a good worker and was extremely kind and loyal, staying with us for 17 years. Joseph simply asked her never to mention her niece to us.

She didn't. Then one day, over 40 years later, we were amazed when Diana walked into the office. She apologised for how she had treated us—and even began to cry. We had to calm her down. I took her out for a coffee and told her that I forgave her, without asking for explanations.

It was not easy running an expanding business while looking after our growing family. While we were still at the Chatswood premises, our son Henry was born.

C.
$9

C. Blazer style suit.
Rayon linen. $9 (90/-)

All Pants Suits in sizes
XSSW to SW

Buckingham's Department Store advertisement in *The Sun* newspaper, Sydney, 29 September 1966, for our pant suit.

A 1966 advertisement for our washable cotton parka,
which sold 6000 pieces at Woolworths.

Top: An order for our blouses from our South Australian agent, Laurie P. A. Lawrence.

Bottom: The Rainbow Productions swing tag was attached to every garment.

14

HENRY

◈

Henry was born at seven in the morning on Thursday 16 June 1960 in the King George V Hospital. I was extremely happy to have a son, and so was the whole family. Lilian and Michelle immediately loved their little brother.

Seven days later I was still in hospital. They were kind enough to let us have a private room for the circumcision, the Brit Milah, to which we invited 20 people. Joseph organised cakes and drinks, as is customary.

We knew that our son would carry the names of his two grandfathers, Joseph's father Chaim and, for his middle name, Schmuel, after my father. Before my father passed away, he asked that if we had a son, we should give Joseph the honour of naming him after his own father. So in English, his name is Henry Samuel Weinreich.

Joseph gave a short speech and lifted his glass to our guests. 'Let us drink: *L'chaim!* (to life!).'

We were very lucky with our new baby. Henry was a good boy, easy to manage and happy to sleep in the corner of our bedroom so that I could feed him every four hours. Joseph helped by changing his nappies.

At the hospital I had met a friendly nurse, Maria, who was originally from Vienna. She asked me whether I might need help at home with Henry who, even as a small baby, had a certain charm. I was delighted and grabbed her offer with both hands. She looked after him during the day and I had complete trust in her, so was able go back to work very quickly. She spoke to Henry in German, and even gave him a German pet name, Harzipinki. 'He appeals to my heart,' she told us. Maria stayed with us for four years.

Lilian and Michelle played constantly with Henry, who adored them. They fed him, bathed him, dressed him and lavished care and attention on him. As parents, we could not have wished for more.

Henry was full of life and energy. He was always running around and was a mischievous child. He was only 16 months old when we moved out of Artarmon to a new house; its full story I will tell later. It had a glass-fronted balcony on the first storey, with a gap between the glass and the floor. One day, Joseph got a terrible fright when he observed Henry trying to slide under the glass. He immediately grabbed him by the legs and pulled him back. As a result, we added protective wire to fill the gap.

When Henry was four, Michelle's birthday party was held in Dunbar House at Watsons Bay, an old mansion in a leafy park overlooking the sea. Henry was in his element, thoroughly enjoying the music, dancing and delicious food—and especially the big grassy space to run around in. It was impossible to hold him back.

As soon as we returned home, we found that he had a high fever. Our children's doctor, Dr Elizabeth Whealy, diagnosed a collapsed lung. We found our son the best medical help and were grateful for Maria's wonderful care of him afterwards, since she was a nurse. It took him several weeks to return to his energetic self.

After he recovered, we enrolled him in a Jewish kindergarten on Glenayr Avenue in Bondi. We thought it better if he attended for only half the day, so Joseph dropped him off every morning and picked him up to return home at lunchtime. On the way he gave him a treat: a nice, fresh slice of cheesecake from the nearby Mendy's Bakery, which our son loved.

One Sunday, Joseph took Henry back to the Watsons Bay park. Delighted, he played on the slippery-dips and swings. Then suddenly he overbalanced on one of the swings, falling face forwards so that the swing hit him on the back of the head, wounding him so badly that he bled. Joseph rushed him back to the doctor, where he was found to be fine. It was my husband who was by this time sweating and shaking.

Henry has always liked to be busy and to take over, so when we took him to the factory with us, he would answer the phone and even have a go at selling dresses to our customers. He loved packing parcels and closely observed how I worked with Mrs Martin to mark in the patterns. It was like a chess game.

Joseph bought his precious son some golden-coloured boxing gloves so that he could learn to box and always feel confident that he could defend himself. Joseph also enrolled him in a soccer academy. I would iron his blue T-shirt and white shorts, while Joseph would polish his boots.

Early on, when they returned from a soccer outing, I asked why Henry had stayed so clean. He had been playing right full-back, with very little contact with the other players unless the forwards from the opposing team ran towards him trying for a goal. Apparently, Henry simply let them through. Like all the other parents, Joseph was following the game by running up and down the sidelines, marking his son. He shouted: 'Henry, stop him! Don't let him through.'

The referee stopped the whole game, came up to Joseph and told him that he was teaching the boys to be good sportsmen. No matter what Joseph tried to do, Henry was just not interested in soccer. We soon learnt not to push our children into things they did not enjoy or in which they had no interest. Henry has many other talents and interests at which he excels. For example, he has always loved music and acting. Whenever musicals were put on by his school, he would play the lead. One successful part was as Tevye in *Fiddler on the Roof.* I made him a Shabbat black satin coat, just like the one his Grandfather, Joseph's father, wore in Poland. My husband taught Henry to put a *gartl* (belt) around his waist, and Henry changed into the coat onstage.

Mrs Darlington, the music teacher, directed the show, with her husband Ken playing piano. On the night of the performance the auditorium was packed, with standing room only. Henry's performance of the famous song was mesmerising. The audience went wild when he sang:

> *If I were a rich man*
> *Ya ha deedle deedle, bubba bubba deedle deedle dum*
> *All day long I'd biddy biddy bum …*
> *I'd build a big tall house with rooms by the dozen*
> *Right in the middle of the town*
> *A fine tin roof with real wooden floors below*
> *There would be one long staircase just going up*
> *And one even longer going down,*
> *And one more leading nowhere just for show …*

The other production in which Henry starred, that we remember well, was *Oliver*. He artfully played the villain, Fagin, who trained orphan boys for theft and other crimes. Henry became so immersed in the role that he was really convincing. He sang the show's big number:

I'm reviewing the situation:
Can a fellow be a villain all his life?
All the trials and tribulation!
Better settle down and get meself a wife.
And a wife would cook and sew for me,
And go for me and nag at me,
The fingers she will wag at me,
The money she will take from me.
A misery she'll make from me...
I think I'd better get it out again.
I'm reviewing the situation:
If you want to eat you've got to earn a bob
Is it such a humiliation
For a robber to perform an honest job?
So a job I'm getting, possibly,
I wonder who the boss'll be?
I wonder if he'll take to me
What bonuses he'll make for me?
I'll start at eight and finish late
At normal rate and all—but wait!
I think I'd better think it out again.

One night onstage, one of Henry's friends forgot his lines. Our son immediately leapt to his aid in such a way that the play continued without people even noticing. This is one of the hallmarks of Henry's character. He always understands, in an incredibly kind and thoughtful manner, when to assist people.

Henry's childhood seemed to pass very quickly. When the time came to prepare for his Bar Mitzvah, a very important event for every Jewish boy and his family, we started his Torah preparations early so that there would be no rush at the last moment.

At Henry's school, Moriah College, Joseph had become a great friend of the headmaster, Mr Harold Nagley. He taught Henry his *parsha* (portion), the extract from the Torah that our son would recite in front of the entire congregation. Seven chapters are recited, though it's not compulsory for the Bar Mitzvah boy to read all seven. But Henry recited them all—plus the *haftarah,* which is a series of selections from the books of Nevi'im (Prophets). A family member goes up to the *bimah* (podium*)* and the Bar Mitzvah boy points to the lines in the Torah he is reciting with a silver pointer, in Hebrew called a *yad.* The person then says a short blessing and the boy recites a chapter from the parchment scroll, in Hebrew.

Mr Nagley's method of teaching Henry his *parsha* was unorthodox. Instead of instructing him to start at the beginning, he began teaching him first from the last chapter. His theory was that a boy can master what he initially studies, but may struggle towards the end. Joseph took our son to Mr Nagley twice a week for lessons. Since Henry had already studied Hebrew at school, he took to this new task like a fish to water.

He also had to sing a traditional melody. After his stage appearances, this was no problem at all for him.

For the great day, we had suits made to measure for Henry and Joseph by the finest tailor in Sydney, Mr Gelb. We also made *kippahs* (skullcaps) for our male guests in silver lurex. Inside the bands they read: *Henry, Bar Mitzvah, 24 June 1973.* We invited all our family and friends to a Sunday reception to celebrate the occasion.

The day approached. Then suddenly something unexpected

happened. On 22 June, Henry lost his voice. We all panicked. Lilian and Michelle gave him gallons of hot milk with honey to drink and all sorts of throat lollies. But nothing seemed to help.

We approached Rabbi Silberman to ask his advice. He asked me to put our son on the line. After a while, Henry passed the phone back to me. The Rabbi told me he had blessed Henry and that everything would be all right on the day.

And it was. After a sleepless night, our son woke to find he could speak normally. He read the verses with great confidence. As he started one particular passage, he raised his eyes and looked straight at me, as if to say: 'This is for you, Mother.'

At the reception we really wanted music that reminded us of our Jewish lives before the War. We wanted to recreate the joyous atmosphere steeped in tradition that we remembered from our past. We included melodies from Poland and songs in Yiddish and Hebrew. We found an Italian singer, Joe Cole, and shared our records and tapes in Yiddish and Hebrew with him. He performed superbly on the day, in spite of never having sung Jewish songs before. After he performed at Henry's Bar Mitzvah, he was in demand for years after at Jewish weddings and other Bar Mitzvahs.

We hosted a reception for about 120 people at the B'nai B'rith, including all Henry's classmates and our family and friends. Lilian and Michelle were the MCs. They brought warmth and personality to their brother's great day.

I had designed my dress in purple velvet, and my girls were also beautifully dressed in a combination of silver lurex and brown crepe fabric. The details of their outfits were also co-ordinated with the décor and the *kippahs*.

Henry loved all of it. He danced, he sang and he spent time with all his friends. The speeches were short, but full of expression and meaning. Our family had a wonderful time, but we were conscious of our dear family members who were not with us. On occasions like this we believe that our forefathers and family members are watching over us.

While Henry may appear to be carefree on the surface, he has a deep soul which is difficult to even describe. His mind is razor sharp and his memory of all sorts of details reaches back many years. He has an innate deep intelligence and understanding. Like our girls, he attended the University of Sydney, completing his Arts-Law degree. Although he did this largely to please us, he now admits that it has been very useful to him in his everyday life, in a career which has been very versatile and taken him on different paths: from John Clemenger (advertising) in Sydney to Harvey Goldsmith (public relations) in London, then back to Sydney, where he set up a very successful retail branch of our business called Bridal and Formal. Then he moved to New York, where he joined Michelle in a bridal business for many years. He has been particularly successful in his relationships with the American media, and has appeared on *Style Court*, E! Entertainment Television, *Starlicious, Fashion Police* with Joan Rivers and *The View* with Barbara Walters, among others. On Australian television, he has worked with *Project Runway, Beauty and the Geek, Australia's Biggest Loser* and *Red Carpet from Hollywood*, to name just a few.

Henry believes in giving back to the industry, to people and needy projects, always with his brand of compassion and authenticity. He lives in Melbourne and his deep-seated feelings towards his Jewish identity and Israel resonate very strongly with us. He cares deeply about the world. He was an ambassador for the charity Make-a-Wish Foundation, an indication of his distinctive brand of humanity. He pours his heart into every task, whether personal or for work. It's 150 per cent or nothing.

Henry's devotion and unrivalled love for us and his whole family is palpable. Everything he does has layers of substance—yet he makes it look so effortless. Henry sees things in advance. He has always been light years ahead of us in his thoughts for our business, our care and our comfort. Sometimes we do not agree about the path he wants us to take, but after considering his persuasive ideas, we see the merit and his tremendous foresight.

Henry's love of his niece and nephew has no bounds. He has a special language and understanding with them, and from his weekly face-time calls to the clothing he selects for them, Henry knows exactly how to reach them with his unique brand of humour and intelligence. They are captivated by him, as he is with them.

For his sisters, I can only speak in hyperbole, as Henry would raise the universe for them. This bond between our children and grandchildren is the jewel of our existence. And it is Henry who has set the tempo so many times.

Henry, one year and four months old with Joseph teaching him boxing, 1962.

Maria, Henry's nurse and nanny from the beginning, with him,
Lilian and Michelle, June 1963.

Henry, Lilian and Michelle in Moriah College winter uniform, June 1964.

Aneta and Henry in Tiberias, Israel, December 1966.

Henry as Fagin in his school production of Oliver Twist, with his proud parents, 28 August 1970.

Henry's Bar Mitzvah, 24 June 1973, a very proud moment for the whole family. From left: Michelle, Henry, Aneta, Joseph and Lilian.

Henry's graduation from the University of Sydney, 28 February 1986, an unforgettable moment in the family's lives and a dream come true. From left: Joseph, Michelle, Henry, Franka and Aneta.

Henry with Michelle on the red carpet at the 55th Annual Primetime Emmy Awards, just before Henry's red carpet comments at the Shrine Auditorium, Los Angeles, 13 September 2003.

Henry, the Judge on the television program *Style Court*, New York City, 2004.
Photo: Courtesy of E! Entertainment Television.

Henry the Mentor in Foxtel's Project Runway Australia, 2008.
Photo: Gina Milicia, https://ginamilicia.com
Henry in the factory at 87 Foveaux Street, Surry Hills, 2012.
Photo: Sue Robbins.

The cover of the bridal book *Your Day, Your Way: The Essential Handbook for the 21st-Century Bride*, by Michelle, Henry and Sharon Naylor, Three Rivers Press, New York.

Cover: Penguin Random House LLC.

247

Henry with Max and Zoe, February 2018.

15

BUILDING
THE BUSINESS

◈

After working in York Street for some years, we decided to move to
new premises at 2 Lacey St, Surry Hills, on the fourth floor with big
windows that flooded the space with light.

It was a good move, since a lot of other textile businesses were also
moving to the area. Our staff liked it because it was close to Central
Station, making it easy for them to get to work. Joseph could park
in the garage on the ground floor of the building. In these larger
premises, we could fit more cutting tables and more shelves to store
fabric. We became so busy that we took on another cutter.

We started to produce a wide range of garments: blouses, dresses,
uniforms, skirts, slacks, trouser suits, culottes, tennis frocks, ladies'
bowls' uniforms, hooded parkas for women and children—and even
plastic hot-pants with matching hats and chokers.

My brother Martin at London Textiles showed me a lightweight fabric in psychedelic and solid colours and I designed some little sleeveless chiffon cocktail dresses. These were instantly successful—and no one else could copy them because our fabric was exclusive.

We decided to try something new, 'mail order', informing our customers about what we were producing by showing a sketch of the dress, stapling a sample of the fabric to it, then mailing it to them. But this wasn't as successful as we'd hoped, so we stopped doing it.

One sunny Monday morning when we arrived at work, we were astonished to find that someone had broken into our premises. Many garments had been stolen, and the thieves had also made a terrible mess by ripping out drawers from our desks and scattering the contents around.

We contacted the police and soon two detectives came to see us. They were cheerful and happily informed us that they had found and arrested a man selling our dresses in the local pub. They asked whether we would like the recovered garments. We said they should donate them to charity. Fortunately, the insurance company honoured their obligations and paid us back their full value.

We had our struggles building up our business, even though our employees supported us. Being well-organised and working hard for long hours has always contributed to our success. But some of our customers were very demanding. Says Joseph: 'We had a customer with eight shops who bought a lot of stuff from us: blouses, suits and skirts. One day I got into the factory late to find Aneta in tears. He had called and shouted at her over the phone because his order was two days late.'

So Joseph called him up and apologised, letting him know that everything would be delivered the next day, adding 'But if you ever speak to my wife again in such a manner, I'll personally come to your office and it won't be pleasant.'

The following day the customer called me, apologised, and said: 'I kiss your hand, Madam.' After that he became an even better customer.

At the same time Joseph and I were building our company, my brother Martin, a brilliant businessman, was selling fabrics at 127 York Street. He was also involved in other businesses, and wanted to pursue some of them. He saw how hard we were working and told us he wanted to help us. He said: 'I'm a first-class organiser and have a lot of business know-how. Joseph is a top salesman. It's the perfect combination.'

We thought this was very decent of him—and it was an opportunity to make our lives easier. Martin had a plan for a different business model: to buy fabrics from the mills, with whom he had strong connections, and sell them to manufacturers and retailers.

We sold everything at Lacey Street and put all the money earned into London Textiles. Martin continued to be involved. Our mother, with her expertise and experience, oversaw the whole operation. For a while it worked well.

After a few months, however, Martin told us that my other brother, Jim, as a medical student had no income, so Martin registered a new company, Paris Textiles, to enable Jim to support himself. This meant that London Textiles would be split in half.

From the time of this division, things didn't really work out. My mother gave priority to despatching Jim's goods, so relations between all of us suffered. Everyone tried to adjust to be fair to everyone else's interests, but to no avail.

After trying to make a go of it for a year, Joseph and I decided we couldn't continue in this way. We wanted to return to what we did best, and start all over again, manufacturing garments.

It was a difficult time: we were mentally and physically exhausted.

Starting from scratch once more meant that we had to look for new premises and new fabrics. I would have to make new patterns. Finally, after four months during which we looked for suitable premises, we found them at 101 Reservoir Street, Surry Hills. It wasn't the most glamorous place. To enter, you had to walk down five steps into a basement. There was a tiny window in front and another at the back. Joseph used to joke that he could recognise which customers were arriving by their shoes.

These conditions were very different from what we'd become accustomed to, but fortunately we were able to build the new business into a success. We employed a new cutter, Mr Kovacs, as well as two more cutters. They were both named Barbara, so we called them Big Barbara and Small Barbara. Mrs Martin, Vicky the clerk and Katherine, another cutter, completed the team.

By this time, we could afford to employ a pattern-maker. She made the originals using thick brown cardboard. Patterns were usually made from thinner paper but I wanted ours to last longer. The first pattern for the dresses was usually made in size 12 for that season's collection; then we cut a few more in that size, which became our selling samples. Once we received orders from the samples, the pattern-maker had to 'grade' the patterns to whatever sizes were required.

When we began in business, the old method of using cardboard patterns was cumbersome. We traced around the patterns with white chalk, directly on to the fabric. Then we knew how long the marker should be; the layer of fabric that had the chalk on it became the marker. We then measured the length of the marker so that we knew how far along the cutting table to lay the fabric. Then we layered the rest of the fabric according to the number of orders we received. We placed the single layer of fabric marked in white chalk on the top of the pile and began to cut with the upright Singer machine.

We soon switched to a new and much more time-efficient process. With this new method, the cardboard patterns were traced with a special pen on to what was then called marking-in paper, and the style number, yardages and sizes were noted on each end of the marker, together with a sketch. Two sizes could fit economically on the paper like a jigsaw puzzle, so as not to waste any fabric. I was by now an expert at marking-in. I taught Mrs Martin how to mark economically on paper, and Katherine especially was fascinated by how I could save three or more inches on a marker. A devout Roman Catholic, she called me 'The Pope' because I could produce miracles and save lots of fabric.

We bought a printing machine for the markers, which could print up to five metres at a time. Joseph fed these markers into the printing machine. These then became our original copies and our library for future orders. This meant we didn't need to mark anything in again if we needed that particular style. We only had to print it again.

The next step was to place plain paper directly on to the cutting table. Step two was to lay up the fabric. Step three was to place the marking-in paper on top of the fabric layers. Finally heavy weights were placed on top of the paper so that it wouldn't move while being cut with an upright electrical machine. This machine, with its knife-like blades, operated so fast you could barely see the blades move. Upon completion, the segments were bundled and tied with some remnant strips of fabric and Nick and Barbara, our contractors, came to pick up the cut work.

We involved the children in the business as much as possible, and they learned not only about business, but about life. They all mastered the process I've just described, and also how to answer phones, take orders from customers, process cutting sheets, and do other necessary tasks, such as marketing and book-keeping. Their school holidays were mostly spent training at the factory.

The printing procedure was revolutionised when a New York company came up with a copying machine similar to a huge photocopier to speed up the printing of the markers. This meant the copying could be completed in minutes. A company called Henmark imported this new machine for us. They also supplied us with the marking-in and printing paper, which came in large, heavy rolls.

Joseph's familiarity with printing newspapers in Kazakhstan helped him to understand the workings of the printer even though the machines had improved tremendously. He was also adept at knowing how to handle the large rolls of paper correctly.

Where previously it had taken a few hours every day to produce the markers, the process now took only minutes—though, for that machine, ammonia was required and it had a very powerful and unhealthy odour, so the printing machine was in a room on its own, and Joseph was the only person in it.

In order to safeguard our employees from the side effects of the ammonia, we always arrived at the factory before anyone else so he could do the printing. In the evening after the day's work when everyone had left, he would print again to prepare for the following day's production.

One morning my husband went to park the car, leaving me on my own on the premises. I was filling the kettle kept on a bench in the middle of the room to make tea, when I heard voices. I went to investigate and caught two men stealing our dresses.

I was petrified. What if one or both of them attacked me? I screamed: 'Joseph, come over—there are some people here!'

The men grabbed as many dresses as they could and ran out. As soon as they left, I locked the door. I was shaking. How could they get away with such an act in broad daylight?

Because of this incident and because we also outgrew this premises, we needed a new space once again. The space simply wasn't big enough. I remember Joseph saying: 'Even a sardine would feel claustrophobic here.' He loves the dry Aussie sense of humour.

We started to look in earnest for a bigger place, with Joseph literally going from building to building. This time we found wonderful new premises at 87-89 Foveaux Street, Surry Hills, on the first floor. Finally, we could work entirely in natural light.

Women's sportswear is smart, keenly priced

VERSATILITY and good fit are the keynotes in a range of women's sportswear offered by an Australian manufacturer, Rainbow of Sydney.

The garments are well made and moderately priced but faithfully interpret high fashion for the budget-conscious woman.

With the recent development of a Crimplene material suited to men's wear, the company has also introduced a range of men's trousers and jackets. In both ranges, the emphasis is on popular, modern styling.

One of the main fabrics used in women's sportswear is an Australian-made filament polyester double knit jersey which is quick drying, non-iron and, if required, permanently pressed.

Suitable for summer or winter, it is in 10 colours or can be dyed to any shade required by a customer.

The fabric is used in two basic lines — well-cut slacks and a front-buttoning midi skirt — and in high fashion garments such as knickerbockers, knee length gaucho pants with wide legs, and hot pants without tops featuring side lacing on the legs.

Another attractive, easy care fabric, polyester viscose jersey, is made into skirts, gaucho one piece suits with slide fastener fronts and midi dresses with front slide fasteners opening from the hem.

The midi dresses combine plain coloured skirts with bodices in a print which emphasises the skirt colour.

Another range of midi dresses is in lightweight terylene polyester. Cool and with the "cling" required by current fashion, this fabric will

● *A Rainbow midi skirt and gaucho, available in polyster/viscose double knit jersey or filament polyester double knit jersey.*

dry outside in only 10 minutes and needs no ironing.

It is also used in pant suits and one piece gaucho suits.

The new range for men comprises trousers in two hipster styles and a conventional style and matching "soft look" jackets with short sleeves for summer and long sleeves for winter. They are washable, non-iron and permanently pressed. The trousers and jackets can be bought and worn separately or together.

INQUIRIES: Rainbow of Sydney, 111 Reservoir Street, Surry Hills, New South Wales, 2010 Australia. (Agents wanted).

1971 article from trade publication *Austral News* with Lilian (left) in Rainbow's 'midi skirt' and Michelle (right) in our 'goucho pants' (also called culottes).

256

'Dream Makers', *Ita* **magazine, October 1992 (page one of four).**
Courtesy Ita Buttrose.

DREAM MAKERS

Australia offered Aneta and Joseph Weinreich the chance to fulfil their dreams. Now they work to make the dreams of others come true

BY VICKI MACKENZIE   PHOTOGRAPHY BY ANDREW FURLONG

ANETA and Joseph Weinreich are hawkers of happiness, dealers of dreams. White, frothy dreams covered in pearls and sequins, lace and bows. You find them spinning their fantasies in a most unlikely place: a small factory in downtown Sydney.

Aneta and Joseph are neither magicians nor jungle analysts but makers of wedding dresses — beautiful, snowy-white creations in hundreds of styles. They have been in business 25 years and reckon they have developed the art of wedding dress design to perfection.

"To us, making a dress is like painting a picture or composing a song. They are wonderful creations that, even after all this time, still give us an enormous buzz," they say, beaming with pleasure.

All of this would be quite unremarkable, saccharine even, were it not for the world they came from. A world so startlingly different from the one they have made that you wonder how they have done it.

Aneta and Joseph lived through the nightmare of the Holocaust. They left Poland for Australia some 40 years ago. With nothing but a bagful of painful memories and an unquenchable zest for life, they began building their dream.

Walk into their factory and you enter a fairytale world. Row upon row of billowing white dresses, boxes of trims and accessories, patterns and, around the walls, their proudest collection of all: pictures drawn by their children from the age of two upwards.

Stacked away in a cupboard are other treasures — the clothes Aneta made for their school plays. This, you soon learn, is very ▶

DEALERS IN DREAMS: ANETA, JOSEPH AND HENRY WEINREICH.

'Dream Makers', *Ita* magazine, October 1992 (page two of four).
Courtesy Ita Buttrose.

much a family story. To prove the point, son Henry, with as much chutzpah as his parents, has had the novel idea of opening a warehouse, selling his parents' wares at factory prices. They're inexpensive and he figures this will keep them on top of the recession, keeping production up, prices down, providing instant feedback to Mum and Dad on what the customer wants. Business is booming.

Aneta, alert and naturally reserved, looks you in the eye when she says: "Australia has given us the tranquility to create the life we wanted and to give our children the opportunities we never had. We are very grateful."

Joseph adds: "We wanted to build a life surrounded by happiness and I think we have managed that. A girl we hired recently left after a few weeks saying she couldn't stand the fact that there was no 'aggro' in the factory. She thought it unnatural. Most of our staff stay with us for years."

They don't like to talk about the past. They don't want to breed hatred. "Let us just say that my wife went through the German horror and I went through the Russian one," says Joseph. But during the interview snippets of that nightmare come out.

Aneta escaped the gas chamber because her mother altered her coat to make her look older and bigger than she really was. She hid in a secret compartment in the Krackow ghetto and then in the forests, always on the run with her mother. She was the only one among her friends who survived.

As for Joseph, he was shipped to a Russian concentration camp with 600,000 other Jews, faced near starvation, escaped, and spent the rest of the war hiding out in a cow shed in southern Russia. Before his father was murdered in Auschwitz he sent Joseph a letter saying he should do two things: learn English and go to Australia. Joseph took him at his word.

Theirs is the classic rags to riches tale. And a romantic one. Joseph

❝YES, WE HAVE DONE WELL. WE WORK EXTREMELY HARD AND HAVE NEVER BEEN GREEDY. SUCCESS TO US IS THAT WE ARE DOING WHAT WE LOVE❞

arrived in Australia in 1947 with the equivalent of $6 in his pocket. His one word of English was "darling." He had heard a Polish uncle call his Australian wife that and for years thought it was a girl's name.

That same uncle offered him a job in his mattress factory. Joseph had ambitions of becoming a doctor but he accepted the job as he needed to make money. Six years later he met Aneta.

"It's a family joke that we met over a mattress, the one I was delivering to her house. We were born only 10km apart in Poland but it had taken until then for us to meet, in a new country thousands of miles away. For me, it was love at first sight. I knew this was the girl I was going to marry."

"For me it took three weeks longer," says Aneta. Making quick decisions, she says, has been the hallmark of all their success. "That's the way we do our business. We make up our minds and do it." The formula

has worked for them personally as well. "We're together 24 hours a day without quarrelling."

Their beginnings were small but audacious. Happy but broke, they decided to try their hand at the rag trade. "I went to Farmers (now Grace Bros) and looked at the blouses they had in stock. There was nothing but a sea of white and very conventional styles. I thought, 'I can do better than that,' and went home and started designing blouses in all the colours I could find," says Aneta.

Joseph chips in: "I took the door off its hinges, put it on the bed and used it as a cutting board. Then, because we did not have a sewing machine, we took them all to a dressmaker. When she had finished, we took our six blouses to the buyer at Farmer's.

"She looked at them and said they were beautiful and gave us an order for 156 more! When she asked what was the company's name I told her honestly we didn't have one. The buyer thought for a minute and said we should call ourselves Rainbow because of all the colours of our blouses. That's how we started."

Joseph put the door back on its hinges and, with an overdraft, took a factory in the Sydney suburb of Chatswood and employed a proper cutter and sewer. They never doubted they would succeed, and they were right.

Their next order from Farmer's was for a 1000 blouses. Aneta moved on to designing and made the first Australian slack suits. "New ideas excite me. We've never stood still."

As their business grew, so did their family. They had two girls and a boy and brought them to the factory with their prams and playpens. "They grew up in the business and they're all still very involved," says Aneta.

One daughter, Michelle, a political scientist based in New York, scours shops and fashion parades for the latest trends in wedding dresses to send her parents. She also shops ▶

'Dream Makers', *Ita* magazine, October 1992 (page three of four).
Courtesy Ita Buttrose.

DREAM MAKERS

for accessories. The other daughter, Lilian, an architect in Los Angeles, advises on colour co-ordination.

The next turning point in the story came 25 years ago when Joseph and Aneta wondered what they could do next. This made them wonder about the most beautiful thing in women's fashion — and the answer they came up with was the wedding dress. They found their true niche. Today Aneta and Joseph are doyens of the business, supplying the most prestigious bridal boutiques around Australia.

"Yes, we have done well," says Joseph. "Our business has grown slowly but steadily. We took risks with ideas but never with money." When pressed on just how successful he and Aneta have been, he remains reticent. "We are comfortable but not what I would call rich. To be honest, we both came from extremely wealthy families in Poland, but lost it all. Everything.

"Now, success to us is that we are doing what we love. My greatest joy was seeing my three children graduate from Sydney University. When I came to Australia I would pass the university on the bus and pray that if I had children they could all go there."

They say their success is due to a simple policy. "We work extremely hard and have never been greedy. Our prices are very competitive but our garments are far from cheap. We make sure the fabric and the finish are top quality." They travel the world buying the duchess satin, mulberry silk, Thai silk, crystal organza, chiffon and taffeta they need. "It took us five years just to get the right white."

Aneta still has the nose for the best-selling styles and says she knows intuitively how many dresses to cut each month. She's also a stickler for fit, remaking every pattern until she gets it right.

But a formula of top quality dresses at low prices is dangerous in the time of recession. It demands high production all the time. A fact not

always possible with people generally spending less. That's when their son, Henry, 31, came up with his Bride and Formal Warehouse. The move has delighted and astonished them.

"We would never have thought of going into retail ourselves. Our thing has always been design and manufacture. When Henry told us his plan we were thrilled. 'Great, another new idea,' we said."

Henry is sure he is on to a winner. "Where else can you get a beautiful wedding dress for $200, $800 or even $1000?" he asks. He's right. They are bargains. Similar dresses in central Sydney cost twice as much for exactly

> ❝COMING INTO THE FAMILY
> BUSINESS WAS MY OWN CHOICE.
> I WOULD NEVER HAVE DONE
> IT HAD MY PARENTS FORCED
> ME. THEY GAVE US FREEDOM❞

the same quality. But Henry is offering more than just dresses.

"We're running a one-stop wedding shop, providing the bride's dress, veil, shoes, hoops, jewellery, flowers and stationery, the bridesmaids' outfits and wedding insurance. We even do Mob and Mog." What? "They are the trade's name for Mother of the Bride and Mother of the Groom. The reaction has been unbelievable."

Henry is a ball of energy, returning to the family firm after graduating in law and then venturing into marketing and promotion in Sydney then in London and Los Angeles. "Coming into the family business was my own choice. I would never have done it had my parents forced me. But they gave all us children absolute freedom to do whatever we wanted.

"I broke the umbilical cord, then thought, 'Who else has a wonderful, family business all set up for them?' Of course, I knew it thoroughly,

having been in it all my life. But my parents are terrific. They have backed me to the hilt."

In return he is offering Aneta and Joseph a fresh, but starkly realistic view of the business climate. "The party's over," he says. "I believe our business is a microcosm of what's going on in the whole country. The entire garment industry has a big question mark over it.

"People generally are buying less and we are all threatened by the cut in tariffs. If those cheap wedding dresses from Asia have their prices slashed, it could be disastrous. There are many losers in this recession but we're not going to be one of them."

Henry is prepared to put himself out. The Bride and Formal Warehouse is open six days a week and Henry has moved house to be within 10 minutes of the shop. He is prepared to open at 3am if necessary. He has also stuck a large sign on his window that reads: "Yes, Yes, Yes. We have change!" It's a service for frustrated motorists looking for dollar coins to feed the parking meters. "It's a real rort, they charge a dollar for just 20 minutes. I'm not having my customers inconvenienced like that!"

Henry's work ethic is "never say no." "The other day some men came in and wanted to hire a bridegroom's outfit for someone who lived some distance away. I said, 'No problem.' Then they said he lived a really long way away and might not be able to get the suit back in time. Finally they told me the groom was in a detention centre. I still said, 'No problem.' Then the bride came in and wanted a dress that wouldn't show her tattoos. That was no problem either.

"My theory is that your wedding is a big event in your life. It's emotional and people must have what they want. My policy is to do everything I can to make people happy."

It's a notion he must have picked up from his parents. ∎

'Dream Makers', *Ita* magazine, October 1992 (page four of four).
Courtesy Ita Buttrose.

Top: The original chiffon sleeveless cocktail dresses.
Bottom: The Rainbow sew-in label used inside the solid blue chiffon cocktail dress. Photos: Jamie Levine Photography, New York.

**Please add to the caption: Aneta in the factory with the outline
of a pattern on a marker and with camera man Kevin May.**
Copyright and photos: Compass, ABC-TV.

16

THE CHILDREN GROW UP

◈

Even before our children were born, there was an unspoken agreement between me and Joseph that if we could have children, we wanted to give them what we hadn't experienced ourselves: an uninterrupted childhood. We wanted to show them an untainted world and teach them to be kind and tolerant. We wanted them to appreciate family and love their sisters and brothers, understanding and embracing their identity. We wanted them to go out into the world without fear.

Both Joseph and I had beautiful early childhoods with our families. Then we were suddenly plunged into a dark and unforgiving place which no child should endure.

From the time our three beloved children were born, Lilian, Michelle and Henry have given us an enormous amount of happiness and pride. Raising children takes a tremendous amount of care, patience and love. We had plenty to give our children.

Each of them has a different personality and character. As parents, we focused on giving them every opportunity in any field they chose. If we saw they had even a trace of talent or interest in a subject, we pursued it. We wanted them to enjoy the childhood activities and opportunities for learning we were not privileged to experience ourselves. We felt an urgency within us to provide lessons we could never even have dreamed of growing up in Poland.

All three took piano lessons from first class teachers, beginning with Mrs Muir, whose husband was a World War I Anzac (a member of the Australian and New Zealand Army Corps, 1914-18) who had survived Gallipoli in what is today Turkey. Michelle remembers his medals displayed in the front hall of their house. Then there was Mrs Kopke, followed by Ms Ryan in Bondi. Michelle and Henry took violin lessons, and Lilian and Michelle went to the dance studio run by Mr and Mrs Rudas in the Haymarket. They learned tap-dancing there as well as contemporary dance with teacher Ronne Arnold and Henry did acrobatics. The girls then went to formal ballet classes with the twin sisters, Joan and Monica Halliday.

Joseph, a dedicated father, took them to all their lessons so I could have a rest. Some of the stories they told afterwards were amusing and we laugh about them even now. During the class breaks at Rudas', Joseph brought them lunch, usually consisting of thick slices of challah and kosher wurst (salami) bought at the deli in Sydney that a lot of Europeans patronised: Cyril's in the Haymarket. After wolfing these down with a Coca-Cola or a Fanta from the red metal dispenser, they were sometimes so full that it was difficult to return to the physical activity required for the rest of the classes.

We also gave them the opportunity to learn drawing and painting. From a very young age Lilian demonstrated artistic talent. We were lucky to find a Polish artist who had taught art at the celebrated

Jagiellonian University in Kraków, Professor Klimek. When Lilian was 14 years old, we arranged private tuition with Polish born Professor Maximilian Feuerring in his Woollahra studio. Feuerring was considered to be one of Australia's key figures in the post World War II émigré modern art movement. He did not teach children but made an exception for Lilian whom he considered a prodigy. Lilian chose Feuerring as the subject in her Bachelor of Fine Arts Honours thesis at Sydney University. Feuerring considered architecture as the discipline that combines all the arts, which possibly influenced Lilian's later career path.

As a result of studying with these gifted teachers, Lilian has created more than 100 paintings. We display her large works in our home, where they greet us every day and constantly remind us of her enormous talent.

After Michelle was discovered to have a strong singing voice as a mezzo-soprano, we enrolled her with Elizabeth Todd OAM[1] in classes at the Sydney Conservatorium of Music. Michelle relished those lessons overlooking the Royal Botanic Gardens. She sometimes sang at Brit Ivrit Olamit, the Hebrew-Speaking Association, at a time when Mrs Siderowitz was its leader.

The children were also attending Moriah College, so naturally we kept all the Jewish holidays, according to tradition. Everyone dressed well for our visits to the South Head Synagogue usually in something new for Rosh Hashanah, Jewish New Year. This was a tradition in Joseph's home city of Chrzanów.

In summer we took the children to the beach, just like all Aussie

---

1   The Order of Australia is an order of chivalry established on 14 February 1975 by Queen Elizabeth II, Queen of Australia, to recognise Australian citizens and other persons for achievement or meritorious service.

kids. They loved these outings to Balmoral Beach so much that they would sing in the car along the way: *Daddy is a good ol' boy...*

To further broaden their horizons and give them an appreciation of the beauty of Australia and the wider world, we took them on trips around our wonderful country. This was also a learning experience for me and Joseph, because we had to adopt and adapt to Australian customs and its way of life. We started with places that were easily accessible, such as Katoomba (Leura Motel) and Blackheath (Karaweera Hotel) in the Blue Mountains. One especially enjoyable trip was to Canberra, the capital of Australia.

In December 1969 we took them to Kosciuszko in the Snowy Mountains, where we stayed in a chalet, Chez Jean, overlooking the sweep of the mountains. The air was crisp and clear and we had a magnificent holiday. We took long walks, went boating on the lake and the children tried riding horses, a novelty for city kids. Once we were caught in a storm in the middle of the lake. It was ferocious, and we were glad to get safely back to the shore.

From the age of six, the children went with us on overseas trips. We wanted them to understand that the world is open and that there are no borders.

We also took them to social events, driving to the wedding of our agent Mr Polonski's son. During our journey to Melbourne, we stopped to refresh ourselves in a coffee shop near the statue of the Dog on the Tucker Box at Gundagai. The story goes that when his bullocky master went to get help after becoming bogged, he left the dog to guard his swag—but never returned. The faithful dog continued to wait and wait.

As the children continued with their schoolwork and other lessons, we always tried to protect them from even the smallest discomfort, such as a disagreement with a friend, or a well-loved teacher leaving the school. Sometimes I reflect that maybe we protected them too much as a direct reaction to being so interconnected with our own families and being vulnerable during the War, as children ourselves, to life's dark side. But now I see how well they have navigated their own lives. Joseph and I are satisfied that the years of love and affection we poured into our children was the only way to do it. We feel we would still take this path in bringing up children.

Family picture in front of the car on the way to the synagogue in new clothes for Rosh Hashanah (Jewish New Year) 1966.

Opposite page:
Top: Michelle and Henry, piano practice, May 1966.
Bottom: The Snowy River, Kosciuszko, 1965.
From left: Michelle, Henry, Aneta and Lilian.

269

On the lake at Kosciuszko, December 1969.
From left: Joseph, Michelle, Lilian and Henry.

Travelling to Kosciuszko, January 1970,
with Henry holding Bijou, our pet dog.

271

17

MY MOTHER
AFTER THE WAR

❖

The memory of my remarkable mother, Franka Baral, is deeply entrenched in my being and my life. After the War it always amazed me that she could cope with normal, everyday life when she had lost her parents, four sisters and two brothers and their families. She never, ever spoke about this tragedy to my brothers or me—or to anyone else. She was adamant about this: no one would have to contend with the after-effects as she did. We knew by her silence and attitude that we dare not approach this bitter part of her life.

I don't know any other woman who, during the Holocaust, personally looked after and saved the lives of six children. She was the ultimate survivor, with depth of character, tremendous instincts and the wisdom that comes only from facing up to life's most horrific and challenging experiences. During the War she showed she had the courage to take enormous risks every day.

She was also a lightning-fast thinker, seeing at once what needed to be done in even the most dangerous situations, and then taking decisive action. Remember how in Hungary she invited the Nazi soldiers into Ilonka's parents' farmhouse and made them tea, while pretending that she didn't speak German? And how she greeted the police as saviours after we had all spent the night in the farmhouse, but been betrayed?

Her husband Samek's early death of lung cancer at 52, on 16 March 1957, completely devastated her. I'm sure she thought often of the sophisticated man-of-the-world whom she had married, and of her charmed life with him in pre-War Kraków. She just couldn't bear to speak of that life with him that had been so completely destroyed. After his death, she threw herself into the textile business, working side-by-side with my brother Martin. She was shown great respect by both employees and clients, because she was a very good businesswoman. This seemed to come naturally. When a particular customer walked into the showroom one day, she not only recognised him but could remember the colour of the fabrics he had ordered—a year before.

My mother Franka was determined to be independent. Without letting us know, she took driving lessons, only revealing this fact when she had obtained her licence. Lilian, who had been staying with her most weekends, had accompanied her grandmother both to her lessons and to the driving test, and was the only one who knew. It was their secret.

When we found out that she had passed her test, my mother told us she wanted to buy a car. Joseph took her to the Truscott showroom on Parramatta Road, where she chose a red Celica. She didn't drive to work in York Street because there was no parking nearby. But on Saturday mornings she did the rounds of the family and came to see us so we could have lunch together at home. We would see her coming down the street in her bright red car.

Because of the loss of her husband, our beloved father, we wanted to devote as much time to her as possible, shielding and protecting her to make her life more bearable. In summer on Shabbat, Joseph would take us to the beach at Nielsen Park before he went to the Synagogue. We spoke for hours about everything, usually about the children and the business—anything except the War years. In winter, if the weather was warm enough, we would picnic under the same tree in the park at Vaucluse House, opposite our own house.

Joseph was completely devoted to my mother. On every drive to Katoomba and every holiday, he spent hours with her, respected and looked after her—even better than other family members. I have never seen this type of loyalty and understanding from any other son-in-law to a mother-in-law—and my mother was not easy to please.

I admired the way she would walk in good weather from Double Bay to her workplace in York Street in the city, summer and winter. This is quite a long way: four kilometres, but she believed in keeping fit through exercise. She also regularly did yoga.

Joseph had the key to her apartment, and one day on a visit he arrived to find her standing on her head, legs in the air, doing the yoga headstand pose. She did not want to be interrupted, so my husband lay on the floor in order to tell her why he had come.

One day when it was raining, she went to a stop in New South Head Road to wait for a bus to take her into the city. The pavement was slippery and she fell over and hurt her arm. But it took more than this to keep her from work. She took the bus anyway.

We were worried about her and called our doctor, Dr Samuel Friedman. He examined her and said we needed a specialist, since she had broken bones. We took her immediately to a specialist in

Randwick. Dr Roden was a high-ranking surgeon who had worked in Vietnam, and had a lot of experience with such injuries. Her arm was broken and she needed an operation.

We took her to the hospital in Kogarah where Dr Roden operated. After successful surgery, she stayed on there for a few days. When she was about to be released, Joseph went to pick her up and the doctor called him in to show how well the arm was healing. He was in the middle of changing the dressings.

But what my husband saw, to his horror, was my mother's arm with the bone protruding and a good deal of blood. He took one look—and fainted.

Dr Roden took this in his stride. 'Go and lie down,' he said, 'while I finish bandaging your mother-in-law. And don't conk out on me. As soon as I'm finished here I'll come and look after you.'

That was a turning point in my mother's life. As soon as I took her home, I saw she could not manage on her own and would need a full-time carer. We took on Krysia Głuszuk, a Polish woman who was kind and efficient and who could talk to my mother in her native language. She was with her for about a year. Before she returned to Poland, Krysia introduced me to another Polish lady, also called Krysia, who then became my mother's carer.

My mother yearned to go back to work. Some mornings we gave her a lift, but on others Krysia accompanied her on the bus, and then took her home around lunchtime.

By this time my girls were living in New York and Jim was also living and working there. He suggested that Joseph should bring our mother over for a visit, since I would be there on business and to see the girls. But my husband observed that my mother was not particularly excited about the prospect of the journey. On the plane, he directed her to the bathroom and then wondered why she was taking so long to return. When he went to investigate he found her completely disorientated. She asked Joseph what she was supposed to be looking for—then told him not to worry, she would find it. Instead of sleeping through the night, she spent hours rummaging in her handbag.

When Joseph arrived at Jim's apartment where Lilian, Michelle and I were waiting to welcome her, she seemed listless, with little interest in seeing the sights of the city or even going shopping. And she looked desperately unhappy.

To cheer her up, I told her that a dear friend of hers from Kraków, Mrs Edzia Kamińska, my Auntie Ela's sister-in-law, would visit the following day. But when her friend arrived, my mother did not even greet her in the normal way, and seemed scarcely to know who she was. She hardly exchanged one word with her.

I was shocked. It was clear to me that my mother, with her razor-sharp memory, who was friendly to people that she knew well, was not the person she had been. To see her losing interest in life and failing to remember what had happened to her was heart-breaking for all of us. Lilian, Michelle and Henry, who had spent years with her, knew her idiosyncrasies and sayings like: 'You know me not from yesterday.' (You know how I am as a person). They understood her reactions, and Henry in particular shared a special language with her. They had lived in her apartment over the years when they wanted peace and quiet while studying for exams. They were particularly upset at what was happening.

When Joseph and I returned to Sydney with my mother, we stopped over in Hawaii for a few days. This seemed to do her a lot of good, both physically and mentally. Relaxing beside the hotel swimming pool, listening to soothing local music and eating delicious food seemed to relax her.

Her disorientation did not improve. One morning Krysia rang us in a panic. Returning to her bedroom from the bathroom, my mother had fallen and was unable to get up. Dr Friedman came at once, and immediately ordered an ambulance. In Emergency at St Vincent's Hospital, Mother was told she had broken her hip. This was a disaster, since the doctors thought she was too old to have a replacement. Instead, a pin was inserted.

Joseph and I looked after my mother through this catastrophe with all our strength and devotion. I advertised in the daily paper in Wollongong, where a lot of Polish people had settled, to find another carer. The second Krysia returned to Poland after looking after my mother so well. Fortunately we found another exceptional person, Wanda Pruchnicki, who lived with my mother for five days a week. For the other two days, we employed another carer, Elizabeth Nowakowska, with whom we are still in contact. Wanda has now passed away.

While my mother was recovering, she was transferred to Wolper Hospital for a course of rehabilitation, including physiotherapy. We hoped this would help her walk properly again. But unfortunately, it didn't.

I wanted her to see a doctor specialising in dementia, and Dr Friedman recommended Professor Henry Brodaty as the top man in the field. When Joseph rang him, he said he didn't do consultations as his work was only in research.

But Joseph continued to pursue him. Now I will go back in time to give a little history: In the early 1950s, a friend by the name of David Knobloch told my husband about a family, a husband, wife and small boy, who had just arrived from Germany and were living in a basement in Cremorne. Apparently they were very unhappy. Joseph went to see them—even though it was the middle of Rosh

Hashanah. He found them all in tears. Joseph brought them food, then suggested where they could find jobs and a better place to live. He was able to find a kindergarten class for the boy, and a job in his cousin Maurice Weitz's knitting factory for the man, where he could be trained to use the machines. The man was intelligent and eager to learn, and worked long hours.

His name was Mr Brodaty—and his little son was named Henry.

In time Mr Brodaty left the factory to open up his own business, which did well. Meanwhile Henry excelled at his studies, first at school and then at university. When his father became sick and began to lose his memory, he changed his speciality so that he could find out more about dementia. That became his field of expertise.

Instead of going to the recommended colleague, Joseph asked Professor Henry Brodaty to call his mother. 'Tell her Joseph Weinreich needs her son's expertise to help his mother-in-law,' he said. Ten minutes later, a call came from the Professor: 'I'll do anything you ask,' he said.

Our problem then was that I knew my mother would never agree to go to any doctor except Dr Friedman for a check-up. So I suggested a plan to Professor Brodaty: we would meet the following Saturday night when we were taking my mother to dinner at the Hakoah Club. I would introduce him by telling her: 'Professor Brodaty is a friend of Jim's, and he's just arrived from New York, where they met.' Her dementia was still mild at this point, and anything connected to her favourite youngest child was always trusted and therefore met with no resistance.

After dinner, the doctor took my husband aside and told him that my mother was suffering the first symptoms of Alzheimer's Disease. She frequently couldn't answer his questions, or her answers were incorrect. He told Joseph that he was part of a team looking for a cure, with generous government funding. Meanwhile, he would prescribe medication for my mother, even though it was certain that the illness would continue to incapacitate her. Each person experienced it in a different way, so he couldn't tell us whether further decline would be slow or fast.

Professor Brodaty emphasised the importance of her carers speaking her native Polish, because skills in languages acquired later often disappeared. We were able to reassure him that we had already dealt with that.

I rang my brothers—but neither wanted to believe the diagnosis. They were unable to accept my mother's mental decline right until the end. They were in denial; it hurt them too much.

This put tremendous pressure on me. Much as I would have liked it to be otherwise, I knew my mother's condition could only get worse and felt the heaviness of this responsibility. Unfortunately everyone went in a different direction in what they thought would be best for Franka.

One day I found out that the second Krysia had been replaced with a live-in Filipino carer, since Krysia was returning to Poland. Of course, she and my mother could not communicate well. An additional problem was that my mother did not like the strange spices in the food this new carer cooked. My mother was mostly vegetarian and always chose her food carefully: fresh vegetables, grapefruit, wheatgerm and polenta.

Her health deteriorated very rapidly. One Friday afternoon when I visited her, I found her in bad shape, crying. 'Help me! Take me away from here,' she begged.

I called Dr Friedman. 'Replace the Filipino lady—or your mother will die,' he advised. I told my brother that we were taking our mother into our home at Olola Avenue. There, in the middle of the night, she fell out of bed. When we called the ambulance they refused to take her to hospital, since nothing had been broken. They simply put her back in her own bed.

After Mother had stayed with us for a few days, I re-employed our Polish carers. Professor Brodaty prescribed stronger medication, to calm her down. He told us frankly that this whole episode had set her back, and that it was time for us to consider putting her into a Montefiore Home, a Jewish old age home.

We organised this even though I felt ripped apart at even the thought of having to place my mother there. She entered the Montefiore Home in Hunter's Hill in 1995, along with our two carers on eight-hour shifts. I bought her a wheelchair, made to measure for her comfort, and a chair for the shower, and visited her during the week after work. Joseph went to the Montefiore Home during the day. My mother by this stage had progressed deeply into the disease. For instance, she called one of the nurses Guscia, thinking she was the manager of one of the hotels we used to stay in at Zakopane.

The children were deeply distressed when my mother moved to Montefiore. Lilian, then in New York, wanted to remember her as a young and vibrant grandmother. It would have been too upsetting for her to see my mother in this condition.

When Michelle and her husband Peter came to Sydney in April 1998, they went to visit her. In the car on the way, I showed my daughter photos so she would not be too shocked when she saw how badly her grandmother had declined.

Not only was Henry deeply involved with everything regarding my mother's care, but insisted on accompanying us before and on the day she was admitted to the Montefiore Home. He took over the situation with a clear-minded plan. He had already explained the family dynamic and my mother's situation to the admissions' officer, clarifying all their queries. His work was critical, as it prepared the groundwork for when she arrived. Henry's Herculean efforts showed the depth of his love and understanding towards my mother and me. He loved Mumusiu (this is the name the family used for Franka; it means Mummy in Polish) with every fibre of his being, and he saw my despair. He wanted to take on all the burden, as is his nature. He also understood the incredible love for her that I had, and the bond we shared. Afterwards he tried to ease this difficult decision of placing my mother in the Jewish aged care facility for me by taking us to Manly, by the water. But my mother's decline affected me deeply, in body, mind and soul.

Henry often went to visit his Mumusiu, and on every visit sang and danced for her, just as he had when he would stay with her while studying for his university exams. He understood all her complexities and layers and brought out the best in her, especially on days when she was sad. But for me, every visit to my mother distressed me and broke my heart.

Franka Baral passed away on 28 July 1998. During the last month of her life, she didn't recognise me and couldn't speak. When I told the children how gravely ill she was, they immediately travelled to Sydney from New York, where all three were living. Cousin Lillie Michael picked them up from the airport and told them what to expect. My mother had passed away during their flight.

The three years my mother was in the Montefiore Home were the most difficult of my life. I couldn't concentrate on any work. I would sit at my desk gazing at the ceiling and constantly crying, wondering if I could do anything more for her. Without my creative input, the business faltered and we began lose money. The entrance fee to the Montefiore Home had been hefty—but even with the business in decline, we covered it fully.

I was grateful during those years that the love I had for my mother was mirrored by my children. I believe they saw from an early age how inseparable my mother and I had become. Joseph always understood this, and then my children embraced her history. This dedication of my family reassured me that they would remember Mumusiu and her life with love. The tremendous support from Joseph and my children was some comfort as it helped me carry my heavy burden.

I couldn't imagine ever having to let go of my mother.

Her memorial service was held at the Chevra Kadisha on 30 July 1998, and was conducted by Rabbi Ben Zion Milecki. Joseph recited the prayer and gave an incredibly moving eulogy encapsulating my mother's life. He highlighted how courageous she had been, and how she had always been the most fiercely protective of mothers, as well as a powerfully compelling woman. She was buried with honour at Rookwood Cemetery. Finally, after 41 years, Franka was united with her beloved husband Samek.

Böruch atöh adonöy,	בָּרוּךְ אַתָּה יְיָ,
elohay-nu melech hö-olöm,	אֱלֹהֵינוּ מֶלֶךְ הָעוֹלָם
da-yan hö-emes.	דַּיַּן הָאֱמֶת

Blessed are You, Lord, our God,
King of the Universe,
the Judge of Truth

Franka Baral, Kraków, 1926.

Franka Baral with sisters, Hela (left) and Mina (right), 1926-27,
in outfits typical of the region.

Franka, Zakopane, 1938.

Franka's only written account of her Wartime experiences,
28 March 1943, in Polish translated into English.

March 28, 1943

The escape from Bochnia to Slovakia took about two
months, under terrible conditions, when right at the
beginning, the smugglers escaped and we were left
alone in the forest for several days. Our nourishment
was a small amount of sugar and grass. Helpless, we
wandered during the night, and during the day we
were hiding under tree branches and leaves. At last
we were found by the Slovakian gendarmes and were
taken to prison. We remained there more than three
weeks. They took not only our valuables but also
our clothing, and were left with whatever we had
on. From there we were bought out by an underground
organization. They also arranged and paid smugglers
to get us to Hungary. Again we were wandering through
forests, often shot at by the border police. And
again the smugglers disappeared and I was left
alone. In the darkness I lost the children. After
two days wandering alone in the forest I reported
to the first accosted police, begging them to help
me find the children. I did not mention that I was
Jewish. Miraculously I found the children; they had
been arrested. I was taken to them and I was also
detained. After a long stay in prison in terrible
conditions, hopeless and sick, again we were bought
out by the underground organization. Ragged shreds
of human beings, on July 24, 1943 we arrived in

Budapest. Out of pity, with help from the Joint,
we were taken to a hotel. After a short stay at
the hotel the Gestapo was searching for us. Each
one of us slept in a different place. I picked up
all the children in the morning, gave each a piece
of bread, sometimes there was only soup for all,
without shoes or warm clothing in the rainy cold
months. We never had enough bread to satisfy our
hunger. Under those circumstances I applied to
the underground organization for help to save the
three children who were in Kraków with Poles, and
in danger. After hard work and effort I managed to
bring the three children. After June 30, 1943 I had
six children to care for. It was a hard struggle.
After many efforts we managed to get into the Polish
camp in Dunamocs. We were there about three months,
constantly suspected about our origins, everyone
avoided us. The ground started to burn under us for
fear that we would be denounced. In the middle of the
night, quietly, we left our abode, an earthen cottage
without a window where the children slept on the
floor and were often sick. We escaped in a fisherman's
boat across the Danube River using the last of our
money. I am now standing helpless on the pavement of
Budapest with six children. It is a fight and fear for
life, and a problem of finding all a place to sleep.
After spending one night we had to move on for fear
of suspicion. After a long time I found a Hungarian
woman, she did not know that we were Jews. She kept
us for some time in a locked apartment, but even so
there was fear because of the neighbours and the
woman's divorced husband who was of German descent.
This was a time when the Germans occupied the city.
At the time, Jewish boys were operated on to erase
that they were Jews. Then the further wandering

with the sick and emaciated children to Nyíregyhaza, which under normal conditions takes 12 hours by train, we were traveling 30 days under bombardment by the Americans and Russians. Solnak [?] everything is in ruins, only one shelter survived, where we are. Constantly in the bombed trains, bullets flying over our heads, without bread, ragged and sick. We wandered like this until the Russians took over till the end of the war. Sick children and I looked like living corpses. Of course this left a physical and psychological impression on the children.

Under those circumstances there was no normal way for the children's healthy development, nor even primitive ways to get an education. The children were constantly sick and feverish. To cool off they were sitting on stone blocks or on the steps of houses, because they never had a home of their own, only a place to sleep which they had to evacuate in the morning.

Under those circumstances we lived in Hungary till the end of the war, May 5, 1945.

Top: Aneta, Franka, Jim, Leonie (Jim's first wife) and Joseph
(with lady on the far right unknown) at a 1960s Bar Mitzvah.
Bottom: Franka and Aneta, Hakoah Club, Bondi, 1978.

18

BRIDAL WEAR

◆

Our new premises had been a high-class furniture showroom. The tenant told Joseph when he first saw him that they would be moving out in a fortnight, so I dropped everything to see the place immediately. We called the agent and signed the lease for the first floor of 87 Foveaux Street, Surry Hills, on the spot. It was 1985.

Moving yet again was hard, but this time we did it with pleasure. It was a corner building, bright and sunny. It is in this new place that we started making our first range of bridal samples. We chose wedding dresses because weddings are always hopeful occasions, and I remembered the promise I had made to myself that if I ever got out of the concentration camp, I would create wedding dresses. We wanted to make people as happy as possible and for women to take charge of how they felt and looked on their wedding day. The symbolism for us was of continuity and life.

At the new place, we were able to spread out over four long cutting tables. We employed a book-keeper, Beatrice, and Michelle also worked with us, starting soon after she finished high school and university. She continued to work on design while learning every other aspect of the business.

Michelle's dream was to work overseas and she did: first in Los Angeles and later in New York City. Only six years after being offered a position at the Australian Consulate at the Rockefeller Centre in 1986, she was able to open her own bridal business.

When Lilian was 19, she suggested she take samples to Melbourne to show to some of the department stores. Joseph phoned a friend there, George Leski, and asked him to keep an eye on her, and to find someone to help carry the suitcases of samples from store to store. He said he would do this himself, with pleasure. He carried both cases but said afterwards that he was just the assistant.

Our first Melbourne customer was the huge department store, Myer, which placed a large order for our skirts. We were at this point still working on our first bridal collection.

George phoned us to commend Lilian on her professional presentation of our samples. She showed them, he said, with such elegance and knowledge, that no buyer could resist placing an order.

The buyer at Myer suggested that we should have an agent in Victoria, and recommended Roy Polonski. When he came to see us in Sydney, we had no hesitation in giving him the agency, an agreement on which we shook hands—no contracts. With Roy's help, we started selling in Victoria.

We worked happily with him for years. He was not only a first class representative, but we also became friends. Even after he retired, we kept in contact.

Then we thought about expanding to other states. Our agents in Queensland were two ex-policemen, huge fellows, Bob Nolan and Jim Beitz. They knew everyone in the trade. One of them told me, 'The customers are too scared of us not to buy.'

Later on we started selling in South Australia through our agent, Laurie P. A. Lawrence. Then Allen Levin in Perth approached us. Both did a terrific job.

When we had a new range, we had showings in different cities. The agents made appointments for the buyers to see the 20 or so samples and to meet us. The customers wanted to meet the principals, and we wanted to meet the customers.

By this time we were producing so many different sorts of garment that we needed to re-name the company. After Rainbow Productions, we became Rainbow of Sydney, because we knew then that Sydney was the capital of style.

We had good luck. One day a girl knocked on our door, looking for a job at a time when we were hiring. When Joseph walked in, he asked me quietly who she was. I told him she had introduced herself as Lucy Nguyen, but had admitted she was not familiar with our sort of work. 'But that doesn't matter,' I confided to my husband. 'Look at her eyes. She looks directly at us. She's obviously extremely intelligent; listen to how she answers the questions. She'll be able to do the work.' We had no hesitation in employing Lucy.

Before Michelle left to work in the United States, she taught Lucy everything she needed to know—and Lucy was a star student, mastering it all. Years later she revealed that after she got the job, she went to night school to learn accountancy.

My judgement of Lucy was spot-on. She is a perfectionist, highly organised, capable and methodical. We have now worked together happily for 30 years. Soon she brought in her sister-in-law, Lee Ung, who showed she was able to handle many aspects of the business. She worked closely with customers in selecting the most suitable styles for their shops, something for which she has real talent. She has now been with us almost as long as Lucy. They operate in harmony and are such a pleasure to work with.

I wanted our wedding dresses to be distinctive and always put a lot of work into meticulously choosing the finest fabrics and laces to make them unique. I worked out that the best way to do this was to purchase novelty fabrics and accessories that could not be found in Australia. I found that good quality satins came from New York, the best laces and accessories from the north of France and the best linings from Japan. I had to match the colours of each, not an easy task. After all, there is more than one shade of white or ivory. We bought the French laces and Japanese fabrics locally from agents in Sydney who represented their home companies, and asked that they should be sold exclusively to us.

When I had pulled together the fabrics and accessories that I needed, I drew upon all the skills I had been taught by my mother to make six sample dresses. I knew they had to be classically elegant in the European way. When a bride tried on one of my dresses, I wanted her to have tears of happiness in her eyes and to call out to those with her: 'I love it! This is my dress.'

I got my first order from Canns' Bridal in the heart of the city next to David Jones' department store. At the time, there were a few small salons providing custom bridal dresses to measure. Canns' was the biggest bridal emporium; it was five storeys high and provided or advised on everything else needed for the ceremony: men's suits, limousines, flowers and venues, as well as dresses.

Joseph made an appointment with Mrs Cann. He put on his best suit with a new white shirt, and polished his shoes to a high shine. Then he took in the six samples.

Before he even showed her the dresses, Mrs Cann said, 'First of all, let's have a cup of tea. I want to find out who I'm dealing with.' Then she viewed the samples.

'They're beautiful,' she said. 'Give me 60 pieces.'

She wanted a certain number of pieces per size in each style: 6 pieces in XXSW, for petite women; 6 pieces in XSW; 18 pieces in SSW; 24 pieces in SW and 6 pieces in W. This was before sizes were indicated by numbers.

Mrs Cann gave her orders verbally, telling me that she trusted us completely.

We loved Mrs Cann. She was friendly and easy to deal with. Canns' were the finest and most decent merchants with whom we had ever done business. We continued to sell to them when her son Bobby and his wife Gennelle took over the business.

At the time, we were still having all our garments made up in the Leichhardt factory and took special pride in the finish of our dresses. Each one was as beautiful on the inside as it was on the outside— which the girls could feel the minute they put them on.

I am satisfied with only the best workmanship, and I made sure that all the ladies we employed worked to my high standards. It's good to know that your staff is capable and that everyone has the same goal. This created an atmosphere of pride and camaraderie.

When Henry returned from working in London, he also became involved in our business. He found a ground floor shop at 17 Foveaux Street, Surry Hills, just down from where we were at Number 87. This was a very convenient location, a short distance from Central Station, through which thousands of people poured every day.

Henry had the shop painted and put up a couple of signs. The store was called Bridal and Formal. He printed flyers to give to passers-by. Early each morning, Joseph took a pile of flyers to Central and handed them out to girls coming out of the train station. It didn't take long for the shop to be full of customers and for Henry to take on salespeople.

The shop succeeded because of Henry's creative ideas, drive, hard work and personality. He worked on the principle of a reasonable mark-up, so his prices weren't exorbitant. He offered gowns in a variety of styles and sizes from 4 to 30, displayed in racks according to price: from 120 to 600 dollars.

Even though Henry was always busy, he made a point of speaking to every bride who walked into the store. He welcomed them and made it his goal to find out exactly what they were looking for. No matter the shape of the gown required, from figure-hugging to extravagant tulle ball gowns, Henry had the knack of directing them to the right dress on the racks.

Sometimes a bride would put on a dress and be very pleased with how she looked. But Henry is known for his honesty. 'Let me choose one more dress for you to try on and compare,' he would say. When the girls put on another, even more beautiful dress, it was not uncommon for them, their mothers, sisters and girlfriends, to become tearful. They know when they've found the right one.

Right from the beginning, people would come in and ask for Henry personally. Many also took the trouble to thank him after their weddings.

Then some of the girls began enquiring where they could buy a formal suit for the bridegroom. Henry found a firm in Newcastle specialising in men's suits, and it wasn't long before they were producing the suits he designed, exclusively for him. When he began it was fashionable for jackets to have wide lapels and for trousers to be flared. Henry ordered narrower lapels in dull satin, and trousers that narrowed towards the ankle, with no cuffs. He began to show the suits in the shop with the gowns. He rented suits rather than selling them, since few men have occasion to wear such a formal outfit again. Bridegrooms began to arrive on their own to select the right suit.

Joseph would visit the shop to watch Henry deal with his customers, running between bride and bridegroom. The atmosphere created was well-mannered with a dash of humour. Everyone was treated the same, no matter how much they had to spend.

One day when Joseph was around there were three big, tall girls in the shop, tattooed from head to toe. They looked as if they would be able to hold their own on the wharves alongside the toughest wharfies. Henry went over to them as he does to all his customers and asked politely: 'How can I help you?'

They told him that all three would soon be marrying. He led them to the rack of gowns for their sizes, and advised them on a couple of dresses to try.

Then one of the girls said, rather quietly, 'We love these dresses—but they show our tattoos, and we don't want to do that.'

Henry had the solution. 'No worries—I'll put in sleeves and fill in the bodice right up to the neck.' They agreed at once that this was the solution.

When they came later to settle the account, one girl suddenly burst out crying. 'Why are there tears?' Joseph whispered to Henry. 'No idea,' he answered. So Joseph said, 'Let me handle this.'

He approached and asked if anything was wrong. 'Why are you crying? Didn't my son treat you well?' They said: 'Before we came to you we went to every bridal shop in Sydney looking for our dresses—but they all kicked us out. They didn't even want to serve us.'

Then they started to describe the other bridal houses and their staff in very colourful language. 'Now, now, girls—no swearing,' Joseph said. 'Were you greeted and treated well by my son Henry?'

'Yes. This is the only place we were treated like everybody else,' they said. 'As if we were actually human.'

They had another request: they wanted to rent suits for the three bridegrooms. They were big boys, they said, with wide shoulders. 'No worries,' said Henry. 'Bring them in. I guarantee we'll be able to find the right suit for them. Tell them they can come any time, incuding in the evening or on Sundays.'

At this the girls burst out laughing. 'They can't come in. They're in Bathurst.'

Bathurst? 'Am I right?' guessed Joseph. 'They're under Her Majesty's protection? In gaol?' All three nodded their heads. They went on to tell him that the Governor had granted them permission to marry— inside the gaol.

Joseph and Henry stepped up to managing this, too. They gave the girls a measurement chart to take to their grooms.

After the business side was sorted out, Joseph and Henry asked the girls more about their prospective husbands. 'They're in gaol for various offences: selling drugs, armed robbery...' they revealed. 'But the police pick on them because they're bikies and wear special leather outfits and ride motor-bikes together. When the police motor-cyclists chase them and try and catch them, they can't. We reckon the cops are jealous. Our boys don't hurt anyone.'

Eventually the marriages took place in Bathurst Gaol with everyone wearing our outfits. Food was brought in and the boys were allowed an hour for the ceremony.

A few years passed. Then one day Henry called Joseph and asked him to come into the shop. In front of it was parked an enormous motorcycle, a Harley Davidson. When he went inside, Henry introduced him to an equally enormous bikie and his little son of about four. Both were dressed entirely in leather. The child's hair was shaved on both sides with a sort of mop in the middle. He was very cute.

Both of them were very polite. The father had come to thank Henry for what he had done for his wedding, and to show off his little son. The father's parting words as he shook hands with Joseph and Henry were: 'Here's my card. Ring us if you fellows have any trouble from anyone. We'll straighten them out.'

So after that, we lived under the protection of our delightful new friends. Joseph joked that Henry should put up a sign: *Accredited Supplier to Royalty and Bikies.*

Another day a young lady from Papua New Guinea, accompanied by her gorgeous curly-haired little daughter, came into the shop. Joseph heard her asking Henry for a nice dress for her wedding, not too expensive.

She was shown a dress that showed off her figure. The price was right too—about $150. Henry told her how good she looked, but then said: 'Let me show you another one.'

When she put on the second gown she looked not just pretty, but stunning. The problem was that it was four times the price. She agreed that it was lovely but insisted she couldn't afford it.

'Don't worry,' said Henry. 'Just let me put the dress aside and you come in and settle the account when you can. We can do a deal for you.' When she returned, he had the dress all packed up and ready for her. As he handed over the box, Henry said: 'Congratulations. Enjoy your wedding. This dress comes with our compliments.'

She was so happy that she cried. When she left with her beautiful dress, Joseph told Henry that he was proud of him.

'If you read about the Japanese occupation of New Guinea during World War II, you'll understand why,' Henry told him. 'Think of how the people, the Fuzzy Wuzzy Angels, helped the Aussie troops. I could see I could thank them a little through this bride.'

Here's another heart-warming story. Crystal, a young woman, was getting married, and needed a beautiful wedding dress. Her mother heard a work colleague talking about a sale being held at Bridal and Formal in Surry Hills. Crystal was on holiday, and by the time she returned, the sale would be over. So she asked her sister Alicia, similar to her in shape and size, to look at the gowns on her behalf.

Meanwhile Henry had engaged a film crew to come to the sale to record scenes for a documentary about the company. Jonathan was one of the crew. As Alicia and her mother entered the premises they decided to take the stairs up to the sale, and so encountered the film people. On the long ascent, Alicia and Jonathan joked together about what good exercise this was.

When Henry heard that Alicia was trying on dresses for her sister, he immediately dubbed her *the virtual bride.* He made her a tempting and generous offer. He suggested she select three or four dresses that Crystal might like, and he would put them aside for her—sale or no sale.

Meanwhile the crew had started filming as the customers tried on the gowns. Jonathan watched as Alicia tried on a number of gowns to select those she thought Crystal would like. He watched very closely; it was clear that he was attracted to her.

Finally he went up to her, looking sad. What a shame that this lovely girl was about to become someone else's bride! 'Of all the girls I've watched trying on dresses today, you were the most stunning,' he told her.

Then Henry stepped forward. First he introduced Alicia to me and Joseph. (We were helping out.) Then he turned to Jonathan and introduced him to Alicia. He took good care to mention that she was *the virtual bride*, standing in for her sister.

Henry had noticed the chemistry between them. 'Alicia, you're now going to give Jonathan your phone number,' he told her. 'Jonathan, you're then going to call her and take her out for coffee.'

Joseph had even bigger plans. 'If after the date a romance blossoms, and if that leads to a wedding, then the Weinreich and

Roth (Michelle's married name) families will provide a beautiful wedding dress for the occasion,' he announced.

Alicia felt as if she were in some kind of surreal fairy tale. But she did give her phone number to Henry, and he duly passed it on to Jonathan.

You can guess what eventually happened. As Joseph said later to Henry, it was fate that brought these two young people together. Fate with a helping hand from the Weinreichs and the Roths!

This story was told at Alicia and Jonathan's wedding at The Gap, Watsons Bay, as she wore the promised gown. Joseph and I were invited, and as we sat in that beautiful venue overlooking the Harbour, the sea sparkled in the sunshine. The wedding was held outside, then everyone went into the restaurant for the reception.

Joseph and I were treated like VIPs and seated with the couple's best friends. To our surprise, up on a big screen came a little film showing how they had met at our showroom. Jonathan invited Joseph to make a short speech, which he did with his usual aplomb. Then both of us were given a standing ovation by the guests.

This was an unforgettable wedding, full of joy, happiness and laughter. We certainly enjoyed every minute of it. We are sure that Alicia's and Jonathan's life together will be long and happy.

After five years of hard work building the business, Henry's shop had to move from Surry Hills when the landlord increased the rent to a figure so high that it was not worth our son's while to stay. We couldn't understand the landlord's thinking. The store attracted so many people to the street that all the other retailers benefited.

Michelle and Henry had been talking for a long time about joining forces. This is when Henry decided it was the right time to join Michelle in New York where he brought a new, vibrant approach to the business. He computerised it, and visited customers across the country at trunk shows. He knew instinctively what would be popular with brides in both big cities and small towns. Michelle and Henry are a powerful combination, each with different strengths.

In 1996, Michelle and Henry also opened their own New York store on 24 West 57th Street. It was a prestigious location, diagonally across from Bergdorf Goodman and elegantly designed by Lilian. Their store was up against significant competitors, but they persevered. They had loyal staff and built a wonderful following.

At this point Henry was travelling between both businesses in New York and Sydney.

The key to the success and longevity of our business is that we always listen to our customers, and try and give them what they want.

The major Australian newspaper, the *Telegraph*, wrote on 2 October 2013:

Seventy angry brides who were left without dresses after a bridal gown firm closed its doors without warning could have found their guardian angel with a well-known designer offering to supply them speedy below-cost replacements.

Twenty of the brides and their families arrived in an angry crowd at the premises of [the failed business], wanting not only their dresses but the deposits they had paid. Nancy Moujalli said that she had already paid $1400. When a friend rang to tell her the business had ceased trading, she couldn't stop crying. When she went to find out what had happened, there were so many other people there who had bought dresses fighting and arguing. 'One girl is being married on Saturday. What is she supposed to do?'

What Nancy did was visit Henry at Surry Hills. He had offered to provide every bride left in the lurch with a below-cost wedding gown:

'I feel very strongly that someone has to go in to bat for the industry. We also want to keep our brides in Australia buying from Australian designers.' He went on to say that he would do anything he could to help the brides-to-be—because it was the right thing to do. 'Overall ours is an amazing industry filled with professional people.'

After an exhaustive selection process Ms Moujalli is beaming in a new dress drastically different to her first, but still 'perfect'. 'I'm over the moon,' she said. 'It's so beautiful. I'm so happy.'

[Article by Simon Black, *Daily Telegraph/Sunday Telegraph*, 2 October 2013. Its use has been licensed by the Copyright Agency; excerpt as permitted by the Copyright Act. You must not use it without the permission of the copyright owner or Copyright Agency]

Many of our customers are now international. One day in 2002 Michelle and Henry received a phone call from Shaunie Nelson, who was planning to marry giant National Basketball League (NBL) star Shaquille O'Neal. She wanted them to design her gown for their huge black-tie wedding, and also the gowns for her four bridesmaids and flower-girl.

Honoured to be chosen above all other United States designers, Michelle and Henry took up the challenge. They realised this was an opportunity to have one of their gowns showcased on TV all over the country—and indeed the world.

Since Shaunie was unable to travel because her third child with Shaquille was on the way, Michelle and Henry took a seamstress with them and flew to Los Angeles. They were placed in the Four Seasons hotel and brought a sewing machine to make any last-minute adjustments. Michelle and Henry were also invited to the wedding.

It was magnificent. In Australia, *The Sunday Telegraph* reported that the gown of platinum silk tulle, beaded chiffon and Swarovski flowers was worn with a silver-embroidered veil and described as 'one of the most extraordinary wedding gowns ever'. The attendants wore hand-beaded sheaths. The wedding cake was shaped like a carriage and the couple exchanged gold rings presented in a box mounted on a crown. O'Neal's mother called it 'the event of a lifetime. Seeing the two of them together and in love is what every mother dreams of for her child.'

These and many other stories filled our days in a business that has brought us a huge amount of happiness plus a share of challenges. The children have also found this to be true. The business has revealed that at the point where dreams and life meet there are myriad possibilities.

Top: With some staff members at Foveaux Street, 1994. From left: Standing: Lee Ung, Joseph, Aneta, Effie and Lucy Nguyen. Henry is centre front.
Bottom: In New York City with the iconic LOVE sculpture by American artist, Robert Indiana. From left: Michelle, Aneta, Henry and Joseph.

Top: **Staff meeting at the bridal salon designed by Lilian at 24 West 57th Street, New York, 2002. Aneta (fifth from right) next to Michelle.**

Bottom: **Henry (centre) conducting a staff meeting with Michelle to the left of him, 2002.**

Henry and bride Nancy Moujalli, *The Daily Telegraph*, **2 October 2013.**
Photo: Justin Lloyd/Newspix.

19

HALOMI

◈

The Hampden Road flat, in which we had our three children, was small. The living room and kitchenette were tiny and so were the bathroom and the two bedrooms. But all the years we lived there, we were happy with what we had: *Hasameach Bechelko* in Hebrew. Despite the lack of space in this small flat, it was still much better than our conditions during the War. Remember Płaszów: my mother and I sharing wooden bunks with dozens of other women and no facilities at all. Joseph also endured terrible conditions in the Russian labour camp. He spent 14 months in the bitter cold of the Urals sleeping on a long wooden bunk with 40 other people. In Kazakhstan he shared a stall with a cow—for a year.

In Sydney, however, as our business grew more prosperous, we dreamed of a spacious house in the Eastern suburbs so as to give our children a rich life filled with education, culture and love in a comfortable home environment. A strong motivation was also to get away from our obnoxious landlord. We worked day and night to save enough money, until we had 9000 pounds—which was quite a substantial amount, since in the early 1960s, you could buy a red-brick cottage in Bondi for 7000 pounds.

We decided to aim higher. Joseph combed through the Saturday house ads in *The Sydney Morning Herald* to see what was on offer. Then he went to the Eastern suburbs every Saturday morning, following up leads. He looked in affluent suburbs such as Double Bay and Dover Heights and was attracted to the more modern homes in Dover Heights, with their views of the Harbour Bridge and the Opera House from their second storeys. Unfortunately, they were expensive—at 12-15,000 pounds, out of our reach.

But Joseph never gives up. Every weekend he looked at houses, often until late in the afternoon.

One Saturday he returned home, disappointed. 'What did you find?' I asked. 'Nothing,' he said in a downcast voice.

'But how is it possible to be out all day and find nothing?' I insisted.

'Nothing for us,' he told me.

Finally one Saturday around 11am he rang to say: 'Drop everything and come to Bondi Road, to a real estate agent called Rudder. I've found us an empty block of land. It's opposite a park and a few minutes from the beach.'

The land was in the prestigious suburb of Vaucluse, on the desirable Olola Avenue.

I met Joseph at the estate agent's office. In those days, everything shut at noon on Saturdays, and I arrived at 11.45am. The agent told us the price was 7500 pounds—not negotiable. I had brought our cheque book with me and we paid the asking price then and there.

Later Joseph filled me in on how he had found this block. After going to the usual suburbs week after week, he had decided to try his luck in Vaucluse. As he drove slowly along the streets, he saw a sign with a phone number on a vacant site. 'I loved it,' he said. 'Both the land and the location. Superb!'

But where would we live? How do you build a house when you don't have the money? We also knew we would have to find an architect to design it.

I had clear ideas from the beginning of the sort of house I wanted. Living in Israel had shown me how attractive modern architecture can be. Through friends we found three architects and I told them the style of house I wanted. 'Impossible,' they told us.

Three weeks passed. Then Joseph showed me an article in the Sunday paper about a young architect who had been commissioned to design a new kind of office block, Australia Square. It would be the world's tallest lightweight concrete building, with 58 floors, and would have fabulous views over the city and the Harbour—while taking up only a quarter of the block, leaving plenty of space and light for people to enjoy below. It would be built in new ways. Construction time for each floor would be five working days: an unheard-of rate of work.

'This man is a genius,' Joseph said. 'Tomorrow I'm going to ring him and make an appointment.'

I simply burst out laughing. But Joseph was serious. He found out that Mr Harry Seidler worked out of a tenth-floor office in Circular Quay.

'You'd better take a parachute in case he throws you out,' I joked.

The following Monday morning Joseph drank two strong cups of coffee and rang Mr Seidler. I was surprised when he was put straight through to him.

'We've bought a beautiful block of land in Vaucluse,' Joseph said, 'and I want you to design our home.' He took a deep breath: 'Mr Seidler, we're Jewish. Both my wife and I are Holocaust survivors.

Since 1939 we haven't been able to put a decent roof over our heads. We've worked hard over the years to build up our business and save so that we can offer our children better lives. Please, at least have a look at our land. You're the only one who can design our house.'

Mr Seidler listened carefully. 'All right—on Sunday I'll go for a drive with my wife and we'll look at the site. Ring me again on Monday.'

All weekend we were on tenterhooks. When Joseph rang on Monday, Mr Seidler said: 'It's a good piece of land,' he said, 'in a good position, even though it's difficult terrain with a steep slope and a water drainage problem in the middle. Does your wife know what she wants?'

'She knows exactly what she wants,' Joseph replied. 'She's a very talented designer of women's clothing.'

We made an appointment to meet Mr Seidler in his office at noon a couple of days later. We arrived at 47 Macquarie St, Circular Quay and were taken into a large office containing nothing but a big dark timber desk on which sat a phone, a yellow legal pad and a couple of pencils. There were three chairs and an amazing view of Sydney Harbour.

Mr Seidler made us feel very welcome. His first question was: ''Did you engage another architect?' We told him we had spoken with three others, but none of them could provide what we wanted.

'Our house should be modern: elegant, with simple lines,' I told him. 'I lived in Israel for eight years and their buildings are very bright inside because their windows reach from floor to ceiling. The other architects told us they can't get glass sheets big enough for that.'

'What?' Mr Seidler said. 'Australia Square is glass from top to bottom of every floor. I can get any size glass I want.'

I then described what I wanted for my house. 'From the front room you enter the living room. Then there's a veranda right across the front of the house. You should be able to go out to it from the main bedroom. The children's bedroom should be on the same side. The dining room should overlook the park, and the children's playroom and the bathrooms and laundry can be on that side too, where people can easily reach the back garden. The kitchen can be small. I'm in business and have no time to cook.'

Mr Seidler invited us to come and have a look at other houses he had designed. We took up his offer and found we had instant rapport with his wife, Penelope, an architecture student. And we loved the houses they showed us.

After a month he called us into his office and presented us with a folio containing architectural drawings of our dream house on Olola Avenue, in detail, down to the last brick. 'I'll give you three copies,' he said. 'Now you have to find a builder to do the work.'

'And the money to pay for it,' I thought.

Joseph didn't know any builders. He immediately asked Mr Seidler: 'Please choose the builder you want to work with.' He gave us the name of Mr Peter Cussel, a Viennese immigrant.

We received a quote by mail from Mr Cussel for 15,000 pounds. Joseph said to me: 'We have the architect, we have the land, we have the builder—but we have no money.' I told him: 'Don't worry. God will provide.'

I always believed we could build the house—and, as you know, I never give up.

Mr Seidler told us that it would take a year to build. The process was that every three months, his office would check the invoice submitted from the builder, which we would have to pay. If we couldn't meet the payments, they would stop working.

We thought these conditions were harsh, but fair.

It was clear that we would have to approach the bank for a loan. At the time we dealt with the Commonwealth Bank at Artarmon. Managers could approve loans without having to consult head office.

After his appointment with the manager, Joseph returned with a big smile on his face. 'Sit down comfortably,' he told me. 'The bank manager read through Mr Seidler's documentation and told me that in all his time as a manager, he had never seen such a precise document —so readable and easy to understand—right down to the last brick.'

There were two ways of arranging a loan, he explained. The bank could lend us the money and have a mortgage on the property. If the agreed-upon repayment, with interest, was not met, the bank would sell the property to recover the money.

But there was also another way. 'Have you got any collateral?' he asked. Joseph didn't even know what that was. 'Meaning other properties, diamonds, valuables,' the manager continued. 'They would need to add up to 20,000 pounds. The bank would keep the goods or the title deeds until the loan is paid in full.'

Joseph said that his father had left him a block of six apartments.

'I don't need all six. Give me the deeds to one. That will be enough. Let me have the address and the bank will value the property and then approve the loan.'

'There's one tiny problem,' Joseph said. 'The apartments are in Chrzanów.'

The bank manager couldn't even pronounce the name. 'Where's that?' he asked.

'It's in Poland—and unfortunately our apartments, like all others, as well as houses and farms, have been confiscated by the Communist regime.'

The manager burst out laughing. 'You have a lot of guts and nerve—so I'm ready to take a risk on you. I'll approve a loan of

15,000 pounds. Come back in a few days and sign all the documents for repaying the mortgage.'

Euphoric, Joseph called Mr Seidler to tell him we had the money. 'Let the building begin!'

Every Saturday we used to take a picnic lunch to the park opposite our new home and watch it growing. It was finished, as predicted, in exactly a year.

But it was a year of worries. When we received all those documents from the bank, Joseph and I discussed how we were going to manage the hefty repayments to them.

'Don't worry,' I said.

In what seems a miracle, 1960-61 was one of the most successful years ever for our business. We had no trouble meeting our instalments in full every three months—and without touching a shilling of the bank's money. The manager was astounded.

We had chosen the right people to create our precious home: Mr Seidler, the brilliantly creative architect and Geoff Danks, the young, talented architectural project manager. Together they managed every aspect. Joseph told Geoff: 'We won't sneeze in the house until you and Mr Seidler approve of any of the requirements, such as painting and other maintenance.'

The builder was also exceptional. Joseph asked him how he could save on the cost of materials, and he managed to find a company in Newcastle to provide the bricks we needed at a saving of 200 pounds. It doesn't seem a big amount, but it gave my husband great satisfaction.

After 12 months, in September 1962, Mr Seidler presented us with the front door key to our new home. We were over the moon. From the beginning, the children loved it too. The girls were delighted to have desks in their bedroom, and Henry ran around in all that space. We enrolled them in Mount Moriah War Memorial College (commonly known as Moriah College) so they would grow up knowing their Jewish heritage. They were taught both Hebrew and secular subjects in the school. One year, I designed the uniforms worn by the Moriah girls and our daughters were proud to wear them to class.

Just before the house was completed, Mr Seidler rang me and said: 'Let's go shopping. You need to get kitchen utensils and other items that fit in with the design of the house. I know a lot of wholesalers and can get you a healthy discount.' He was such an incredibly busy man—with many residential and commercial projects—yet he found the time to help me to make the house and all its contents perfect. As I reflect on this today, I realise what an incredible gesture this was from Mr Seidler. He had a clear vision for our house, from the exterior design to the smallest interior details. His vision encompassed Modernism and the visual principles of the Bauhaus School. He was the first architect in Australia to fully realise these.

With Mr Seidler, I chose Arzberg dinner sets, stainless steel baskets by Alessi, cutlery, pots and pans and placemats. They look as modern today as they did 57 years ago, and we still use them.

Mr Seidler also designed all the furniture in the house. In his office, there was a painting by John Coburn that he told me would look good there, too. He even arrived to hang it himself, to be sure it was placed in the right spot.

The second set of keys handed over that day we returned to our landlord.

'You're losing a good tenant,' Joseph told Mr Webb.

'I know—I've seen your new house in Vaucluse,' he said. He had obviously used his investigative skills as an ex-policeman to snoop around and find out all about it.

The finishing touch was a name for our home. We decided on 'Halomi', which means 'my dream' in Hebrew:

H for Henry
A for Aneta
L for Lilian
O for Olola Avenue
M for Michelle
I for Iosef (Joseph)

All our private cards and letterheads now include the name.

Later Joseph pulled Mr Seidler aside and asked, joking, 'How long will this house last?'

His answer was: 'For the next 100 years.'

We settled quickly into our wonderful new home. Everything was harmonious, full of love and respect, with the children developing well. They absolutely love our house, which was one of our goals in building it. They proudly grew up in it, appreciating its modern and timeless beauty.

Some of the friends who had not been supportive during difficult times, clearly wanting to have a look, rang and invited us to go out with them. But we found we were simply too busy.

Instead we became friends with the Seidlers. Joseph remained in contact with Mr Seidler. Every time he read something about his work, he would call his office and speak to him. When he was designing the Australian Embassy in Paris in the 1970s, Mr Seidler showed us the plans. He also showed us plans in the 1990s for affordable workers' apartments on the banks of the Danube in Vienna.

Recently Woollahra Council has honoured us by calling our much-loved home the Weinreich House, and listing it as an important heritage house.

Joseph standing with the For Sale sign on the land
at 11 Olola Ave, 1960.

Halomi exterior and the dining and living room, 4 February1962.
Photos: Max Dupain, https://www.maxdupain.com.au, © Penelope Seidler.

317

20

BACK TO OUR ROOTS WITH THE CHILDREN

❖

When our children started going to school at Moriah, they were vaguely aware that some of their friends also had parents who had similar backgrounds to ours. They were Holocaust Survivors, though the children never used this terminology. Our philosophy, however, was not to tell Lilian, Michelle and Henry about our pasts until they were adults. When they were children, Joseph and I discussed how the time would come when we would give them the full details of our survival and our journey from Hell to this Lucky Country.

When they were growing up, we wanted them simply to enjoy their lives as happy-go-lucky Aussie kids. We wanted them to have everything we had been denied because of the War and to benefit from all that Australia could offer: piano, singing and violin lessons; sports, ballet, acrobatics, painting and—most importantly—a good solid education which would lead to a profession in which they would be happy.

It was December 1993 when we decided to tell them our full story. The girls were then working in New York, and told us they were going to the film *Schindler's List*, based on a book about the Holocaust by the Australian author Thomas Keneally. Joseph and I, by coincidence, had planned to visit the girls in New York. We saw the film together. What they didn't know was how much of it overlapped the real stories of my life. As we sat with our daughters watching the film, I found myself whispering to them when what I had personally experienced came up before us on the screen. I would say, 'I was there,' and 'I walked over that bridge.'

After it was over, we all went to a coffee shop where, in a low, gentle voice, I said to the girls: 'Remember the scenes in the Ghetto in Kraków?' They did. 'What about those in Płaszów camp? I was there.'

They started to cry. 'But you never told us! Why?'

'We wanted to wait for an appropriate time when you were adults,' said Joseph. 'We've decided that's now, since you took the initiative to want to see the film. Next year, we'd like to take you and Henry to Kraków and to Chrzanów, where your mother and I were born and lived. Then we can show you our roots, and tell you the stories of where we—and you—come from.'

So began our incredible journey together. This was my and Joseph's first trip back to our birthplace since we had left Poland in 1939 and 1940. Lilian and Michelle accompanied us back to Poland. Henry felt he was not ready for this heavy journey, and was not to visit my birthplace until years later. When we arrived in Kraków, we took a taxi to our hotel, the Forum, a pleasant place where our two rooms overlooked the River Wisła.

On the way from the airport to the city I felt overwhelmed, as all my emotions were unlocked. I became agitated and worried because I couldn't recognise anything in that part of Kraków. Lilian tried to reassure me and pointed out that I hadn't left the city of my birth by plane.

We did a quick tour and I started to calm down. I gave instructions to the driver to visit where I had been born, my school, and where we had lived when my father ran his fur business. Even after all those years away, I could find the places easily.

Joseph and I still speak Polish fluently, and that helped us discover the new Kraków. I began to feel at home as soon as I saw the block of flats where our family had lived. Lilian noticed that my memory became 'crystal clear' after that, as 'my mother walked along the path of her earliest girlhood.'

We also looked for some of the documents of our past. When we had watched *Schindler's List* in New York, I had been shocked to see that the man shown as Schindler's accountant and adviser was Itzhak Stern, who used to visit my parents when both he and my father were living in Tel Aviv after the War. They had worked in the camps together, but never, ever mentioned any of this in my presence.

On Schindler's List we found my father, Samuel Baral, at No. 41. Mr Stern was there too, as *Bilanzbuchhalter*, at No. 659.

On the first morning we went for breakfast at our hotel, we sat at a huge window with a wonderful view of the river. I pointed out to the children that I could see across to my grandfather Juda Baral's house. I also showed them the two bridges across the river. The one on the right I called 'the bridge of happiness', since it led towards where my family had lived. The second I thought of as 'the bridge of tragedy'. That's where we crossed to enter the Ghetto.

I found it difficult to describe to Lilian and Michelle the acute sadness of being forced out of our home, grabbing just a few possessions, and then finishing up in the Hell of the Ghetto and the camp.

After we had finished breakfast the following day, I took Joseph and the girls for a walking tour to show them where our murdered families had lived. Joseph was amazed by how much I could remember after all the years that had passed. He said that I seemed to know every stone in the city.

I took my family to:

- 2 Paulińska Street, where my grandparents, Juda and Rachela Baral, had lived;
- 20 Na Groblach Street, where I was born;
- 7 Krakowska Street, where my grandparents, Juda and Jenta Baral, had lived;
- 27 Stadomska Street, where my father and grandfather had their fur warehouse;
- 5 Brzozowa Street, my Hebrew school;
- 4 Morsztynowska Street, where my parents, my brothers and I lived;
- 7 Bonerowska Street, where my uncle, aunt and cousins, the Susskinds, lived;
- 16 Floriańska Street, where my Feuer grandparents and their children lived;
- 18 Tomasza Street, where my grandfather Matias Feuer ran his retail menswear shop;
- 28 Starowiślna Street, where my uncle and aunt, the Ehrlichs, lived with Ada and Olga;
- 18 Zielna Street (now Monte Casino) Street, where my uncle and aunt and cousins, the Hirsch family lived;
- 6 Janowa Wola Street, where we first lived in the Ghetto; and
- 3 Józefińska Street, where we next lived in the Ghetto.

Lilian noticed that the only place I hesitated was at my Jewish day school. We all walked into the building, then operating as a technical college. Joseph found the caretaker, who took us to the headmistress.

He asked her permission to go up to the first floor because, as he explained: 'My wife attended this school. It was a Jewish school, and we've come all the way from Australia to show our girls their mother's classroom.'

Her reply was, 'This was never a Jewish school. We don't know anything about that subject—so I don't give you permission to go up to the first floor.'

We all left the building. I was shocked. Joseph asked: 'Are you sure this is the Hebrew school building?' I said I was 100 per cent certain that I had attended school there. Joseph turned around, looked up, and located two large plaques nailed high up on the stuccoed corner of the building, prominently facing the centre of the street. One was in Polish and the other in Hebrew. He saw that they were dedicated to remembering the martyred souls of the Jewish students who had attended this school, most of whom had perished during the War.

Joseph indignantly told us that he was going back to tell the headmistress she was lying. We didn't want him to do this, but he insisted. With Michelle, he went straight into her office and said: 'You're lying. You must have seen the plaques on this building a thousand times. You're not dealing with Jews from before 1939 now. Today we're a proud nation, with the best fighters and the best Air Force in the world—stationed in our own country.' He was so incensed he was shaking.

After this confrontation the headmistress had no choice but to give us permission. I sneaked up to see my classroom. The corridor was still painted exactly the same gold colour as when I was a little girl.

We also went to eat at my mother's favourite restaurant, Hawelka, in the elegant part of the city known as Główny Rynek. As we sat there, it seemed as if Mother was next to us, after all those years.

Before we left for Kraków, Auntie Ela had sent us from Tel Aviv the names of a Christian family she said we should meet. We rang them and Adam Benedykt Bisping and his wife Barbara invited us round for a cup of tea. As soon as we met them, we felt very happy in their warm company. Since that meeting in 1994, we have been in constant contact with this charming couple—the sort of people you meet once in a lifetime.

Mr Bisping offered to take us in his car to the places we wanted the girls to see, the most painful places of my life. He even took time off from work. First we went to the Ghetto, and I showed Lilian and Michelle where I had hidden in the loft. Next door at 18 Plac Zgody was the famous pharmacy, Apteka Pod Orłem, where in the Ghetto Martin had been to get the medication and where we met Mrs Anna Pióro, who showed us everything and explained in detail the museum and its photographs. She was most interested in finding out how my mother had saved six children. I promised to send her a tape and family photos. Now that tape is constantly played in the museum and thousands of visitors have learned of my story. In my mind this tape is a definite antidote to the Holocaust deniers and that's the reason I want it to be viewed. We are also still in touch with Anna.

When we went to Płaszów, we found that the barracks had been destroyed and that only the building where the murderer Amon Goeth (shown in *Schindler's List*) lived among the other executioners, had survived. There is a memorial erected there to the dead, which greatly moved us.

During the following week we went to Chrzanów, where Joseph was born. The house where he grew up had been destroyed, but he was able to show us his father's business premises and his school. He could even remember where he sat, and gave the current class a talk about Australia. The children loved hearing about kangaroos and koalas. When we returned home, we sent them a package of little toys, including koalas and kangaroos.

This was a happy day. But then we went on to Auschwitz. It was a gloomy, cold day. As we passed through the entrance under the notorious *Arbeit macht frei* arch, we saw, on the left, the building where people's arms were tattooed with a number upon arrival. It also contained a register of names of those who had passed through this dreadful place. Joseph couldn't find the names of his father and brother. For Joseph's father, this meant that as soon as the transport had arrived from Chrzanów on 18 March 1944, he was immediately gassed in the crematorium. His brother had been a big, strong young man and had been working on the railways in Germany as a slave labourer. It was only when he became ill from starvation and over-work that he was sent to the camp to be killed. He was only 22 years old.

His friend Aron Gerstner, who was also in Auschwitz, survived the War. In Sydney, years later, Mr Gerstner told Joseph that he had seen his brother suffer terrible dysentery. One day he had simply leaned against a camp wall, keeled over and died. He also told Joseph that the barracks where his brother died was next to the place where the butcher-doctor Mengele worked.

Since Joseph knew exactly where his brother had died, he sat down there to honour him and to tell him he had not been forgotten. We also went into the building where the crematorium had been, Joseph said Kaddish and we lit a *yahrzeit* candle in memory of his father and brother.

Remembering these stories and seeing the pain on Joseph's face is indescribable. It brought home the realisation that I and our children never had the chance to know my father-in-law and brother-in-law and that the torment of this place saw so much suffering and brought death to so many beautiful lives. It is impossible, even today, to absorb what happened there.

Joseph's mother had told him that her own father, Simche Sofer-Schreiber, had been born just over the border in Czechoslovakia in the Carpathian Mountains, in a village called Pilchów. During our visit to Kraków, Mr Bisping remarked one day that we were so close to it that we should go there. It was just three hours away.

As we drove, Joseph told us how his grandfather had operated a tavern selling not just drinks but meals too, seven days a week. They could open on Shabbat because the food for that day was pre-cooked and bills were settled the following Sunday. The tavern had a file system with coloured cards containing the menu prices, so that there could be no cheating. The card was simply filed next to the customer's name.

We decided to visit Pilchów to see where Joseph's grandfather had been born. When we arrived at the Polish border, we found passport control in a long wooden building which led into the Czech side. We produced our Australian passports and were told that we needed a visa to enter Czechoslovakia. However, they had a convenient facility whereby our passports could be stamped—for a fee of $US100. Mr Bisping, of course, had his Polish documents.

We crossed the border into countryside of great beauty. The pristine white snow reached our knees when we got out to walk and admire the trees dressed in white. There was no one else about and no signs of habitation. We kept driving to reach the municipal council building where Joseph hoped to find historical documents proving that his family had actually lived there.

We seemed to drive for hours. Then we saw some old men walking along the side of the road and stopped to question them. Joseph asked if anyone remembered a man called Schreiber who ran a tavern. One old man's face lit up and he pointed to the place on the side of a mountain where it had stood.

Mr Bisping let Joseph out to climb up the steep slope while we waited in the car. As he disappeared from view, I began to worry that he might get lost. Then all of a sudden a figure appeared at the very top—on a sled. It shot down the slope at tremendous speed, delivering my husband at our feet.

Then we saw two boys running down the mountain after him.

How had Joseph persuaded them to let him use their sled? He had simply asked, saying he hadn't had the opportunity to ride one for many years. As a boy himself, he had owned a sled on which two could ride, and another for three people, and he used to play on them with his friends. That day the boys at first refused—but they didn't know Joseph. He had a business proposition. He told them he would slide down the mountain on the sled, and then would re-hire it so that his wife and daughters could also have a go. Afterwards he would return the sled to them.

A deal was struck with the money upfront. Lilian and Michelle went half-way up the mountain and slid down, amid much hearty laughter. Then I went up, sat on the sled and simply let go. As I was happily descending the slope, I heard Joseph shouting *Stop, stop, stop!* and saw him running towards me. But it was too late. He threw himself in front of the sled and stopped it that way.

He told me later that if he hadn't stopped me, instead of going straight down the slope the sled would have veered to the right and tipped me out into an icy mountain stream.

The girls and Mr Bisping were roaring with laughter watching all this and it was a moment of relief from the feelings of despair and sadness we had been experiencing revisitng our past.

On the way back to Kraków we stopped for dinner at a lovely country restaurant. Despite not finding the tavern or any documents, we felt it had been a day well spent. Joseph had enjoyed the opportunity of returning to his family place. We had enjoyed ourselves and breathed the cold, pure mountain air, just as his forefathers had. It was an unforgettable time.

Riding on the sled also brought back my own childhood memories. When my mother had taken my brothers, me and our nanny to the winter resort at Zakopane in the Carpathian Mountains, not far from where we had revisited Joseph's past, we had a great time. The three of us had piled on to the sled and my mother and nanny had pulled us along.

After our trip to the places of my childhood, both Michelle and Lilian wrote to us about how deeply it had affected them. Lilian spoke of how she was left with 'overwhelming grief for members of a large, pious family and a deeply-rooted culture that I will never meet and never know.'

She said that her earliest childhood memories were, at two-and-a-half, being taken to see her Grandfather Samuel Baral on his deathbed. 'He kissed me, told me to be a good daughter and sister and gave me a large doll. Throughout my childhood I received a doll every birthday.'

Lilian didn't play with these dolls—I did. I yearned for those lost years of my childhood when I could have played like other children.

My daughter also noted that the young Poles they had met were courteous and pleasant, 'as if they want to make up for the horrendous past'.

Michelle wrote that the trip had 'gone deeply into my heart and soul'. She said that being able to be with us as we travelled back to 'a very painful part of your lives is *so* precious and has given me a better understanding of your backgrounds and those of my grandparents and great-grandparents.' She noted how much of our history we had been able to cover. 'Your sharing with us even the most difficult times has put so much into perspective. It will ensure that these wonderful stories about both families will be preserved and held warmly in our memories forever. They are now recorded as an important part of our Jewish heritage and are the pillars upon which our family has been built ... I am now a true Krakowska/Chrzanów girl with parents who are the most exceptionally humane and wonderful people that I will always admire, respect and love.'

Lilian summed it up: 'I wish you both a loving and healthy life, enjoying every moment of your freedom.'

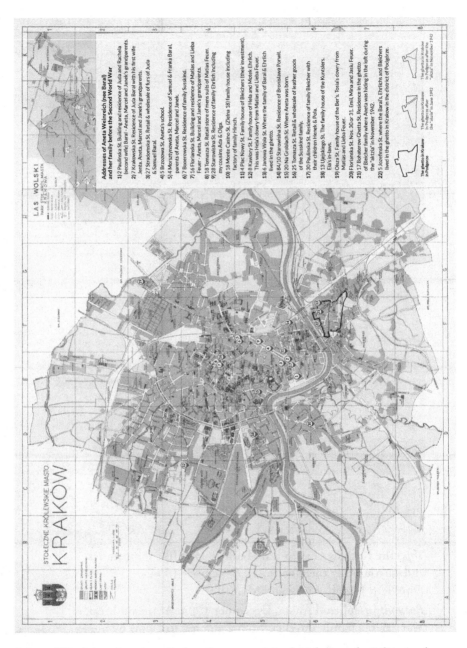

Map of Kraków, showing all the places we visited with Joseph, Lilian and Michelle in 1994. Map: Adam Launer, Opracował.

Top: The Kraków Ghetto wall, built to look like tombstones, and surrounding the Ghetto, 12 December 1994. From left: Joseph, Aneta and Michelle.

Bottom: Joseph and Aneta, December 1994. At the outbreak of War Aneta's family travelled from Zgłobień to Lwów by horse and cart similar to this.

Aneta standing in front of her school with Joseph at 5 Brzozowa Street
with the two plaqes above her, December 2006.

Close-up of the two plaques at Aneta's school and the translation
(opposite page).

THESE BUILDINGS IN 5 BRZOZOWA ST AND 1 PODBRZEZIE ST
HOUSED THREE SCHOOLS
OF THE JEWISH SOCIETY
FOR COMMUNITY AND SECONDARY SCHOOLS:

THE HEBREW PUBLIC SCHOOL
THE CHAIM HILFSTEIN JUNIOR SECONDARY SCHOOL
THE SCHOOL OF TRADES AND CRAFTS FOR MEN

AFTER 35 YEARS OF OPERATION (1904 – 1939)
THESE SCHOOLS WERE CLOSED DOWN
BY THE GERMAN INVADERS,
WITH THE TEACHERS AND STUDENTS HAVING SUFFERED
THE SAME FATE AS KRAKÓW JEWS.

THIS PLAQUE WAS MOUNTED IN 1987 BY

THE ASSOCIATION	THE COMMITTEE
OF FORMER KRAKÓW	FOR THE PROTECTION OF
RESIDENTS IN ISRAEL	JEWISH CULTURAL HERITAGE

Top: At the Bispings' apartment, Kraków, 13 December 1994.
From left: Adam Bisping, Aneta, Michelle, Lilian and Joseph.

Bottom: Aneta, Michelle and Joseph at Amon Goeth's house in
Płaszów, 12 December 1994. It was common knowledge that from
the second floor, where he used to sit sunning himself, he aimed a
telescopic rifle at 'labourers', taking pride in never missing.

Sledding at Pilchów, a light-hearted diversion on the December 1994 trip.

21

SHOWING THE CHILDREN THE WORLD

◈

Because the War prevented Joseph and me from having normal childhoods, we wanted to make sure that Lilian, Michelle and Henry had every opportunity to see our beautiful country, Australia, as well as the rest of the world. We hoped to expand their horizons. From the time they were small we went on breaks and vacations with my mother in the lovely Blue Mountains.

We started slowly, so they could absorb everything. We loved the crisp, fragrant air and the spectacular rock formations known as the Three Sisters. The children enjoyed finding the woody fruits of the red, flowering 'mountain devil' plant and making figures with them. The mountain devil 'heads' were placed on pipe-cleaners of different colours which were bent into different shapes to make legs and arms.

We would stay in a comfortable hotel called Karaweera at 132-74 Govetts Leap Road in Blackheath, run by a Hungarian couple, Mr and Mrs Mandel. They served traditional Jewish food and had a huge yard in which the children could run wild and play on the swings and slippery-dips.

At the beginning of every month, we would pick my mother up from her business to go to Blackheath, Katoomba or Leura. Joseph would drive into York Street around lunchtime to meet her at 1 o'clock. Her favourite saying was 'You don't have to wait for me'— but since there was nowhere to park, my husband had to constantly circle the block until she was ready. Often this was an hour after the arranged time, during which he had frequently been pursued by traffic policemen and parking attendants.

When the Hungarian place in the Mountains closed, we stayed at the Leura Hotel instead. Joseph and I kept this up even after the children left home, going once a month for a refreshing weekend break. We always went to Cyril's, the European delicatessen in the Haymarket to buy the food we required for the weekend, since my mother didn't like what was served at the hotel. We bought Estonian black bread, white farm cheese and other yellow cheeses, wurst, sour cucumbers, smoked fish, scumbria (sardines in tomato sauce) and roll mops (herring). Eating these delicious familiar foods always felt festive.

When they were still children, we also took them to Canberra so that they could see Australia's capital. They loved exploring Parliament House and the other grand public buildings, and walking around Lake Burley Griffin. We also went to the mountains around Kosciuszko to see the huge hydro-electric scheme. The children revelled in the green summer landscape, the wildflowers, the horse-riding and the boats on the lake. When we drove all the way to Melbourne for the wedding of our agent Mr Polonski's son, we all enjoyed riding the trams and strolling in the Botanical Gardens by the Yarra.

These trips brought their country and its history alive for the children.

For many years I dreamed about taking them back to Israel—when they were a little older. I wanted them to meet my grandfather, Juda Baral, other family members such as Jacob and Toni Feuer and their children, as well as Ada, Olga and Pola with whom I had experienced so much during the War. Motek Ehrlich, Ada's and Olga's father, was also living in Israel, as well as Pola's mother.

Just as I was finally booking the first trip with the girls, I received the sad news that Grandfather had died, on 12 April 1964. But I was still determined to take them to Israel.

On the way we stopped over in Hong Kong, where the girls were fascinated with the rickshaw rides, part of a completely different way of life, new customs and another language. They loved the hustle and bustle of the business district and the neon lights of Nathan Street. I took them to a Chinese opera where shark-fin soup was served, and we travelled to the New Territories and on a cable car to The Peak, from where we could look down on the whole of Hong Kong stretched before us.

In Israel we received the warmest, most heartfelt welcome, with so much love from family and friends. Lilian and Michelle bonded immediately with their cousins and other family members. I took them to all the places I had lived and introduced them to our neighbours at 124 Ben Yehuda Street, the Bernstein family. Unfortunately, no one was home in the apartment where I'd lived. Around the corner was the home of the Prime Minister, Ben-Gurion, on Keren Kayemeth. It had become a museum, so we were able to go in and experience its atmosphere.

I took the girls to lunch at my favourite restaurant, the Roval, where I used to go with my friends when I lived in Tel Aviv, and we sat outside watching the passing parade. It seemed as if everyone in the world was represented in Israel: from Russia and other parts of Europe to Africa and the Americas. When we saw young people in the uniforms of the Israeli Defence Force, this dramatised for the children my time in the Army as a sergeant. After lunch, we walked the short distance to my high school.

We took a special trip to Jerusalem and saw the Knesset, the Jewish Parliament, and of course the celebrated Wailing Wall, the Kotel. We went for a few days to stay in Tiberias, an interesting town with a lake, on which we went boating. Looking up, we could see the Golan Heights. We also went to the Dead Sea and bathed in the hot springs.

Back in Tel Aviv, we always went to Auntie Ela's for Shabbat dinner. Ela cooked a feast and Moshe always sang special songs. Whenever I visit, I can still smell the fragrance of her baking and cooking.

Before returning to Australia, we spent hours at get-togethers with family and friends in different homes. This was an unforgettable trip, which introduced the girls not only to the country, but to the family. Both Lilian and Michelle have since kept contact with their Israeli relatives.

There were so many other places we wanted to visit. When Joseph and I went on business to London and Paris to see the latest trends, it was just a short hop to Israel and Poland. In 1970, when Joseph went on a business trip to Los Angeles, he stopped over in Hawaii. He was so excited by what he saw that he called me and said: 'Aneta, come to Paradise! It's called Hawaii.'

I was on the plane the next day. I loved the warmth, the relaxed atmosphere and eating breakfast where you could touch the sand on one of the beautiful beaches. Our room in the 'Pink Palace', the Sheraton Waikiki, had a splendid view of the ocean from its balcony—especially spectacular at night-time. We also had dinner at the hotel next door, and saw hula girls dancing under soft lights. The raised outdoor flares provided a wonderfully warm glow. Everything was done out in the open air, and we swam in the sea twice a day: once in the early morning and then at lunchtime.

It was all so magical that we decided to show it to the children. We visited Pearl Harbour, where American warships were destroyed by Japanese bombers in December 1941, bringing the United States into World War II. Then we took them to Los Angeles before flying on to New York. We stopped over again in Hawaii on the way home.

Henry and Michelle were later to return to Los Angeles to open a showroom for our business in the prestigious California Mart building, to sell our dresses to the American market. Although they were well received, after a year-and-a-half, they felt it was time to return home. Henry had been attending UCLA, and had to make a decision whether to stay there or return to take up his place at the University of Sydney. When he decided to return to Australia, all three children were then back in Sydney.

As the business became increasingly successful, we would travel to London and Paris to study the new trends. They gave me ideas so that I could experiment with my designs. On each trip, the children not only learned different aspects of our business but also came with us to art galleries, musicals and ballet performances.

It gave us a lot of pleasure to travel overseas twice a year, in June and December. We would go first to the United States to spend time with the children as they moved out into different worlds and took new opportunities. In New York, where we bought the finest supplies of laces and accessories, I would love to see my brother Jim and spend time with him. He was making his way as a dermatologist, much in demand by New Yorkers. He had a well-appointed surgery in a prime position opposite Central Park, at 210 Central Park South.

We believe that because of the opportunities these trips offered, our children's eyes were opened to a wider international world. Our goal was to immerse them into a mindset of possibilities, incorporating their Australian roots into a borderless world.

Top: Michelle (left) and Lilian (right) in a rickshaw, Hong Kong, February 1965.
Bottom: Michelle, Aneta and Lilian, Israel, 1965.

Top: Lilian in London, December 1974.
Bottom: A wonderful family trip to Hawaii, 1977.
From left: Henry, Lilian, Joseph, Aneta and Michelle.

343

22

CELEBRATING OUR CULTURE

◈

I find it very comforting when I make the long trip back to Kraków to steep myself in my childhood memories and my Jewish culture. There I feel close to my parents, my brothers and all my lost family members. I enjoy repeating some of the simple experiences that marked my childhood, such as feeding the pigeons in the main market square, Rynek Główny.

I always visit Apartment 12A, 4 Morsztynowska Street, where our family lived on the third floor. When I first asked the present tenants if we could come in, I explained who I was and they graciously agreed to let us enter. That meant my own family could stand in what had been my parents' bedroom and the dining and sitting rooms, in the actual spaces I had described to them. I found that the bedroom which I had shared with my brothers had been used to enlarge the neighbouring apartment.

At the annual Jewish Culture Festival held in Kraków, the brochure says: *Life is what interests us—its astonishing capacity for rebirth and flourishing anew. It is an unending celebration of Jewish life*, paying tribute to the past but always looking to the future. Jewish people attend from all over the world, and Polish people also participate. It's interesting to see this.

The Festival is now in its 27th year. We visited Kraków for the 15th festival, which started with Friday night prayers ushering in the Shabbat, with talented cantors such as Yakov Stark and Benzion Miller from the United States singing our ancient melodies in the fully-restored Tempel Synagogue at 24 Miodowa Street. These heavenly songs are in Joseph's DNA since his father, brother and grandparents all sang them.

During the Festival, Leopold Kozłowski, known as the Last Klezmer of Galicia, sang Jewish songs accompanied by his five singers. His concerts were so popular that we would arrive an hour early to stand in the long queue to get good seats. Kozłowski even taught four Christian girls to sing the songs in Yiddish. Their performance was word-perfect and with the correct Yiddish accent.

On Saturday morning the Tempel Synagogue or Remuh Synagogue was packed with visitors from overseas, including schoolchildren from Israel. In the evening, Polish people joined us. On this happy night there were prayers, drinking and singing. Everyone joined in with the Chief Rabbi of Kraków to sing spirited choruses of the great traditional song, *L'chaim, To Life*. Joseph was in his element, even dancing with the Rabbi. At prayers that morning, my husband had been given the great honour of being called as witness to the reading of the Torah. This is known as *Aliyah*, to ascend or rise.

We met some interesting—and surprising—people at the Festival. While queuing for the Kozłowski concert, we began to chat with

Mr Edward and Mrs Ursula Sieprawska Śliwa. Joseph, as inquisitive as always, asked why a Polish couple was coming to listen to Jewish songs. Also, he wanted to know why there were so many others who were not Jewish who were also waiting in line for the performance.

Mr Śliwa told us that they loved klezmer music, 'the sound of the Jewish East'. They enjoyed all the singers, but their favourite was Marta Bizoń and her group, who sang first in Yiddish, then again in Polish.

After the long concert finished it was quite late, but the Śliwas accompanied us back to our hotel. We had a long and interesting conversation with them, and found them to be super-intelligent. As they were leaving, Joseph gave them his card, but after they left, I noticed they had dropped it. He knew where they had parked, so he ran out to see them again.

This was the beginning of our long friendship. The Śliwas took us to Ojców, an attractive town famous for its white cliffs. We hired a horse and cart and Lilian insisted on taking the reins. I posed for a picture on a scooter in which Joseph says I look *sporty and elegant*.

Mr Śliwa passed away on 19 October 2013, but we are still in contact with Ursula.

On one of our Kraków trips, our friend Mr Bisping had, by coincidence, mentioned my name to Mrs Barbara Oleksyn, an acquaintance of his. She had actually been our neighbour during the War in Lwów! We met and were delighted to see one another after 64 years. With great emotion, she told me that her father had been arrested by the Gestapo in October 1941. His family had been shattered when he was taken away. My father had worked out a plan to get him out of gaol by bribing one of the guards, and gave Barbara's mother his gold watch. She told me how touched she had been by this gesture of kindness and generosity. Unfortunately, it did not succeed, she said, and her father is thought to have died in January 1944.

One of our most memorable moments on a Kraków visit was when Professor Aleksander Skotnicki invited us to a commemoration of Oskar Schindler's 100th 'birthday'. The Professor was aware that my father was No. 41 on Schindler's List, and in his address he mentioned that I was in the audience. He asked me to stand—and I did. I was standing for my father as if to say: 'You suffered here and we will remember.'

We also visited the Emalia factory where Schindler saved 1200 Jewish people, including my father. At the factory they produced pots, pans, cups and plates, to show the Nazis how useful they were. The irony is that these products were not useful; the factory was merely a way to save its workers. It is well known now that Schindler risked his own life by employing them, at the same time drinking with, and bribing the Gestapo to keep them from discovering the futility of the work being done there.

On the wall of the museum which now stands where the factory did, the name of every worker is listed. Samuel Baral, my father, shows right at the top of the wall.

On one trip, Joseph and I returned to the holiday resort at Zakopane at the base of the Tatras Mountains. This brought back many happy memories of winter vacations with my mother and brothers, since we were taught to ski there on wooden skis. I was even able to show my husband the slope where I had my first lessons.

Our hotel had spectacular views from the windows and balcony of the top floor room where we stayed. The whole landscape was dressed in white, like a bride. We enjoyed walking to the market and buying embroidered sheepskin waistcoats for our grandchildren. Joseph was especially pleased we could do this, since his family also made these waistcoats before the War, when they were made for men and women as well as children.

We also took the opportunity on that visit to go to a famous sanatorium, Słowacki, in Busko-Zdrój. Its main attractions include hot springs and a spa, and their gardens are very beautiful.

Back in Kraków it was a great pleasure to meet up with a famous Israeli author who, like me, was born there and suffered during the Holocaust. Moshe Plessner was my Auntie Ela's husband, and Miriam Akavia was their niece. Miriam's great life project was to unite the Polish and Jewish people, something she fostered by writing books, giving lectures in Kraków and Warsaw, and being interviewed frequently on TV as well as in a specially-made documentary. Her stories of the War were beamed across the country. Written in Hebrew and translated into Polish by Moshe, they were also translated into many other languages.

On another trip to Poland, we went to Wadowice to see the family home of the Roman Catholic Pope, Jan Paweł (Pope John Paul the Second). As Jewish people, we have tremendous respect for this Holy Father. At the end of the War, when many who had survived the concentration camps were being forced on death marches by the Nazis, he was out on his morning run and came across a woman hiding in a bush. She was weak and begged him for help. He picked her up and carried her on his shoulders for two kilometres to a village where she could hide with a kind farmer until the War was over.

Years later, on 26 March 2000 when the Pope made a pilgrimage to the Holy Land, he received a tremendous welcome in Jerusalem. Among the crowds thronging to see him was a woman waving and screaming to attract his attention. He asked the driver to stop his car, then stepped down and embraced her. It was the woman he had saved from death.

On his visit he also went to the Wailing Wall and inserted a letter (called a *kvitel*) in a crack. It read:

God of our fathers,
You chose Abraham and his descendants
to bring your Name to the Nations:
we are deeply saddened
by the behaviour of those
who in the course of history
have caused these children of yours to suffer,
and asking your forgiveness,
we wish to commit ourselves to
genuine brotherhood
with the people of the Covenant.

John Paul II
Jerusalem, 26 March 2000

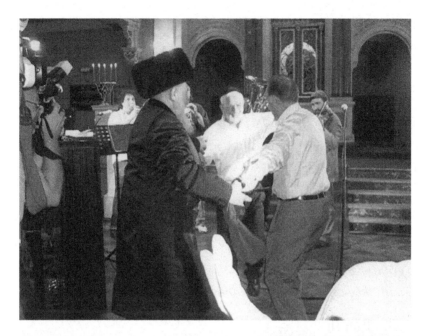

Top: Jewish Culture Festival, Kraków, 2008. Joseph (right) dancing with the Chief Rabbi of Kraków at the Tempel Synagogue.

Bottom: With our friends the Śliwas, Kraków, 2009. From left: Aneta, Mrs Śliwa, Joseph, Mr Śliwa.

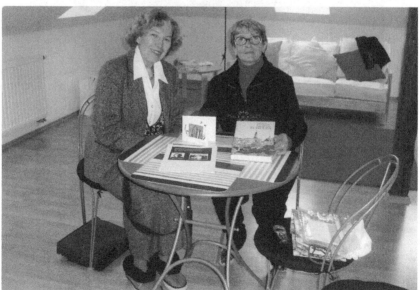

Top: Aneta on a scooter, Ojców, Poland, 2006.
Bottom: Meeting with Barbara Oleksyn, Kraków, 31 December 2005.

The Oscar Schindler factory. This building was used from 1948-2002 by Krakowskie Zakłady Elektroniczne Unitra-Telpod, later renamed Telpod SA, a Polish manufacturer of electronic components. The picture was taken in December 1994 before, in June 2010, it reopened as a branch of the City of Kraków Historical Museum. It now has a new plaque with the name Oskar Schindler Factory-Emalia.

Top: Aneta and Joseph at the Emalia Factory Museum, Kraków, 2010, showing pots and pans produced there.
Bottom: Aneta at the gardens in Busko-Zdrój, 2010.

Aneta, Zakopane, December 2009.

Top: Aneta with famous Israeli author, Miriam Akavia, Kraków, 2010.
Bottom: Pope John Paul II at the Wailing Wall, Jerusalem, March 2000.
Photo: Vatican Media, Vatican City, Rome, Italy.

23

NEXT YEAR
IN JERUSALEM

◈

Few cities have attracted more love and controversy than Jerusalem. It is a powerful lightning rod and spiritual centre. The Jewish people always turn towards the East, to Jerusalem, from every synagogue around the world, to pray for peace and for the triumph of humanity and the human spirit. As a Jewish nation we have seen it destroyed twice, and captured and recaptured 44 times. Yet throughout those years, wherever Jewish people have lived, we have never ceased to face Jerusalem, pray for Jerusalem, speak its language and remember it in every home, at every wedding and at all the high points of the Jewish year.

We have travelled to Israel many times since I lived there in my youth. As soon as we reach Tel Aviv and our regular room at the Sheraton, family and friends crowd in to welcome us. There is an abundance of emotion. When Auntie Ela was alive, I fully devoted myself to her and these visits gave me the opportunity to plan all her requirements for the year, anticipating what she would need for the present and future. I adored her and wanted to make her life as comfortable as possible.

We were such frequent guests of the Sheraton that they went out of their way to give us a good room on a top floor with a view over the Mediterranean on one side. My daughter Michelle observes that I always prefer a clear, unobstructed view with light everywhere. I believe this stems from days during the War when I felt I was always in darkness and surrounded by walls.

I always look forward to Israeli breakfasts, which include freshly-baked bread rolls, salads, cheeses, herrings, olives, eggs and fruit: a feast. They remind me of the fresh fruits and vegetables that were so readily available when I first arrived there—the beginning of hope, sunshine and freedom.

In the evenings we often invited family members over for supper. The food at the hotel was also delicious, and the night views even more spectacular.

On our first trip to Tel Aviv, in 1966, we took a bus to Jerusalem. As we drew near, we were moved to see the city spread before us in all its ancient glory. Our final prayer at Rosh Hashanah is always: *next year in Jerusalem.* But once again, our holy city was under attack. We saw the burnt-out remains of jeeps and tanks and memorial plaques for soldiers who had died. I was reminded of the human sacrifice that accompanies every struggle for what you believe—and also that the battle for freedom is constant.

Our first stop on one of our first visits was Yad Vashem, the World Holocaust Remembrance Centre and also the world centre for Holocaust research. We researched the names of family members which re-opened this cruel wound as my mind turned back to all the beloved family members I had lost during the War. It is a wound that never heals; it just pains me with varying degrees of intensity. When I read the plaques carrying the names of righteous people who had risked their lives to save Jewish people, I made a pledge that I was going to continue to look for members of the two Christian families who saved our own lives: the descendants of Bronka Porwitowa and Ilonka Nemes. We wanted to honour them.

We then made our way to the Wailing Wall, to give thanks that we were still alive, against all the odds. In his darkest hours, Joseph had promised himself that if he survived he would visit the Eiffel Tower in Paris, the Statue of Liberty in New York and the Wailing Wall in Jerusalem. He inserted a *kvitel,* a note with a prayer, into the Wall, and we prayed for the health of our children. He recited Kaddish, a prayer for those taken from us.

Our third port of call was the Knesset, the impressive building housing the Israeli Parliament. It was even grander inside. We went to the public gallery to listen to the debates of the day, and I translated the Hebrew for Joseph so he could understand what was going on.

Our last stop in a crowded day was the boarding school at 60 Rashi Street that I had attended for a year. This building is now used for a different purpose.

As we boarded the bus back to Tel Aviv, we reminded ourselves of the words of Psalm 137:

If I forget you, oh Jerusalem, may my right hand forget its skill.

אִם-אֶשְׁכָּחֵךְ יְרוּשָׁלָם- תִּשְׁכַּח יְמִינִי.

Top: Family get-together on a visit to Tel Aviv, January 2005.
From left, seated: Zvi Bar Lev (Bleicher), Margalit Bar Lev (Zvi's
wife), Aneta, Olga and Joseph. Standing: Ada, Hila (Ada's daughter),
Hagai (Ada's husband) and Abir (Ada's son-in-law).

Bottom: Aneta in Haifa, Israel 2006-07, with her best friend, Pola,
cousin of Ada and Olga.

Joseph and Aneta breakfast at the Sheraton Hotel, Tel Aviv, December 2009.

Opposite page:
Cousins Yaffa and Tova, daughters
of Uncle Jacob Feuer, Tel Aviv, 2007.

361

Top: Ada, Olga and Aneta in Tel Aviv, Israel, July 2017.
Bottom: Bibi, Aneta, Sylvia (Zvika's wife) and Zvika in in
Petach-Tikva, Israel, July 2017. See the picture of Bibi and
Zvika 71 years ago on page 132.

24

AUNTIE ELA

◈

My first recollections of my dear paternal Auntie Ela are from the time I was a small child. After the War, I don't ever recall her as happy. From her childhood on, her life had been difficult, because she and my father had lost their mother, Antonieta Jenta, on 31 July 1923 when she was only 45 years old. This, of course, made an enormous impact on 10-year-old Ela. Everything became more difficult for her when her father married Rachela Brawmann a few months later.

My father was ten years older than Auntie Ela. My own mother was able to give him emotional support after my parents married on 13 February1928, but Ela grew up hating her stepmother. My mother stepped in to make peace between them and didn't give up until she was successful—which was so characteristic of her.

In 1937 Ela married a stately young man from a good family, Moniek (Moshe) Künstler. They ran a wholesale leather business at 44 Dietla Street in Kraków, together with Moshe's three brothers, Leibish, Hirsch and Alfred and their father. These years of Ela's life were very happy, which is evident in the picture of her with her husband.

But sadly her newfound happiness was not to last. In 1941, both she and Moshe were forced to leave their home at 13 Ujeńskiego Street and move into the Kraków Ghetto. From there they were taken to Płaszów, before they were separated. Ela was transferred to Auschwitz and tattooed with the number A176-52. She managed to survive the long, hard years of imprisonment until the camp was liberated by the Red Army.

Moshe was taken to a different camp. At the end of the War, Ela searched desperately for him and discovered, to her horror, that the day after the camp had been liberated, he had died. Jewish welfare organisations in the United States, upon hearing that the camps had been opened, immediately organised hundreds of doctors and nurses to bring food to survivors, and to take to hospital those who needed extra attention.

The food delivered was not necessarily the kind suitable for starving people. Moshe's first reaction at seeing the food was immediately to eat a huge meal. But his ravaged body couldn't cope with so much nourishment. He died almost at once.

Because we were by then already in Israel, a heartbroken Auntie Ela asked if she could join us. But she was unsuccessful in obtaining the right papers for Palestine, ending up instead in Cyprus. There she met our family friend, Henek Bleicher (Zvi Barlev). It took them many months to reach Tel Aviv, where Zvi joined his mother, Sala Bleicher, and sister Pola. Ela moved in with us at 124 Ben Yehuda Street.

She didn't take long to decide how she would earn her living. In memory of her husband, she decided to train as a dietician. She was smart, and rose to become a director in a big Haifa hospital. She even took an Israeli name, Aliza.

On a visit to the family in Tel Aviv, she met her second husband, Moniek (Moshe) Plessner. After their wedding, they lived at 6 Herzl

Street, Ramat-Gan. On my visits to Israel, seeing both of them happy together gave me a lot of pleasure. Her new husband was a translator. He was also a spiritual man, steeped in knowledge of Judaism. When he and Joseph met, they would discuss religious questions together for hours.

My children loved Auntie Ela as much as I did. I think they saw what a huge part of my life she was and how much I loved her, and followed my affection. Michelle used to call Ela and Moshe special names: Eloingkem and Moingkem. They loved these nicknames.

Joseph remembers one evening when, at Shabbat dinner at Ela and Moshe's apartment, Moshe sang all the Shabbat songs in his beautiful voice, reminding my husband of similar evenings at his own parents' and grandparents' homes.

Such happiness didn't last for Ela. On the eve of another of my visits to Israel, she told me that her husband was not himself. His behaviour, she said, had become strange and erratic. I had taken the latest *Time* magazine to read on the plane, and by chance looked at an article on Alzheimer's disease. The symptoms described were very like Moshe's.

Ela took her husband to their doctor. He confirmed that Moshe was in the first stages of Alzheimer's, the dreadful illness that will always worsen and for which there is still no cure. The doctor provided medication, but the outlook was grim.

Ela did everything she could to keep her husband at home for as long as possible. However, it only took a few months for him to become worse. Soon he required full-time care. Fortunately she was able to get him into a top health care facility, called Lichtenstein.

I made a point of ringing her every day during this difficult period of her life, to keep her spirits up as much as possible. In the 1990s, the telephone rates from Australia to Israel were very high—but this would never have stopped me from ringing Ela. I knew how much she appreciated and depended on being able to talk with me.

Her life contracted to daily visits to see Moshe. Otherwise, she was sad all the time. I went to Israel especially to see her, to find out what could be done to improve her life. Having spent time in her company, I decided that a home catering to the needs of elderly people was what she needed, as she was in her late seventies.

It took me a while to find the right place. Finally I found a facility called Mediterranean Towers, in Jaffa. When the director showed us round, she said that Ela would need to buy her own apartment, but that she could furnish it herself. There was 24-hour medical assistance and a bright dining room which served first-class food three times a day. Residents could enjoy lectures and films, play cards together and go on excursions.

When Ela put down her deposit, we requested an apartment that was high up, with views over the Mediterranean. After a couple of months, one became available and she moved in. Since her windows had no curtains, I quickly bought some suitable fabric in Australia, which I sent to her. She had them made up and they made the room look like a cozy home.

Meanwhile Moshe's health was deteriorating further. He passed away on 16 October 1991. On my next visit to Israel, I decided that Auntie Ela needed a carer to help her get up, bathe, prepare for the day and take her down to breakfast. Most importantly, this person could also accompany her on walks in the fresh air. We were lucky to find Fanny Peresido, and I was also constantly in touch by phone with Ela's doctor, Dr Fira.

On 13 June 1999, I received a phone call from Israel early in the morning telling me that Ela had passed away after a heart attack. I had promised her that we would attend her funeral, so Joseph and I left for Israel a few hours later.

On the plane I took time to remember all the different facets of her personality. Ela was such a character. She had a distinctive laugh, a high-pitched cackle, and a very determined answer to everything. Once when I was staying at her apartment with Michelle, she called out *Layla* before we went to sleep. This is a shortened Hebrew word for 'good night,' and this was to become our mantra. I remember when she kissed Michelle, she would always breathe in her scent as if to capture her time with her forever. All our conversations were in Polish, and they always started with 'What do you think?' She would ask me this same question and I always told her that whatever it was would turn out well, and that she shouldn't worry.

I contacted the Rabbi who would officiate at her funeral and asked him for permission to recite the Kaddish, the ancient mourning prayer. This is not usually a task that women perform, and it's not easy, since the language used is Aramaic. Only the last two lines are in Hebrew. However, I was coached to perfection by my cousin Yaffa's husband, Menachem, who also presented me with a prayer book.

We woke on 16 June to find it was a sunny, very hot day, after we had flown in from a chilly Sydney winter. I contacted those members of my family who were not related to Ela, and was gratified to see that they all arrived for the funeral, which was held in Hulon. There were also many people present from Mediterranean Towers. We were guided to a spot where four pillars supported a roof, and it was quite shocking to see Ela's tiny body enveloped in white cloth, lying on a cart with wheels. This was slowly moved towards the grave, as the Rabbi chanted Tehillim prayers.

Ela was lowered gently into her grave, to join Moshe. She was at last reunited with her beloved husband.

This was a long, heavy day for me. The enormity of Ela's passing and the tremendous sadness of seeing an era fade away before my eyes; saying goodbye to the last member of my father's family; remembering Ela's devotion to me and mine to her, was overwhelming. I clung to Ela all her life. She was my last link to a past that was once so beautiful and then so cruel. Through Ela I could still feel the bond to my father. She was another precious witness to an inhuman era of history.

She is irreplaceable.

Top: Ela (left) with her stepmother Rachela Brawmann (also known as Rózia), 2 June 1924.

Bottom: Aneta's grandfather, Juda Baral (left), Auntie Ela and her second husband, Moshe Plessner, Tel Aviv, 1954.

Ela and Moniek Künstler, her first husband, Kraków, 1937.

Aneta (front) with Ela standing behind her, in front of the hospital in
Bat-Galim, Haifa, 18 March 1950, where Ela worked as a dietician.

Auntie Ela and Aneta at Mediterranean Towers,
Bat Yam (near Tel Aviv), 1998.

25

CANDLES
FOR OUR SAVIOURS

◈

In 2004, to mark the sixtieth anniversary of the tragic deportation and annihilation of Hungarian Jews, I was invited by the Jewish Board of Deputies in Sydney to participate in a memorial service. The Moriah College hall was packed with people. There were six candles to represent the six million Jews who perished and one candle to honour those who sacrificed their lives to help Jewish people despite the threat of certain death to themselves. I was invited to light this candle for the Righteous Among the Nations.

This was particularly meaningful for me, as my family was saved by two incredible women whose stories I have told earlier in the book. They were the brave Hungarian woman, Ilonka Nemes and the courageous Polish woman, Bronka Porwitowa. The actions of both were crucial to the survival of my mother and the six children in her care.

In my speech that evening I told the audience that I was a survivor and the child of survivors of the Holocaust. 'During the long night of the Holocaust, among the few points of light were the actions of those men and women who risked their own lives to save those of Jews. Their actions show us that compassion, courage and morality were not totally extinguished in those dark days.'

After paying tribute to the courage and enterprise of my mother, I continued: 'Living as Roman Catholics, we were helped by a Righteous Gentile, Ilonka Nemes. From Hungary we crossed to Romania where my mother eluded the Gestapo.' Then I said that we went on to Israel, 'where my Jewish identity was restored... and reunited with my father as a family.'

'Tonight I light a candle to honour those who cared enough not to stand by when innocent Jews were being persecuted.'

The evening finished in a very solemn manner. There was complete silence in the hall and Cantor Deutsch, a Hungarian survivor of the Holocaust, sang *El male rachamim*, a prayer for the departed: 'Merciful God in Heaven, grant perfect repose to the souls of the *Kedoshim* (holy ones) who have passed to their eternal habitation.'

This was followed by *Hatikvah*, the Israeli national anthem.

When my brother Jim visited Sydney from New York, also in 2004, he and I, with Martin, decided that we had to find the families of both our saviours, so that they could be honoured at Yad Vashem for the Righteous Among the Nations. During the years I was away from Poland in Israel and Australia, I had always carried in my mind and heart memories of Ilonka and Bronka.

We started with Ilonka. In a video, my nephew, Edward Baral (Jim's youngest son), interviewed the three of us in Henry's apartment. This was fortuitous, since it turned out to be the last time all three of us were together. A few months later, on 16 March 2010,

Martin passed away—and six weeks later, on 30 April, Jim did too. Martin was 78 and Jim was 75.

It was my nephew Edward who spearheaded the entire process. He took it upon himself to find any close relatives, and his persistence and tireless diligence have been invaluable.

In 2009, he sent the video to Yad Vashem in Jerusalem, saying that we hoped her descendants would be honoured and Ilonka recognised as one of the Righteous Among the Nations, an official title awarded on behalf of the State of Israel and the Jewish people to non-Jews who had risked their lives to save Jews during the Holocaust.

The process of recognition takes time, since a review board made up of former Israeli Supreme Court Judges must research the testimony and evidence, and compare it with the historical facts, to be sure the applicant is truly worthy.

The staff at Yad Vashem asked us to find Ilonka's closest descendant so he or she could be presented with a medal.

Edward continued looking for Ilonka's desendants. His efforts included contacting the Red Cross, searching Hungarian genealogical websites and posting messages to Facebook. He tried every possible Google search term.

Finally he found a blog called Régi Nyíregyháza or Old Nyíregyháza, and found that it was connected to a Facebook page of the same name. He posted a notice in both English and Hungarian, using Google's translation features and included a photo of Ilonka. He asked people to share it and to contact him if they knew the family.

Many people did share what he had written. Within a few hours, he received a message from Ilona Vaskó, a Hungarian woman who, by coincidence, had the same maiden name as Ilonka Nemes but was not related to her. Ilona had written an article for the blog (which is why it came up in Edward's search) and she asked him for more information.

Within ten days an article Ilona had written was published in the *Nyíregyháza News* (http://www.kelet.hu/helyi/2015/04/26/eleteket-mentett-keresik.kelet). Ilona had also spoken to the Mayor of Nyíregyháza to see if he would open the city's archives to enable her to research the family.

Within 24 hours of the article appearing, Ilonka's grand-niece, Katalin, came forward—and the day after that, Ilona received a call from Ilonka's granddaughter, Anna Ottóné Körmendi.

Edward wrote a letter to Anna and to the grand-niece via Google Translate, asking for photos of her grandmother, her mother and herself to show me, to make sure that this was indeed the correct family.

I felt both relief and sadness when I received the photos. When I saw the picture of Ilonka's parents I cried, since I knew we had finally found the right family.

The people at Yad Vashem wrote to Anna:

We are pleased to announce that the Commission for Designation of the Righteous has decided to award the title of Righteous Among the Nations to your late grandmother, Nemes Ilonka (Vaskó), for help rendered to Jewish persons during the period of the Holocaust at the risk of her life.

As Psalm 118 says:

Shouts of joy and victory resound in the tents of the Righteous

It had taken Edward 11 years, starting from the meeting with my brothers, to find her. In 2011, Yad Vashem, in recognition of Ilonka's and her family's actions in saving our lives, inscribed her name on the

Wall of Honour in the Garden of the Righteous in Jerusalem. They agreed that Ilonka should also be remembered with a medal.

I will always be more than grateful to Edward. In his search to locate this Hungarian family, he displayed the characteristics of his father: tenacity, unswerving belief and smart planning. He was driven by the emotional connection he had to his family history and to his father's memory. I am so proud of him.

I must also mention the beautiful heart of Ilona Vaskó. She was as dedicated to finding Ilonka Nemes' descendants as if she were one of our own family. Now it feels as if she is! She answered every email and question before we arrived in Budapest for the honour ceremony, at any time of the day or night, despite the fact that she was busy with her own job. She really took a personal interest in us and our story.

Receiving the invitation from Yad Vashem for the ceremony to present the medal to Anna, her granddaughter, was overwhelming. Honouring Ilonka on behalf of the family was finally within my reach.

The ceremony was to take place on 29 October 2015, at 3pm at the Ministry of the Interior in Budapest. We immediately booked our trip. To my regret, Joseph could not join us in Budapest since his health prevented him from travelling such a long distance.

First, however, Lilian and I decided to go to Kraków. We carried a photo of my Polish saviour, Bronka Porwitowa. I was determined also to find her closest descendant. I gave the photo of Bronka and her family along with all the information I had to our good friend in Kraków, Adam Benedykt Bisping, hoping he would continue the search while I was in Budapest.

Lilian and I arrived in Budapest on the evening of 26 October 2015, and Michelle joined us the following morning. Being in Budapest gave me a strange feeling. There I was after 71 years, with no fear, anticipating an official ceremony.

My first arrival there had been on foot through the border. This time I was an adult tourist as opposed to a Jewish child refugee disguised as a Polish Roman Catholic. On the way from the airport on a smooth and modern highway to the Budapest City Hilton, I could not help comparing the enormous differences between my first trip and this second one.

Months before, as soon as Edward let me know that he had found Anna, he had set everything in motion. There had been a barrage of excited emails between us, the great-granddaughter of Ilonka, her grand-niece Katalin and between us and Ilona Vaskó. We were all to meet in the lobby of the hotel, with a translator.

This meeting was very emotional, full of the feeling shown in our faces. We sat down to coffee and I told Anna, Ilonka's granddaughter, that I remembered her when she was only 18 months old. Now she is 75, a kind, soulful and dignified woman. We exchanged photos. She had brought me a photo of herself as a baby with her grandmother, and another photo of her great-grandmother and great-grandfather taken in Nyíregyháza.

She told us what she knew of our story through her grandmother Ilonka. This was a story of what people do to help one another, rather than just a survival story. One sweet anecdote was that the girls (me, Ada, Olga and Pola) loved to play with her, and that we called her *cudna Ancika* (which in English means gorgeous Ancika).

We sat for two hours going over and over the story, each of us filling in parts we didn't know or were unsure about.

We continued to wait in the lobby for Ilona Vaskó, who had been on a work project and who arrived directly from the airport.

From the moment this meeting started, I felt I was travelling back to 1944. Now I could fully explain to Lilian and Michelle the history of this part of my life. I wanted Ilonka Nemes to come alive for them so that they could imagine my mother's fortitude and the conditions and situations we endured. They had heard me talk about what I knew of the story for so many years—particularly about the bravery of Ilonka.

Before leaving Sydney, Michelle had planned with me how we would spend all of the days we were in Budapest: where we would go and those we would visit. Now this moment had arrived.

I will list the names of all those involved, as it can be confusing: Aneta; Lilian; Michelle; Anna Sr, the granddaughter of Ilonka Nemes, our saviour; Anna Jr, the great-granddaughter of Ilonka Nemes and the daughter of Anna Sr; and Ilona Vaskó the translator.

All of us went to visit Ilonka Nemes' first-floor apartment at 17 Pongrácz út, where we had been hidden. We knocked on the door on the first floor, but unfortunately nobody was home. Granddaughter Anna Sr told us that the apartment had one-and-a-half rooms. I was mystified that we could all have fitted into such a small place—because there were also two other Jewish men in the apartment, 'Kapusta' and 'Wiśniewski' (their made-up names). Ilonka was so kind that she accommodated us all. It never seemed a burden to her.

As we left the building, I noted that it had been painted off-white, but was now pink. Granddaughter Anna Sr told me my memory was correct. We saw a train passing by, reminding me that the train station from which we left for Nyíregyháza is nearby.

From Pongracz Street we went to the cemetery to pray and pay our respects to Ilonka Nemes at her grave. The cemetery was bustling in preparation for All Saints' Day, a Christian festival in honour of all the saints in Heaven. It was a huge place, and it took time to find the grave. We bought a beautiful wreath of flowers from one of the dozens of flower shops lining the cemetery, with money that Edward

Baral had found in his father's wallet after Jim passed away. Edward wanted his father's soul to be present at Ilonka's grave. It was very moving. To see our saviour's name on her grave was the culmination of a yearning that for years had been deep in my, my mother's and my brothers' being.

After we all left the cemetery, I took a taxi with Lilian and Michelle to see the pension where I, my mother and my brothers had stayed for three days. It is no longer a hotel, but a block of apartments. But the wide street was familiar, and I could remember the address: 34 Teréz körút. Lilian and Michelle were amazed that I recalled it.

The next day was Thursday 29 October: Medal Ceremony Day. It was hosted by the Hungarian Ministry of the Interior, Yad Vashem and the Israeli Embassy. When we got up in the morning, we found it was a beautiful sunny day. This was a good omen.

The ceremony was scheduled to begin at 3pm sharp. We were asked to arrive earlier, at 2pm, to familiarise ourselves with the procedures. Both Anna Sr and Anna Jr had been asked to arrive even earlier. Great-granddaughter Anna Jr was given the honour of speaking on behalf of her family.

When I arrived with Lilian and Michelle at the elegant, olde worlde, imposing building of the Ministry of the Interior, I felt a solemn sense about what was going to unfold. We were greeted by the lovely, ever-efficient Edit Kiss, who was in charge of Public Relations at the Israeli Embassy, and walked through to the central room where the ceremony was to take place. 300 chairs were lined up, with the Israeli and Hungarian flags on either side of the platform and an orchestra assembling. There was a table with the eight medals lined up perfectly, in rows.

We were gently guided towards a room just off the hall. It was decorated with tables covered in blue-and-white tablecloths, the colours of the Israeli flag. In the room there were seven other saviours who were also being honoured and receiving medals. I was the only Holocaust survivor.

As each dignitary arrived in the room, they graciously introduced themselves, welcomed us and shook our hands. From the Ministry of the Interior came the charismatic Dr Sándor Pintér and from the State of Israel, the stately Ambassador, Ilan Mor. We also met the very competent Israeli Consul, Mordechay Waller, and the kind and professional Deputy Chief of Mission, Chad Nakash Kaynar. We had a wonderful conversation with each of these gentlemen. I was delighted to speak a little Hungarian with Dr Pintér and we also had the assistance of an interpreter.

I spoke in Hebrew to Mr Waller and Mr Mor. To Mr Kaynar, I spoke in English. Michelle later wrote letters of appreciation and thanks to them all.

Edit Kiss briefed us on how the ceremony would proceed. At 2.45pm we lined up and walked in single file to the main room, where all the guests were already seated. I was placed in the first seat in the first row, an honoured position.

Everyone stood for the National Anthem of Hungary, then the *Hatikva* of Israel, beautifully played by the ENS Ensemble. To hear the Israeli anthem sung in Hungary was beyond anything my imagination could embrace. When my daughters and I sang the National Anthem of Israel, the main message for me was that *tikva* (hope) is never lost and that we would be a free nation. I shivered, realising that I *am* free physically but that all my memories are needed for the next generations. They must consider what hope means to them and what is required of them. I considered the enormous contributions of the others, from my mother to my saviour, Ilonka, who made it possible for me to remain alive.

The guests were invited to remain standing while I was introduced: 'Aneta Weinreich, currently living in Sydney, Australia, a Holocaust survivor.' These words echoed in my mind as I moved forward to light a candle in memory of the six million martyrs *(kedoshim)* who had been murdered during World War II. As I lit the candle, I felt the presence of my mother and brothers and quiet satisfaction that Ilonka, after all these years, would now officially receive the recognition and love she deserved. Her family would know how hard we had searched for them so that Ilonka would never be forgotten.

Ilonka Nemes received two posthumous medals. The second was the Hungarian Medal for Bravery.

Following the speeches in Hungarian by the dignitaries (also read in English), the recipients went up, one-by-one, to receive their medals.

Great-granddaughter Anna Jr's speech on behalf of her mother and great-grandmother was particularly impressive. In addition to other pieces, the ENS orchestra played the theme from *Schindler's List*. Each note seemed to reach the core of my being.

Dr Sándor Pintér said in his speech: 'We remember those who did not turn away their heads and bravely stood by the persecuted. They did not let themselves be intimidated and did not want to become accomplices of a terrible era with their idleness. They have shown what ordinary people can do for their fellows. They have shown us an example that is still valid when they hid their peers, sentenced to death. They have given examples for both today's and future generations.'

Ambassador Mor brought the historical context into our modern world. He said: 'Europe has come a long way from the horrors of the Shoah. Today is not 1939, but freedom is once again under attack. Radical Islamists are marching across the Middle East and North

Africa. Elsewhere and also across Europe, we face challenges that are both age-old but at the same time quite new. Destruction and deadly evil forces, which include vicious rising anti-Semitism, coupled with vicious anti-Israel sentiment, re-appear in different contexts and ideologies across Europe.'

When the historic ceremony was concluded, we gathered again in the room off the hall, where we met the rest of the Vaskó family.

Ilonka Nemes' great niece Katalin made great efforts to be there with her son. We also met another precious member of the family, someone I never thought I would see again, Elizabeth (Erzsébet Margaret Muri), who had come with her daughter Judy Wright and their husbands from Canada to the ceremony.

It had taken 71 years for me to find the names of those we called 'the village children' in the photo on page 97. Elizabeth told me she was the little girl in the photo, along with her brother, József Muri.

We returned to our hotel completely exhausted.

That evening Ilona Vaskó had organised for us all to meet at a local pizza restaurant to enjoy a leisurely evening with Annas Sr and Jr. Great-granddaughter Anna brought her sister. The idea was to relax and appreciate our happiness at finding each other in the name of Ilonka Nemes. The atmosphere was lively, with loud music and spirited conversation.

We went to bed late. The next morning, we had to get up very early to go to Nyíregyháza.

Top: Aneta was invited by the Jewish Board of Deputies in Sydney to light the candle for the Righteous Among Nations, Moriah College, 2004. This was very significant for her and the family, since they were saved by two Righteous women.

Bottom: From left: Aneta, Martin (seated), Dahlia (sister-in-law, married to Martin), Jim and Joseph, Sydney, December 2009.

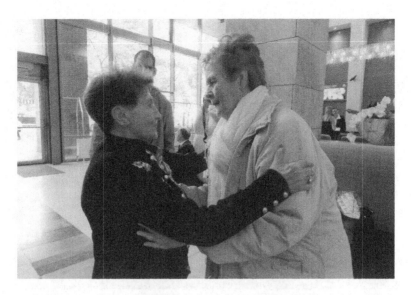

Top: The emotional meeting with Anna Körmendi (Anna Sr), granddaughter of Ilonka Nemes, Hilton Budapest City Hotel, Budapest, Hungary, 28 October 2015.

Bottom: Anna Sr and Aneta exchanging photos of their families, Hilton Budapest City Hotel, October 2015.

Top: Aneta with Ilona Vaskó, so instrumental in connecting the family with the descendants of Ilonka Nemes, meeting for the first time in October 2015 at the Hilton Budapest City Hotel.

Bottom: Paying our deep respects at the grave of
Ilonka Nemes on All Saints Day, 28 October 2015.
From left: Ilona Vaskó, Anna Sr, Aneta, Anna Jr, Michelle and Lilian.

Aneta standing outside the building at 17 Pongrácz út where Ilonka Nemes lived and where she hid Franka and the children, 28 October 2015.

Aneta in October 2015 outside the building where the pension was located, 34 Teréz Körút, Budapest.

Top: The hall at the Ministry of the Interior where the ceremony took place, with Aneta and Lilian seated centre front, Budapest, 29 October 2015.

Bottom: Aneta was given the honour of lighting the candle in memory of the six million Jewish people murdered in the Holocaust, Ministry of the Interior, 29 October 2015.

Photos: Gergely Botár/Miniszterelnökség.

Top: Israeli Ambassador to Hungary, Ilan Mor, giving his speech, with Edit Kiss, in charge of Public Relations at the Israeli Embassy in Hungary, 29 October 2015.

Bottom: On stage at the medal ceremony, 29 October 2015. The first four people at left are saviour honorees who also received medals, then Dr Sándor Pintér (Minister of the Interior), Aneta at the centre, Ilan Mor, Anna Körmendi, and two more saviour honorees.

Photos: Gergely Botár/Miniszterelnökség.

390

Top: Dr Sándor Pintér with (from left) Anna Sr, Anna Jr, Lilian, Aneta, Michelle, 29 October ceremony.

Bottom: After the ceremony, from left: Erzsébet Margaret Muri, the little girl in the picture on page 97 at the back of the house in Rozsrétszőlő, Lilian, Michelle and Aneta. Here Aneta meets Erzsébet again after 71 years.

Edward Baral visitng the graves of his great-grandparents Juda and
Rachela Baral in Israel, 2017.

26

NYÍREGYHÁZA
1944-2015

◈

On Sunday morning, 1 December 2015, we woke up very early to travel to Nyíregyháza. This was the place I had yearned to visit again in my lifetime. Over the years Nyíregyháza had taken on an unreachable, almost mystical quality in my memory, so that the emotion was kept close inside me. Now I would see the actual place where I had lived with my mother and the other children as refugees from Poland, as we pretended to be Roman Catholics.

I knew that Sunday mass would begin at 10am, and I wanted to be on time. We arranged for both Annas Sr and Jr as well as Ilona Vaskó to come to the hotel, and we all travelled for two hours together by van. During the trip, I was lost in my thoughts, wondering what I would find. Would I recognise places from 71 years ago?

We arrived practically on the doorstep of the church. I recognised it straight away, and this gave me a sense of relief. The church was called Magyarok Nagyasszonya. Ilona Vaskó had advised the local newspaper of the history behind our visit, and we were greeted by a photographer who took pictures of us outside and inside the church.

Before entering, I made sure that Lilian and Michelle knew that every Sunday morning I walked five kilometres through the fields from Rozsrétszőlő to this church in Nyíregyháza, along with Martin, Jim, Ada, Olga and Pola.

It was packed. The importance of All Saints Day meant the atmosphere was electric. I entered as if in a trance, heading to the same row and the same seats as all those years ago. Anna Sr joined us and sat on my right, with my daughters on my left. I would have loved to have had my two brothers and two cousins and Pola with me, all sitting together, as we had sat as children with a lifetime ahead of us.

It was a very moving experience to sit in this church again after so many years. It was at this moment, amidst the chanting, the incense, the worshippers, the communion and the symbols for the 12 apostles in front of us on the altar that I felt the acute pain of missing my brothers. I remembered it all. Our feeling in 1944 was that we felt safe in this church.

When the service was over, people filed out so that the next mass could take place. My daughters were also feeling the gravity of this experience. Michelle turned to me and said; 'Mummy, we can't leave this church until we find the priest and tell him what happened here.' This was not in our plan but Michelle told Ilona Vaskó her thoughts.

We left the church and walked over to another building approximately 30 feet away, where the priests were gathered to honour another priest who had passed away. Ilona knew one of the church dignitaries and briefly explained to her our desire to speak to a priest.

Father Tóth László came out to speak with us. Through a translator, Michelle told him the whole story. He listened, transfixed, and was visibly moved. He told us that he would tell this story to the Bishop, and asked Michelle to send the story so he could enlighten what he called 'his believers', meaning the congregation. Then he majestically raised his arms and blessed us. I think that this was his way of honouring and acknowledging what he had just heard. He walked us to the entrance and elegantly bid farewell to us.

We took a break and went to a restaurant. We were happy a translator was with us so we could easily converse with the two Annas and Ilona Vaskó. The atmosphere was relaxed and I felt a sense of accomplishment. We were approached by a journalist from a local newspaper and our story was later printed on the front page, with a photo.

After lunch we travelled to Rozsretsezolo, a suburb of Nyíregyháza because I wanted to show my daughters the actual hut where we had lived. I wanted to see it again with my own eyes.

We travelled on a long dirt road. On our left we saw house after house, and on the right were simply fields. Anna Sr knew exactly where the hut was. When she spotted it, I could see that it was almost the same as I remembered. The fence in the front was now iron, locked with a chain so you could not simply walk in. I remembered a wooden fence. What I also remember was that there were two steps to enter the hut. Now they were missing. Anna Sr verified that there had been some steps but that they had been removed. She also confirmed that that there had once been a wooden fence.

There was no one home. I very much wanted to go in. We saw a car approaching in the distance, then it stopped at the house next door. We asked for their help. After we had explained why we were there, the man let us into his yard so we could see the side and back of the hut. The roof was still the original thatch. It no longer belonged to the Vaskó family, and was in poor repair. We ploughed through the mud to where horses, goats and cows were kept, through decaying vegetables underfoot.

More memories were surfacing. I remembered a hill behind the house. There had been a bunker where we played and a well. All 'facilities' were outside.

All six of us had helped by working on the farm. I found where I had sat on the steps and held a goose between my legs so he wouldn't run away, stuffing his beak with the corn, water and salt that was slippery from being mixed with oil.

We stayed for more than an hour. By then the sun was setting and it was cold. I was very disappointed not to be able to enter the hut. Then suddenly, out of nowhere, two elderly ladies appeared. They were afraid to see so many people outside their house. Anna Jr spoke to them and, after some hesitation, one of the women rummaged under layers of clothing and removed a key from beneath her skirt. She opened up the fence but only to let us into the yard, not the house.

After a little more time, the ladies finally opened the front door to the hut. But they let us into one room only. The ceiling was very low. This was their small kitchen, which also contained a mattress on the floor, covered with bedding. They asked us to close the door quickly so the heat coming from a wood-burning stove would not escape. At last we were inside the hut.

When we had lived there as children, there had been no electricity, no water and no bathroom, only the outside well. Yet the beauty of the hut was that we were safe, very well treated and well fed. The Vaskó family were generous and kind. It was only after the ceremony I found out that the Vaskó family slept in the outside barn because they believed that as 'guests' we were to be treated with priority. Franka, myself, with Ada and Olga, slept in their hut. Martin and

Jim went upstairs into the loft and slept on bags of hay covered with a sheet. Nagypapa purposely gave us chores to do to make it appear as if we were a part of their family. Ilonka, our brave and courageous saviour, risked her life so that we could live.

We travelled back to Budapest in silence, everyone lost in their own thoughts.

On 2 December, we left for New York. Our trip to Budapest had fulfilled every aspect of what I had set out to do. I had represented those no longer alive: my mother, brothers and Pola. I would no longer have to guess at, or imagine the past. I had come full circle and met history eye to eye.

Ilonka's family now became *my* family again.

With Father László Tóth at the rectory of the Magyarok Nagyasszonya Church, 1 November 2015. From left: Lilian, Aneta and Michelle.

Opposite page:
The church Magyarok Nagyasszonya, in Nyíregyháza, 1 November 2015. From left, front row: Michelle, Katalin Vaskó, Aneta, Anna Sr, Lilian. Back row: Anna Jr and Ilona Vaskó.

KELET

2015. NOVEMBER 2., HÉTFŐ

A megmentőre emlékeztek

Aneta 70 év után tért vissza Nyíregyházára, hogy köszönetet mondjon a megmentőjüknek.

Aneta (jobbról a második) a két lányával ugyanabba a padba ült le, ahol 70 éve is kérte Isten segítségét, balszélen Anna néni, a megmentő unokája a római katolikus társszékesegyházban
FOTÓ: RACSKÓ TIBOR

NYÍREGYHÁZA. - Soha nem hittem, hogy lehetőségem lesz még egyszer Nyíregyházára jönni, és mindent áthato érzés kerített a hatalmába, amikor beléptem a római katolikus templomba - mesélt az érzésiről Aneta, majd vasárnap délelőtt ugyanabba a padba ült be a két lányával, ahol 70 évvel korábban imádkozott a testvéreivel, unokatestvéreivel Istenhez, hogy mentse meg őket. - Ahogy akkor, most is biztonságban éreztem itt magam, de nagyon hiányoztak a szeretteim - tette hozzá az idős asszony, majd megelevenedett a múlt, több mint hét évtized távlatából emlékezett vissza arra: hogyan és kinek köszönhetően élhették túl a holokauszt borzalmait, kinek lehetnek hálásak az életükért.

Gyalog a templomba

A család története 1942-ben, Lengyelországban, a plaszówi koncentrációs táborban és a tarnovi gettóban kezdődött; Franka Baral és három gyermeke, Janek, Aneta és Martin, valamint húga, Hela gyermekei, Ada, Paula és Olga meg tudtak szökni, s 1943-ban érkeztek Budapestre.

Nemes Tiborné, született Vaskó Ilona itt találkozott az éhező és bújkáló családdal. A nyíregyházi származású Ilonka néni gondolkodás nélkül cselekedett: magához vette Frankát és a hat gyermeket a másfél szobás lakásukba. Budapest 1944 júniusában rendkívül veszélyes hellyé vált, a német megszállás miatt Ilona féltette a pártfogoltjai életét, ezért a lelkükre kötötte, hogy ha bárki kérdezi, ők lengyel katolikus menekültek. A lakása közelében lévő síneknél várakozva, egyesével rakta fel a családot Nyíregyháza felé tartó vonatra és elindultak Rozsrétszőlőbe, Ilonka néni édesanyjához, aki magyar nyelvtudás híján, lengyelországi katolikus menekültként mutatta be őket a családjának. Franka és a hat gyermek a felszabadulásig a tanyán maradt.

- Nehéz fapapucsunk volt, de minden vasárnap öt kilométert gyalogoltunk a római katolikus templomba szentmisére, imádkozni Istenhez, hogy mentsen meg minket - mesélte Aneta. A vágyuk teljesült és 70 év után a római katolikus társszékesegyházban szentmisén mondott köszönetet a megmentőjének.

Megható, örök élmény

Lapunk áprilisban írta meg „Életet mentett, keresi" címmel, hogy a Baral család szeretné megtalálni a megmentőjüket. Akkor már tíz éve hiába kutattak Nemes (Vaskó) Ilona után, ám a csupán névrokon Vaskó Ilona, akinek írásait lapunk Tollpróba rovatában rendszeresen olvashatják, mindent megtett annak érdekében, hogy a megmentettek álma végre valóra válhasson.

A Világ Igaza posztumusz kitüntetést október 29-én Nemes Tiborné, született Vaskó Ilona unokája, Körmendi Ottóné vett át.

- A nagymamám említette, hogy laktak nála, majd a Maminál zsidó menekültek, de nem beszélt erről sokat. Volt egy időszak, amikor nem is lehetett - mondta el lapunknak Anna néni, aki mindössze pár hónapos volt, amikor a Baral gyerekek és unokatestvéreik a rozsréti tanyán éltek, őt pedig csak Ancikának hívták. Anna néni szemébe könnyek csillognak, amikor arról kérdezzük, milyen érzés találkozni Anetával, a lányaival, s tudni, a ma már több mint ötven, Amerikában, Ausztráliában és Izraelben élő leszármazott az ő nagymamájának köszönheti az életet. - Ezt nem lehet szavakkal elmondani - válaszolja, ahogy a Világ Igaza elismerés átvételének pillanata, az ünnepségen elhangzottak is meghato, megrendítő, örök élményként élnek tovább mindannyiukban. **KM**

> **Soha nem hittem, hogy lehetőségem lesz még egyszer Nyíregyházára jönni**
>
> ANETA BARAL WEINRICH

Article in Hungarian and translated into English (following page), from Kelet-Magyarország, Nyíregyháza newspaper, 2 November 2015, about Aneta's story and visit to the church after 70 years.
Translated from Hungarian by Katarina Duzdevich for Hungarian Translation Services of New York Co.

KELET   Monday, November 2, 2015

Remembering the Rescuer

Aneta returns to Nyíregyháza after 70 years to give thanks to the rescuer.

Aneta (second from right) sits with her daughters in the same pew in the Roman Catholic cathedral where she asked for God's help 70 years ago. To the far left, Auntie Anna, the rescuer's granddaughter.   Photo: Tibor Racskó

NYÍREGYHÁZA – "I never thought I would have the chance to come back to Nyíregyháza once more. I was seized by an all-pervading feeling when I stepped into the Roman Catholic church," said Aneta about her feelings. On Sunday morning she sat with her two daughters in the same pew as she did 70 years prior when she, along with her siblings and cousins, prayed to God to save them. "I felt safe here, just as I did then, although I missed my loved ones very much," added the elderly lady. Then, the past became vivid. She thought back to seven decades ago about how, and thanks to whom, they were able to survive the horrors of the Holocaust and to whom they can be grateful for their lives.

To the Church on foot

The family's ordeal started at Płaszów concentration camp and the Tarnów ghetto in Poland, in 1942. Franka Baral, her three children, Janek, Aneta, and Martin, as well as her younger sister Hela's children, Ada, Paula, and Olga managed to escape; in 1943 they arrived in Budapest.

Mrs Tibor Nemes, born Ilona Vaskó, met the starving family in hiding. Auntie Ilonka, originating from Nyíregyháza, acted without hesitation: she took in Franka and the six children to her one-and-a-half bedroom apartment.

By June of 1944 Budapest had become an exceedingly dangerous place. Due to the German invasion, Ilona feared for the lives of the ones she was protecting. So, she had them promise that if they were asked anything by anyone, they would say they are Catholic refugees from Poland. Waiting by the tracks near her apartment, she put the family one by one onto the train heading towards Nyíregyháza. They were on their way to Rozsrétszőlő to Auntie Ilonka's mother, who did not know the Hungarian language, and introduced them to her family as Catholic refugees from Poland. Franka and the six children remained at the farm until liberation.

> "I never thought I would have the chance to come back to Nyíregyháza once more."
>
> **ANETA BARAL WEINREICH**

"We had heavy wooden clogs, yet we still walked five kilometers every Sunday to the mass at the Roman Catholic church. We prayed to God to save us," said Aneta. Their prayers were answered, and after 70 years she gave thanks to her rescuer during the mass at the Roman Catholic co-cathedral.

A moving and lifelong experience

In April, our paper published an article titled "Saved a Life, Seeking" that the Baral family would like to find their rescuer. At the time, they had been futilely searching for Ilona Nemes (Vaskó) for ten years. Ilona Vaskó who is simply her namesake and whose articles can regularly be read in our *Tollpróba* column, did everything possible to bring the saved family's dream to life.

On October 29th a posthumous Righteous Among the Nations Award was received by Mrs. Otto Körmendi, the grand-daughter of Mrs. Tibor Nemes, born Ilona Vaskó.

"My grandmother mentioned that Jewish refugees were living with her and then with her Mom, although she did not speak a lot about it. There was a period of time when you simply couldn't," Auntie Anna told our newspaper. She was no more than a few months old when the Baral children and their cousins lived on the farm in Rozsrét. They simply called her Ancika. Tears glisten in Auntie Anna's eyes as we ask her how it feels to meet Aneta and her daughters and to know that there are more than fifty descendants alive today in America, Australia, and Israel who owe their lives to her grandmother. "This cannot be expressed in words," she responds. Just as the moment when the Righteous Among the Nations Award was accepted, the words said during the ceremony will live on as a touching, moving, and lifelong experience in all of us. **KM**

Top: The house where Franka and the children lived during the War in Rozsrétszőlő, Hungary, a suburb of Nyíregyháza, in this 1 November 2015 photo.

Bottom: The back of the house in Rozsrétszőlő, November 2015.

Top: Standing with Ilonka's granddaughter, Anna Sr, after all these years, Rozsrétszőlő, 1 November.

Bottom: The two elderly ladies who now occupy Ilonka's parents' house on the same long dirt road the family knew. Left foreground is Ilona Vaskó and partially obscured is Anna Jr, explaining to the ladies why they had visitors on that November 2015 day.

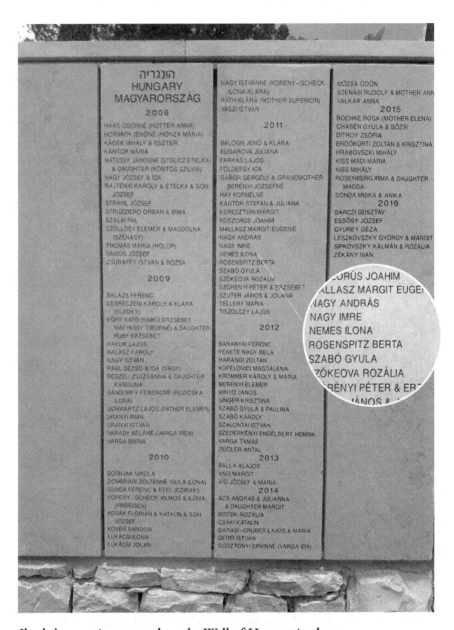

Ilonka's name is engraved on the Wall of Honour in the
Garden of the Righteous at Yad Vashem, Jerusalem.

Inset: A close-up of the name Nemes, Ilona recognised in 2011.

27

HONOURING BRONKA

◈

As I have been writing this book, with each passing day I have waited to receive news that our Polish saviour, Bronka Porwitowa, would receive recognition from Yad Vashem. This was a goal that I and my brothers, Martin and Jim, had agreed we would reach. When my brothers passed away in 2010, this quest for all three of us and for my mother, Franka, fell on my shoulders.

Everything depended upon finding Bronka's descendants. I had very little information to use to find her relatives, since correspondence between my mother, myself and Bronka stretched so far back: to 1943, 1946, 1964 and 1965. But I was determined. Eventually I found Bronka's niece, Pani Elżbieta Kołodziej.

After I submitted all the papers required to Yad Vashem in December 2015, I waited until May 2017 to receive a letter confirming that Bronka Porwitowa was indeed worthy, by virtue of her dedication to saving us, and through her acts of bravery knowingly placing herself in danger and certain death if ever caught by the Nazis.

The last time I saw Bronka was in the cottage she had arranged for us in Bochnia. She had travelled from Kraków to meet us, bringing with her a letter from my father, who was still in Płaszów concentration camp. My mother asked Bronka to find smugglers who would take us through the Polish border to Czechoslovakia and then to Hungary, which was not yet occupied by the Nazis. I thought all over again how incredible it was that my mother decided to embark on such a long journey on foot, with three children. I remembered that I was only 12 years old, Martin was ten years old, and Jim was only eight.

It was a heart-breaking moment when we farewelled our 'angel'. I remembered that Bronka handed me a locket containing a miniature of St Anthony, the patron saint of children. She told me it would bring me good luck and keep me safe. She was right. I wore the locket on a chain from 1943 to 1945 and I believe it helped save my life.

Receiving this letter from Yad Vashem gave me a feeling of completion. I wanted to accomplish what my brothers and I had agreed to do so many years ago. I wanted to have Bronka acknowledged forever for her incredible deeds, and to include this chapter in my book so that my children and grandchildren will have a full picture of my and my family's ordeals, without anything missing.

It was, however, also a bitter moment. Although I wanted desperately to ring my mother and brothers and tell them we could be satisfied, that finally the moment for Bronka had arrived—I couldn't. Her next of kin, her niece, Pani Elżbieta Kołodziej, could learn that we cherished her memory and that we always remembered what she did for us. Now others will know of her righteous acts and her name will last forever on the Wall of Remembrance at Yad Vashem in Jerusalem.

We were given short notice for the date of the Medal Ceremony. It was to be held on 30 June 2017 at the Galicia Jewish Museum in Kraków.

We received an email from the highly efficient Emil Rene Jezowski, representing the Education Department at the Righteous Among Nations Department at Yad Vashem. Emil seamlessly co-ordinated the entire ceremony.

He asked if I would like to say a few words. Michelle immediately answered *yes* on my behalf. It is far outside my comfort zone to speak in public on a topic that slices into my heart like a knife, and with the same intensity as though it happened yesterday. I had done it once before in Sydney at the ceremony to light a candle in memory of the Hungarian Righteous Among Nations—and that had taken 'mind over matter' to achieve. I told Michelle that I had dug my fingernails into the palms of my hands to distract myself. Now I had to confront my memories, speak about Bronka, and rise above my fear. I knew I had to do it. I wanted to do it. I am the only witness and survivor left in my family. If I did not speak up there would be no link, no eyewitness to record what happened to us and to honour people like Bronka, who risked everything.

My family knew the extent of my feelings. Henry took the reins and helped me so much by practising my speech with me. He gave me full confidence to go forward with a strong voice. The speech would be in Polish.

Lilian and Michelle flew in from New York. Henry and I travelled together from Sydney to Poland, a couple of days ahead of them. We all met in Kraków. Joseph could not travel.

I wanted very much to meet Elżbieta Kołodziej before the ceremony. Our meeting was full of emotion. Imagine the reaction of meeting face-to-face the closest relative of your saviour, who also knew your story. Elżbieta had the letters and pictures that my mother and I wrote to Bronka. She was so dignified and warm—an exceptional and humble person. We talked as if we had been friends for years, with Bronka bringing us together.

Although I had spoken to Elżbieta from Sydney prior to my arrival in Kraków, it was a completely different ambience meeting in person. It was extraordinary. I have so much respect for Elżbieta and now we are in contact forever.

When my daughters arrived, we all had a feeling of nostalgic happiness. It was a precious time with all my children together reminiscing about the stories they grew up with, about Poland and my life there. It was a tribute and acknowledgement that family members past and present were all with us. Everything seemed to culminate in this wonderful meeting.

We went out to enjoy really authentic poppy-seed cake. On this trip, the children ate this cake for breakfast, lunch and dinner. I was telling them that I was not nervous. But as the day of the ceremony approached, I felt I had the weight of my family pressing on my heart.

Friday 30 June was a beautiful windy day. We were to arrive at the Galicia Museum by 1pm. Henry did another practise run-through with me and declared: 'Mum you're ready. Excellent.'

We were greeted beautifully at the Museum where three of the Righteous Among Nations would be honoured. My nephew, Steven Baral, Martin's son, had arrived from Seattle. How wonderful for him to represent his father! I was so pleased he was with us. Our friends Mr and Mrs Bisping and Mrs Śliwa arrived and I was most grateful for their presence.

As we entered, a Polish radio station was interviewing Elżbieta. At once they began to ask me questions too. Security people were everywhere.

I could feel this was a momentous day.

There were some impressive people in attendance: Mr Yuli Edelstein, Speaker of the Israeli Knesset, Ms Ruth Cohen Dar,

Deputy Ambassador of Israel to Poland and Mr Marek Kuchciński, Marshal of the Sejm, the Polish Parliament. Ambassador Anna Azari was not able to attend, as she had just broken her leg.

As the hall filled with people, the atmosphere was exhilarating. Television and newspaper reporters were there to record the occasion, and Henry was recording everything on video and social media, Michelle and Lilian sat with me in the front row. The introductions began with Emil René Jeżowski explaining the importance of the medals and who would be receiving them.

Those who spoke had significant things to say. Their world view focused on the Saviours and the lessons to be learned from their heroic actions. Everything was in Polish but there were headphones for simultaneous English translation by Marta Kostyk.

I looked down at the program and saw that on the last page was a picture of Bronka with the Polish words *Odznaczona Bohaterka*, which means Decorated Heroine. Directly under this was the Polish word *Ocaleni,* which means Survivors—and there in print were our names. (The only name not listed was my mother's—in error):

Aneta Baral

Marcel Baral

Janek Baral

Pola Bleicher

Ada Ehrlich

Olga Ehrlich

Then my own name was called. I was the last speaker and only survivor. I went to the stage for my speech. A large picture of Bronka formed a back-drop behind me. From the corner of my eye, I could see Henry crying. Michelle came to the stage with me to adjust the microphone, but it was difficult for it to stay in place, so she took it in her hand and held it for me to speak.

I began by greeting the dignitaries and then said:

I am Aneta Weinreich. I was born in Kraków, and my soul will always be in Kraków, as it was for my mother, Franka Baral, my father Samuel Baral, and my brothers Martin and Jim Baral, who are no longer alive.

Today is not an ordinary day. With the pace and immediacy of the world, we are here to pause …Why?

We are here to reflect on the extraordinarily brave deeds and selfless courage of Bronka Porwitowa. During the German occupation of Kraków from 1941 to 1945, Bronka saved the lives of seven family members—not just once, but in many ways and many times. Bronka manoeuvred her way through the perilous streets of Kraków for us. For example, she protected my brothers, who escaped the Kraków Ghetto and were wandering the streets. They landed on her doorstep. Bronka arranged everything and sent them to the Bochnia Ghetto, where they could be safe until we were reunited. She made plans for my mother and me to escape the Tarnów Ghetto. She organised the place where we would live when we escaped. She collected and posted communications between us and my father, who was working in Oscar Schindler's factory. She knowingly stepped in harm's way each and every time. I understand Bronka did this not just for us, but also for others.

I continued:

In the context of the world today, it is even more important that these torches of light, hope, ethics, and bravery are recognised as the beacon for tolerance—to follow what you know to be the moral path even under extreme duress and under the threat of sure death.

It is with 100 per cent certainty that I say that we would not have survived the War if not for Bronka. And now I am here with my children, the next generation: Lilian, Michelle and Henry, and my nephew Steven Baral, who all have been hearing about Bronka since they were children. Together with my husband Joseph, who is in Australia, we wanted to guarantee that Bronka's actions would not just be in *my* memory, but that they would be passed down to the children and grandchildren, with the hope of recognition for Bronka. This goal is fulfilled today with the extraordinary Medal of Valour … May the light continue to shine for eternity on Bronka … You are a shining example to humanity… We honour you, we bless you. You are a global inspiration.

The ceremony concluded with flowers being given to the Saviours and many photos taken. In the lovely courtyard of the Galicia Museum, light refreshments were served. As we spoke with the dignitaries I felt the hot sun shining down on us. I removed myself mentally from everything around me and felt that Bronka heard us, Bronka saw us, and so did my beloved mother and brothers.

Now I had come full circle, retracing my life journey. A few days later, I arrived with Henry in Tel Aviv.

Elżbieta (married name Kołodziej), Bronka Porwitowa's niece, shown on the left at her first communion, then Bronka and Mr Skoczylas, her brother-in-law (standing). Seated are Mrs Skoczylas, Bronka's sister, and Józiu, Elizabeth's brother, Kraków, 4 June 1949.

Opposite page:

Top: Aneta giving her speech at the Galicia Jewish Museum, Kraków, 30 June 2017, with a large backdrop picture of Bronka behind her, as Michelle holds the microphone and Henry records the ceremony.

Bottom: Elżbieta Kołodziej (third from left) with other honorees on stage, 30 June, with Aneta, the only survivor.

Top: Aneta and Elżbieta after the medal ceremony for the Righteous Among Nations organised by Yad Vashem in Jerusalem and the Embassy of Israel in Kraków, Galicia Jewish Museum, Kraków, 30 June 2017.

Bottom: The medal made for Bronka, whose inscription in French says: 'Whoever saves one life saves the world'.

Photos: Paweł Kula.

Top: Mr Yuli Edelstein, Speaker of the Israeli Knesset, with Aneta and Henry at the ceremony.

Bottom: In the courtyard at the Galicia Jewish Museum after the ceremony. Front row, from left: Lilian, Aneta, Mr Marek Kuchcinski (Marshal of the Sejm) and Elżbieta Kołodziej. Back row, from left: Henry, Steven Baral, Michelle, Mrs Śliwa and Ewa Król (friend and neighbour of Elżbieta).

415

POLUB NAS NA FACEBOOKU
WWW.FACEBOOK.COM/DZIENNIKPOLSKI

DZIENNIKPOLSKI24.PL
SOBOTA–NIEDZIELA, 1–2 LIPCA 2017
DZIENNIK POLSKI

Łzy wzruszenia płynęły w żydowskim muzeum

Pamięć. Potomkowie Sprawiedliwych wśród Narodów Świata odebrali izraelskie medale

Piotr Subik
piotr.subik@dziennik.krakow.pl

Od lewej: Ruth Cohen-Dar, ocalona Aneta Weinreich, Elżbieta Kołodziej i Juli-Jo'el Edelstein

Doktor Adam Janik u progu wojny ukończył Wydział Lekarski Uniwersytetu Jagiellońskiego, pracował jako lekarz w gminie Trzciana. W 1942 r. do jego domu w Ujeździe przybyły Pesia Penczyna Galińska z córką Dvorą, Żydówki z Sandomierza.

Lekarz przyjął je pod swój dach mimo sprzeciwu żony, Niemki. Pesia zajmowała się gospodarstwem, a Dvora bawiła się z synem doktora Janika Robertem. Matka i córka przeżyły okupację, później razem wyjechały do Izraela. Dvora Strich nie mogła wczoraj przyjechać do Krakowa ze względu na zły stan zdrowia.

W Żydowskim Muzeum Galicja zjawiła się za to Aneta Weinreich z domu Barel, która okupację przetrwała dzięki mieszkance Krakowa Bronisławie Porwit. To jej udało się wydostać z getta sześcioro dzieci z rodzin Barel, Bleicher i Ehrlich. Część z nich przerzucono z Krakowa do Muszyny, część do Bochni; wszystkie ostatecznie zostały ewakuowane w 1943 r. z Polski przez Węgry do Rumunii.

– *Bronka uratowała nam życie nie jeden raz, wiele razy. Cieszę się, że wszyscy ludzie dowiedzą się o jej niewiarygodnych*

czynach – mówiła Aneta Weinreich o nieżyjącej już Bronisławie Porwit, nazywając ją „świetlistym przykładem dla ludzkości". Ze łzami w oczach rzuciły się sobie w objęcia z odbierającą medal „Sprawiedliwy wśród Narodów Świata" siostrzenicą bohaterki – Elżbietą Kołodziej.

Z kolei honory dla śp. Adama Janika odebrała jego córka Małgorzata. – *Myślę, że ojciec bardzo by się ucieszył z tego odznaczenia* – mówiła Małgorzata Janik-Trella.

– *To był normalny, ludzki odruch* – tak skromnie o czynach

Marii i Wincentego Kwiatkowskich mówiła ich wnuczka Mariola Nowak. Kwiatkowscy żyli w Przeworsku, przez ponad dwa lata ukrywali na swoim strychu Mojżesza Kestena, u którego ojca Wincenty, malarz, kupował przed wojną farby. O ukrywaniu przed Niemcami Żyda nie wiedziało czworo z pięciorga dzieci Marii i Wincentego Kwiatkowskich. Wczoraj do Muzeum Żydowskiego Galicja przyjechały ich trzy córki – Janina Rosołowska, Jadwiga Rupar i Barbara Kałamarz. Dziękowała im Tamara Blumberg, córka Mojżesza.

Medale za ratowanie Żydów podczas wojny wręczyli potomkom sprawiedliwych przewodniczący parlamentu Izraela Juli-Jo'el Edelstein i wiceambasador tego państwa w Polsce Ruth Cohen-Dar. – *Być może wasi ojcowie i dziadkowie uratowali jedną osobę, ale przez to uratowali ich setki* – mówił Juli-Jo'el Edelstein.

Instytut Yad Vashem w Jerozolimie medalem „Sprawiedliwy wśród Narodów Świata" uhonorował dotychczas ok. 26,5 tys. osób, w tym 6,7 tys. Polaków.
©℗

Article in Polish, translated into English, in the Kraków newspaper, *Dziennik Polski*, 2 July 2017, about Aneta's story and those of the other honorees at the medal ceremony.

Tears of emotion ran in a Jewish museum

Remembrance. Descendants of The Righteous Among the Nations collected Israeli medals

Piotr Subik
piotr.subik@dziennik.krakow.pl

On the eve of World War II Doctor Adam Janik graduated from the Faculty of Medicine of the Jagiellonian University, and worked as a doctor in the Municipality of Trzciana. In 1942, he was visited at his home in Ujazd by Pesia Penczyna Galińska, a Jewish woman from Sandomierz, and her daughter Dvora.

From left: Ruth Cohen-Dar, the saved Aneta Weinreich, Elżbieta Kołodziej and Juli-Jo'el Edelstein.

He lodged them, despite his German wife's objection. Pesia carried out household duties, while Dvora played with Dr Janik's son Robert. The mother and daughter survived the period of occupation and later left together for Israel. Dvora Strich was unable to arrive in Kraków yesterday due to ill health.

But Aneta Weinreich née Baral was present at the *Galicja* Jewish Museum. She survived occupation thanks to a Kraków resident, Bronisława Porwit. It was her who succeeded in getting six children from the families of Baral, Bleicher and Ehrlich out of the ghetto. Some of those children were moved from Kraków to Muszyna, others to Bochnia; all of

them were eventually evacuated in 1943 from Poland through Hungary to Romania.

"Bronka saved our lives not just once, but many times. I'm happy to know that everyone will find out about her unbelievable acts," said Aneta Weinreich about the late Bronisława Porwit, calling her a 'shining example for humanity'. With *The Righteous Among the Nations Medal* being collected by the heroine's niece, Elżbieta Kołodziej, and with tears in their eyes, they threw themselves into each other's arms.

As for the honours for the late Dr Janik, they were collected by his daughter Małgorzata. *"I think my father would*

have been very happy to receive this honour," said Małgorzata Janik-Trella.

"It was a normal human reaction," said Mariola Nowak in these humble words about the acts of her grandparents Maria and Wincenty Kwiatkowski. The Kwiatkowskis, who used to live in Przeworsk, kept Mojżesz Kesten hidden in their loft for more than two years. Before the war, Wincenty, a painter, used to buy paints from Mojżesz's father. The fact of the Jew being hidden from the Germans wasn't even known to four of the five children of Maria and Wincenty Kwiatkowski. Yesterday, their three daughters, Janina Rosołowska, Jadwiga Rupar and Barbara

Kałamarz, came to the *Galicja* Jewish Museum. They were thanked by Tamara Blumberg, Mojżesz's daughter.

The Medals for saving Jews during the war were handed to the descendants of The Righteous by the Chairman of the Israeli Parliament, Juli-Jo'el Edelstein, and the Deputy Ambassador of this country to Poland, Ruth Cohen-Dar. *"Your fathers or grandfathers may have saved one person, but by doing this, they saved hundreds of people,"* said Juli-Jo'el Edelstein.

Awarding *The Righteous Among the Nations Medal*, the Yad Vashem Institute of Jerusalem has so far honoured about 26,500 people, including 6,700 Poles.

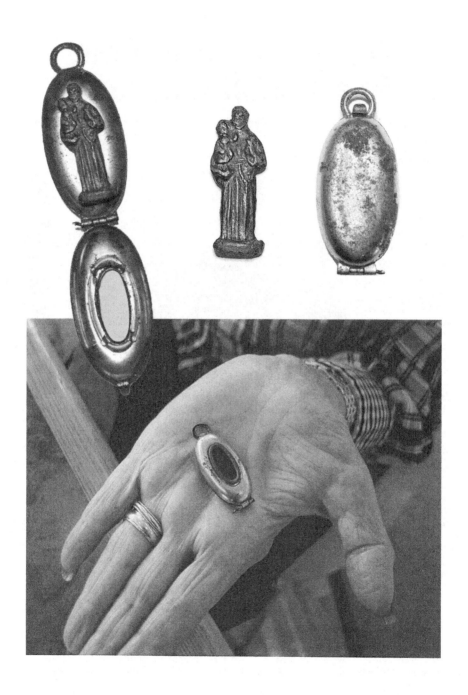

In July 2017, a few days after the medal ceremony in Kraków, Aneta arrived in Tel Aviv with Henry, having come full circle in her life.

Opposite page:
Top: Left: The locket showing Saint Anthony given by Bronka to Aneta in 1943 to wear to keep her safe during the War.
Right: The back of the locket.
Bottom: Aneta holding the locket.

28

TRIBUTE TO ELŻBIETA KOŁODZIEJ

❖

Our family knew Elżbieta Kołodziej, Bronka's niece, for a short time, from July 2017 until March 2018.

It was such a shock to hear she had passed away, since we had remained in contact after I returned to Sydney and called often.

I was able to reminisce with her about her auntie, our story and our lives. Our emotional meeting seemed to span a lifetime. When Elżbieta and I spoke, we had an understanding and deep connection which was different from that with anyone else. We cherished the fragile link between our past and the present and were the keepers of these precious memories and the truth of this time in history. It had been such a comfort to me to find Elżbieta. Our relationship gave even more weight to the memory of Bronka.

I wish I could fully explain the tone of her kind dignity and soulful presence. She was such a humble and elegant woman. Throughout her life, she was steadfast in her belief that we would one day find her.

Now with a deeply sad heart we are forced to say good bye to a human angel.

Elżbieta, I miss you with all my heart. Thank you for believing and keeping memories of Bronka alive.

May light shine eternally on you both.

Funeral of Elżbieta Kołodziej, Kraków, 7 March 2018.

The Wall of Rememberance at Yad Vashem in Jerusalem
with the name of Porwit, Bronisława engraved in perpetuity.
Inset: A close-up of the name on the Wall of Rememberance.

W imieniu cioci odebrała odznaczenie „Sprawiedliwy wśród Narodów Świata"

▼ Pierwsza Komunia Św. Elżbiety. Za nią stoi ciocia Bronka. Na zdjęciu także rodzice i brat

Taka dumna jestem z mojej cioci

Elżbieta Kołodziej

Nie byłoby nas, gdyby nie Bronka

Zawsze gdzieś biegła. Nie mogła usiedzieć na miejscu. Tyle spraw było do załatwienia. A to trzeba było przywieźć świeże jarzyny do sklepiku, a to potem stanąć za ladą i zachwalać je klientom. Miała do tego dryg, więc warzywniak przy ulicy Starowiślnej w Krakowie funkcjonował znakomicie. Podobnie jak restauracją Pod Kogutkiem, tuż obok końskiego targu, gdzie zatrudniono ją, kiedy Niemcy zajęli miasto. Jednak tam dla Bronisławy Porwit nie liczył się już tylko utarg. To miejsce dawało szansę na ratowanie żydowskich dzieci.

Aneta Barel, dziś Weinreich, miała wtedy dwanaście lat. Przeprowadzka do getta była dla niej szokiem. Wychowana w zamożnym, żydowskim domu dziewczynka razem z rodzicami i dwoma młodszymi braćmi, dziesięcioletnim Marcelem i siedmioletnim Jankiem, miała teraz mieszkać w dwupokojowym mieszkaniu, które z przydziału dostały... trzy rodziny. Jednak nie tłok był najgorszy.
- Najgorszy był głód - mówi Aneta Weinreich. - I to, że nikt nie wiedział, co się jutro z nami stanie.

Na dany znak włożycie kapelusze

A w getcie działy się rzeczy straszne. Ludzie z głodu i wycieńczenia padali na ulicach jak muchy. Niemcy dobijali ich strzałami. Gdy zaczęła się akcja likwidacji getta, wpadali do domów, każąc natychmiast je opuszczać i ustawiać się w szeregu na Placu Zgody, dziś Bohaterów Getta. Stamtąd droga prowadziła prosto do obozu koncentracyjnego w Płaszowie, gdzie na wielu czekała śmierć. W tej sytuacji Franka Barel, mama Anety, postanowiła działać. W pierwszej kolejności trzeba było ratować najmłodsze dzieci.

Nawiązała kontakt z Bronką, którą poznała jeszcze przed wojną. Bronka, pracując w restauracji Pod Kogutkiem, skąd dowożono do getta pieczywo, mogła zorganizować ucieczkę Marcela i Janka. Jak to zrobiła, nie wiadomo. Wiadomo tylko, że pewnego dnia chłopcy stanęli przed drzwiami domu Bronki przy ulicy Dekerta. - Problem polegał na tym, że były tam już inne wyprowadzone z getta dzieci, które ciocia ukrywała w piwnicy, za taką niewidoczną na pierwszy rzut oka ścianą. Ja wtedy nic o tym nie wiedziałam, bo byłam małą dziewczynką. Pokazała mi ją dopiero po wojnie, jak podrosłam - opowiada Elżbieta Kołodziej, siostrzenica Bronisławy Porwit.

Następnego dnia Bronka, nie bacząc na niebezpieczeństwo, wzięła chłopców za ręce i udając, że to jej dzieci, zaprowadziła na dworzec kolejowy. Tam kupiła dwa bilety do Bochni, gdzie chłopców odebrał wcześniej umówiony człowiek.
- Bracia byli bezpieczni. Ja z rodzicami poszłam do obozu w Płaszowie. Tato pracował w fabryce Schindlera, dostał informację, że szykowany jest transport kobiet do fabryki Madritscha w Tarnowie. Mama uznała, że w tam będzie łatwiej przeżyć, więc zapisała mnie i siebie na listę - opowiada pani Aneta. - Do fabryki, w której pracowałyśmy, przychodzili Polacy sprzedawać nam jedzenie. Pewnego dnia przyszła... Bronka. Przez chwilę rozmawiała z moją mamą. Ustaliły plan działania. Mama po cichu miała uszyć dla siebie i dla mnie kapelusze. Konkretnego dnia miał przyjść do fabryki pewien pan i stanąć przy oknie. Wówczas miałyśmy założyć te kapelusze i wyjść z nim przez bramę. Byłam na to przez mamę przygotowywana, ale bałam się potwornie. Prawie nie mogłam się ze strachu ruszać. Na szczęście strażnicy byli opłaceni i udało się nam przejść bez przeszkód.

Z więzienia wróciła strasznie odmieniona

Aneta z mamą pojechała do Bochni. Tam już czekała na nie Bronka. Pomogła im się ukryć na obrzeżach miasta, gdzie szczęśliwie przetrwały wojnę. Ona sama nie miała tyle szczęścia. Jeden z sąsiadów musiał się zorientować, że raz po raz w jej domu zjawiają się jakieś dzieci. Doniósł na gestapo, a Bronka wylądowała w więzieniu przy ulicy Montelupich. - Nie chciała mówić, co tam się z nią działo. To musiało być straszne, bo wróciła bardzo odmieniona. Nigdy przez to nie mogła mieć dzieci, choć była młodą mężatką - opowiada Elżbieta Kołodziej, którą większość dzieciństwa spędziła u cioci.

Po wojnie Bronisława Porwit sprzedawał obwarzanki na dworcu autobusowym w Krakowie. Uratowana przez nią Aneta, jej mama oraz dwóch braci wyjechali do Palestyny. Dołączył do nich ojciec, który znalazł się na liście Schindlera i dzięki temu przeżył wojnę. Potem rodzina Barelów przeprowadziła się do Australii. Udało im się nawiązać kontakt z Bronką. Franka przysyłała jej listy i paczki z sukienkami dla jej siostrzenicy Eli, która przechowuje je do dziś. - Jednak gdy ciocia zmarła, korespondencja się urwała - mówi pani Elżbieta.
- Przez wiele lat poszukiwaliśmy krewnych Bronki, bo chcieliśmy powiedzieć im, jak bardzo ją szanujemy. Nie byłoby nas, gdyby nie ona - powiedziała Aneta Weinreich podczas uroczystości przyznania Bronisławie Porwit dyplomu i medalu „Sprawiedliwy wśród Narodów Świata". W jej imieniu medal odebrała Elżbieta Kołodziej. Dla niej spotkanie z Anetą Weinreich z domu Barel, która przyleciała z tego powodu z Australii do Krakowa, było jednym z najbardziej wzruszających momentów w życiu. MS

18 | ŻYCIE NA GORĄCO

Interview in the local paper with Elżbieta Kołodziej and Aneta, July 2017. *Opposite page:* The interview translated into English.

WE WOULDN'T BE HERE IF IT WASN'T FOR BRONKA

She was always on the run. She just couldn't stay still. There were so many things to take care of. For a start, fresh vegies needed to be brought to her little shop and then she had to stand behind the counter to show them off to customers. She had a knack for it, so her greengrocery in Starowiślna Street in Kraków did really well. So did the *Pod Kogutkiem* [Under the Little Rooster] restaurant, just next to the horse market, where she was employed when the Germans took the city. But it wasn't for Bronisława Porwit all about takings there. That place gave her a chance to save Jewish children.

Aneta Baral, now Weinreich, was twelve at the time. A move to the ghetto was a shock to her. Having been raised in a well-to-do Jewish home, the small girl, together with her parents, ten-year-old Marcel and seven-year-old Janek, suddenly had to live in a two-room flat, which had been allocated to … three families. But the squeeze wasn't the worst thing to contend with. "The worst was hunger," Aneta Weinreich said. "And the fact that nobody knew what was going to happen to us the next day."

At the given sign, you will put your hats on

In the ghetto itself, some horrible things were going on. People would drop like flies in the streets due to starvation and emaciation. The Germans would just shoot to finish them off. When the ghetto began to be liquidated, the Germans would charge into houses, ordering people to leave them immediately and line up in Zgoda Square, now Bohaterów Getta [Ghetto Heroes] Square. From there, the path led straight to the concentration camp in Płaszów, where death awaited many. In that situation, Franka Barel, Aneta's mum, decided to act. First of all, the youngest children had to be saved.

She established contact with Bronka, whom she had met before the war. Working at the *Pod Kogutkiem* restaurant, which supplied bakery products to the ghetto, Bronka was able to organise an escape for Marcel and Janek. Nobody knows how she did it. It's only known that one day the boys turned up at the front door of Bronka's house in Dekert Street. "The problem was that there were already other children there who had been led out of the ghetto and hidden away by my auntie in her cellar behind a wall, which appeared invisible at first sight. I knew nothing about it then because I was a small girl. It was shown to me only after the war when I was older," said Elżbieta Kołodziej, a niece of Bronisława Porwit.

The next day, Bronka, disregarding the danger, held the boys' hands, pretending they were her own children, and took them to the train station. There, she bought two tickets to Bochnia, where the boys were picked up by a pre-arranged man.

"My brothers were safe. I went with my parents to the Płaszów camp. My dad worked in the Schindler factory, where he got information about the transport of women to the Madritsch factory in Tarnów being under way. Mum thought it should be easier to survive there, so she put my name and hers on the list," said Mrs Weinreich. "The factory we worked in was regularly visited by Poles who would sell food to us. One day … Bronka came. She talked to my mum for a few moments. They worked out a plan for action. Mum was supposed to secretly make a hat for me and one for herself. On a specific day, a man was supposed to come to the factory and stop by a window. At that moment, we were supposed to put our hats on and walk away with him through the gate. Mum kept preparing me for that, but I was still scared stiff. I was so terrified I could hardly move. Luckily, the guards had been paid, so we managed to walk through without any trouble."

She came back from the prison awfully changed

Aneta and her mum went to Bochnia. Bronka was already waiting for them there. She helped them hide on the town outskirts, where they luckily lived through the war. She wasn't herself so lucky though. One of her neighbours must have noticed that some children over and over again would turn up in her home. He reported her to the gestapo and Bronka ended up in prison in Montelupich Street. "She didn't want to talk about what was happening to her there, but it must have been dreadful because she came back completely changed. Because of that experience, she could never have children of her own, even though she was a young married woman," said Elżbieta Kołodziej, who spent most of her childhood at her auntie's place.

After the war, Bronisława Porwit was selling pretzels at the bus station in Kraków. Aneta, her mum and two brothers she had saved left for Palestine. They were joined by her father, who was on the Schindler list, which is why he survived the war. Later, the Barel family moved to Australia. They succeeded in re-establishing contact with Bronka. Franka would send her letters and parcels with dresses for her niece Ela, who keeps them to this day. "When auntie passed away, though, all correspondence stopped," said Mrs Elżbieta Kołodziej.

"For many years, we kept searching for Bronka's relatives, because we wanted to tell them how much we respected her. We wouldn't be here if it wasn't for her," said Aneta Weinreich during the ceremony at which Bronisława Porwit was awarded the Righteous Among Nations Diploma and Medal. The Medal was collected on her behalf by Elżbieta Kołodziej. Meeting Aneta Weinreich née Barel, who for that occasion flew from Australia to Kraków, was one of the most moving moments of her life. **MS**

Captions and insets – Polish	Captions and insets – English
Taka jestem dumna z mojej cioci: Elżbieta Kołodziej	I'm so proud of my auntie: Elżbieta Kołodziej
W imieniu cioci odebrała odznaczenie "Sprawiedliwy wśród Narodów Świata"	She collected the Righteous Among Nations award on her auntie's behalf
Pierwsza Komunia Św. Elżbiety. Za nią stoi ciocia Bronka. Na zdjęciu także rodzice i brat.	Elżbieta's First Communion. Her auntie Bronka is standing behind her. Her parents and brother are also in this photo.

29

LESSONS OF A LIFETIME

◈

I believe everyone's life story carries weight and authority unique to their experience, so I want to share what I've learned with my children, extended family, and with the world at large. I have been mulling over the eternal question: what can I convey to my children and grandchildren—even a word, a feeling, or a sentence—that will remain in their minds and memories to encourage and help them in their own lives when they meet challenges, both ordinary and extraordinary?

I have divided my thoughts into two distinct time periods: Firstly, the War years, and then my life in Australia. Each required different forms of strength from me. In the first, I was a child and the second, an adult. During the war years, I felt I was forced to move through a deep, dark tunnel, and in Australia, I had to obliterate that dark tunnel in order to forge and turn towards a new life. I struggled to merge these two separate periods of my life. I realise now that they cannot be blended, but rather, they are separate and are to be accepted as distinct units, with the first fuelling the second.

But I never lost my vision: to persevere and see the light at the end of that tunnel. This willfulness and optimism kept me going, and so did the people around me. You may find yourself on a confusing, uncharted, and unpredictable journey, but if you hold fast to a vision of where you want to end up, it will help guide you through and keep you steady-- along with ingenuity, intelligence, and instinct. Hope and support from those around you are also essential. You are not an island.

Secondly, while living my life in Australia, I was busy with everyday life, family and business. The idea of writing a book was never on my horizon. After the War years I had to create another type of life. I certainly wanted to impart as much as possible of what I had gone through to my children, but with some intuitive caveats or boundaries: how much is right for them to know, and how much is too much? When is the right time to speak to them, and how would these topics best arise? Will this knowledge affect their happiness?

I found that speaking about the pre- and post-war years was a comfortable way to introduce the children at a young age to how I grew up, and in what type of environment. In the meantime, they had other input from Joseph, my mother, Joseph's mother and their uncles. This was a layered process. The goal for me was to impart how important being from a different country can be in shaping your goals. It was a subtle message. Learning about the merits of having a strong work ethic, through example, was the other. The children definitely saw how Joseph and I approached making a living, so all three children have this drive deeply embedded in them.

Life went on in a steady and busy rhythm until the moment in 2012 when I was really sick. Then a dramatic change occurred in the way I approached everything. It was at this moment I felt an urgency for the children to know everything—to have in their hands a road-map, not only of facts about my life, but an example of conviction that never gives up. I want them to know that you can count on your own enduring and unwavering vision, creativity, wit, and intelligence when you have to muddle through confusion, powerlessness, and circumstances beyond your control. Sometimes you have to desperately search for the elusive thread that will lead you to better knowledge or solutions, and you won't be certain if you'll find it. Carry on. Persevere. Have faith that you will find it in time. This conviction will propel you through both the minefields and the magnificence of life.

Here are my 12 life lessons:

1. **Learn how to fuel optimism.** Only determination and focus have propelled me forward throughout my life. Through dark times, challenging moments and seeming dead-ends, it was my mind that was my most powerful weapon—and I always had a goal and reasons for my actions. I tried not to waste time on self-doubt. Once I made up my mind to do something or approach a problem in a different way, I felt satisfied that I had an underlying plan that felt right to me. For example, during the War, when I sewed German uniforms, I promised myself that someday I would create a product that would make people happy. I stored this in my mind and it gave me a sense of relief. During tough times in business, I always said to Joseph: 'Things will get better.' When my mother's health was declining and she could still speak to me, I would end our conversations with 'tomorrow must be good.' I believed my own words.

2. **Value your children.** There is only one thing that children want from parents: they want *you*. Children want you to be with

them. They want your time, your attention, your love, and your patience—and you, in return, need to offer as much love and attention as possible. How is this balanced against the backdrop of earning a living, and teaching your children to be loving and independent people? Though technology was of little consequence when my children were growing up, the notion of balance still applies. I see with my grandchildren that the tug-of-war between schoolwork, technology, competition, after-school programs, weekend activities, hobbies and playdates leaves parents depleted and children exhausted. Joseph's mantra was always 'nicely, quietly'. This was applied throughout our parenting. No voices were raised, ever. We respected our children. There was never any 'baby talk'. Know your child and know his or her capacity while still leaving enough room for discovery. Block out the noise of other people's opinions and really observe your children. Create a safe haven, a comforting environment within your home. Make them feel loved there. Have dinner together as much as possible with both parents, one parent or another family member. You will be astounded what you can learn from their silence or what they say. Create one weekly ritual that you all share together. They will remember this forever. Do one less activity, playdate or after-school program—even for a semester—so your children can relax when they get home. Let their minds 'breathe' and catch up. Family and community strengthen our human bonds and render the world a happier, safer, better place.

3. **Show your children how to respect others.** This is a major component of family happiness. Show them what respect looks like, feels like and how it manifests. It begins by example— your example. The way we treat others each day, even in small

exchanges, has a ripple effect in the world and impacts other people's feelings.

4. **Teach good manners.** Always say 'please' and 'thank you' and don't shout across the apartment or house to get someone's attention. Address your parents gently and respectfully. Offer women and older people seats, open doors and allow them out of a lift first. Help grandparents in and out of a car or into your house by holding their hand. Learn to anticipate what your grandparents will need to make their visit comfortable. Write thank-you notes for gifts or if someone has assisted you. When visiting grandparents or someone else's house, clean up after yourself when you've had a snack or played with toys. Show your gratitude for your home by cleaning your room and putting things away. Your children will only learn these lessons and embed them in their minds if they see their parents, relatives and friends acting in these ways. Never underestimate the power of your example. If everyone in society treated each other with respect and courtesy, from leaders of governments and industry, filtering all the way down to young children, it would be easier to work together as a society to collectively build a bright future for future generations.

5. **Mother comes first.** At every step in our lives, Joseph placed me on a pedestal. The children saw how their father treated me. The 'placing women first' principal has shown my daughters that they are valuable and that there is no difference between our daughters and our son, Henry. They were given equal love, equal education, equal support and they never ever felt that we favoured one child over the other. Henry saw how women should be treated and I have heard him explaining to Michelle's son Max how he

should treat his sister Zoe. Lilian and Michelle are also keenly aware of this approach. Societies who value women are the most progressive. Valuing women benefits everyone.

6. **Inculcate entrepreneurial principles so that your children know how to build success.** Think outside the box, know your financial position every day and exhibit the chutzpah of self-belief. In the 21st century, good ideas have to be followed up with hard work. Whether you have borrowed from family members or raised funds through investors or the bank, the key to success can often feel elusive. Joseph and I would never have started our business again if we hadn't believed we could achieve our goals. We had to walk through a wall of fear out of necessity. Identifying, understanding and empathising with your market is a key component. Don't be fooled that conditions will ever revert to those of former times. Change is change—and there are always better and more efficient ways of doing things. There is also more competition in all fields. Be innovative, be aware and continue to progress in new ways. Don't be afraid to make mistakes – creativity is the basis for everything new, and is a trial-and-error process.

7. **Embrace difference.** Use your unique qualities like powerful tools—and be proud of them. Difference is 'the spice of life'. I have repeated to my children many times: *Es gibt nur einen Sie*—There is only one you. When I first arrived in Australia, I was self-conscious about being different—from my accent to the way I looked. With a heavy Polish accent, a European way of dressing and a serious outlook on life, I felt I did not fit into my new country, and that I was not understood. Sometimes I felt very hurt by inconsiderate comments. I had quickly to apply

myself to this new life. Eventually, with Joseph's help, I decided not to worry, got my balance back and forged ahead. I believed I would find my way through all obstacles while remaining true to myself. The world would be dull and boring without diversity. Even nature requires diversity. Imagine the world without its broad range of spices, flowers, trees, animals … human beings should be celebrated for their differences and uniqueness.

8. **Always stand up for what you believe.** Stand up for yourself against peer pressure. This is not an easy path. Going against the grain is unpopular. It creates ripples and comments, and you might even lose friends—but you have to live with yourself and your conscience. Which is more important? You alone must decide this. I have been back to Poland many times and made friends with non-Jews there. For many Holocaust survivors, this is the last thing that they would want to do. But I believe that not everyone is evil. I cannot hate everyone. Make peace with yourself and break the cycle of hate. History has shown us that there are crucial moments in politics and societies at large when people of conscience must take a stand, speak out, and be unafraid to champion basic human values of respect, inclusiveness, freedom, and dignity.

9. **Be single-minded.** Whilst in the ICU, unable to speak due to the intubation, I was completely silenced—and afraid. I focused on the clock on the wall opposite my bed, using it to take my mind to a different place. I knew when Joseph, Lilian and Henry were allowed to see me; I knew the routine of the staff; I knew the time Michelle would call from New York to find out from the nurses how I was progressing; and I knew when the doctor would

visit. I decided to focus on this single object, the clock, and block out everything else. My only goal was to count each passing day through its workings, excluding my emotions outside this narrow focus. I also told myself that I would leave the hospital by walking out. Having a laser focus to the exclusion of all else is sometimes a necessity. The human spirit is persevering and creative. We find ways to solve problems that are borne of necessity—and sometimes that best way to thrive is to temporarily become single-minded, much like a microscope with various useful settings.

10. **Give everyone a chance.** Joseph and I are acutely aware of this from our own lives. When we were interviewing people for jobs in our factory, we didn't see colour or race, we saw people. We rewarded earnest willingness with jobs and promotions. Looking beyond a person's eyes to what they are really saying will reward you. No group of people is entirely alike, so presumptions based on race, religion, physical attributes, location, income, upbringing, and gender will always be proven false.

11. **Don't be overcome by emotions.** During the War we often had to show 'blank' faces. I learned not to react outwardly to alarming news, sad happenings or disappointment. This doesn't mean that I didn't acutely feel emotions. Now I always internalise what I have heard rather than reaching for the panic button. A couple of years ago when Joseph suffered a stroke, my children, having heard the news, called from New York before boarding their flight to Sydney. They were distraught. I told them: 'No, we must remain calm—otherwise we won't be able to think clearly about the best way to help your father.' I have trained myself to over-ride the immediacy of wanting to fall apart. From the conditioning of the

War I think on my feet, taking into account what is happening at that very moment in order to find a way through. Remaining calm and in control of your emotions enables you to make better, more constructive decisions – whether it's a life-or-death situation or a typical daily interaction.

And finally:

12. **Never, ever give up on yourself.** Never lose courage. Never lose faith. This is the unshakeable mantra on which my life stands. As I always say to my children: 'Sometimes the wheel is up and sometimes the wheel is down, but the wheel is always turning.' Life is a gift, and we must never lose sight of that fact. It's the reason we carry on, grateful to be here—and ideally, to make a positive impact on the world while we are.

These are some of the mind-sets and strategies I want to share with my children and grandchildren. I pray that even one of them will trigger something within them so they can hold on to it securely for the rest of their lives—and maybe I can indulge myself and hope that generations after them will do the same. I hope they will discover comfort, insight and understanding.

My dearest Lilian, Mike, Henry, Michelle, Peter, Zoe and Max, every page now belongs to you and is your family history. You stand on the pillars of those that came before you as described in this book. Speak up against intolerance, injustice and hatred. Be proud of who you are and where you came from. Carry your heritage proudly, protect it and let it prevail in your own unique way.

Above all, I hope that you know how much I cherish you and how grateful I am for your abundant love—love you have shown me so many times, in so many ways, over so many years.

Top: Family reunion, August 1982. Front centre: Martin Baral. From left, seated: Ignacy Feuer, Phyllis Feuer, Aneta, Jim, Randolph Baral (Jim's middle son). Standing: Steven Baral (Martin and Dahlia's eldest child), Dahlia Baral (Martin's wife), Jonathan Baral (Jim's eldest son), Joseph, Michelle, Franka, Henry, Liane Baral (partially obscured; Martin and Dahlia's youngest child), Edward Baral (Jim's youngest son) and Naomi Baral (Martin and Dahlia's middle child).

Bottom: Family photo, February 2012. From left: Max, Michelle, Henry, Aneta, Zoe and Joseph (Lilian, Dr Mike and Peter were in New York at the time this photo was taken).

Family photo, Villanova, Pennsylvania, Passover, April 2017.
Front row, seated, from left: Dr Mike Ezekowitz, Lilian and Zoe.
Back row: Max, Michelle and Peter Roth.
Photo: Susan Scovill.

436

Family photo at Olola Ave, Sydney, February 2018.
Front row, from left: Zoe, Aneta and Max. Back row, from left: Henry, Michelle and Joseph. (Lilian, Dr Mike and Peter were in New York).

APPENDIX

CHEVRA KADISHA, SYDNEY
30 JULY 1998

HESPED (Yiddish for Eulogy) FOR FRANKA BARAL
Written and delivered by Joseph Weinreich

With a heavy heart, I stand in front of you, as a representative of the family, to pay tribute to a remarkable lady, our mother, grandmother, great-grandmother, sister, auntie and great-auntie, Franka Baral, affectionately known as Mamusiu.

Her life almost spanned this century. Franka was born on 27 January 1906 in Kraków, Poland. Her parents, Lieba and Matias Feuer, were respected, orthodox and well-known in Kraków.

Franka had four sisters and four brothers so this was a large household, happy, loving, carefree and you could describe it as idyllic. Franka grew up in this atmosphere and her childhood was happy.

At a very young age, she met and married a young man, Samuel Baral. Samek was dynamic, refined, an exceptional businessman and substantial importer and exporter of furs. He travelled extensively to England and was a man of the world.

Samek adored and worshipped his young bride, they had a wonderful marriage and Franka blossomed.

Franka was happy. Three beautiful children were born: Anetka, Marcel and Janek.

Their whole world revolved around their three children. Life was magnificent. Franka was chic, elegant and participated, together with

Samek, in the high social Jewish milieu of Kraków. They had an open house and were very hospitable. Her family was her crown.

Summer holidays with the children were taken on the Baltic Sea, winter holidays in Sopot, Zakopane, where she skied with the children.

Then all of a sudden, the first bombs hit Kraków and World War II started. Her life at 33 and the entire Jewish world in Europe was turned upside down.

The Nazi regime took hold and life became unbearable. Franka rose fearlessly to the situation.

Allow me to share with you some examples of her heroism.

One of the first edicts by the Germans was that you had 24 hours to surrender fur coats. Samek defiantly burnt his entire stock, knowing the possible consequences, but Franka's brother, Emil, unaware of the edict, was arrested and imprisoned in the Gestapo headquarters, in the infamous Montelupich. Nobody ever left that prison alive. What did Franka do? She went straight into Montelupich to try to save her brother. This was a suicide mission. She actually saw her brother behind bars but he signalled to her not to approach him but simply to leave.

Second example. The Germans established the Ghetto in Kraków. Just imagine, Franka was able to get permission to leave the Ghetto daily. Under threat of death, she removed the white armband with the blue Star of David, to establish a millinery business in her father's former residence at 16 Floriańska Street. Franka, who never had to earn a living, started selling hats, mainly to the Gestapo for their girlfriends and in this way, she was able to buy and smuggle food, again under the threat of death, to the Ghetto for her family. By listening to the officers who came to the shop, she had first-hand information as to when the next *Aktzia* would take place.

One of her customers was the notorious Kunde, a high Nazi commander of the Kraków Ghetto. In another selfless act of extreme bravery, Franka approached Kunde after seeing her sister Bala and her family being rounded up for deportation. She grabbed their ID cards and begged Kunde to stamp them in order to save their lives. He did stamp them, but it was too late. Kunde drew his revolver and said to Franka—*Ich habe nicht gawust, das sie eine juden sind.* [I did not know that you are Jewish.]

The Ghetto in Kraków was then in the process of being liquidated. Franka was somehow able to have Martin and Jim escape the Ghetto to Bochnia.

When Franka, Samek and Aneta were marched to the inferno of Płaszów, where men and women were separated, Franka was frantic. How did you get out of Płaszów? The Germans called for women volunteers to go to the Tarnów Ghetto, to sew uniforms for the army. Franka made a critical decision. She volunteered and together with Aneta went to the Tarnów Ghetto.

From the workplace outside the Ghetto, Franka decided that she must escape. She made a hat for herself and Aneta to appear like Polish folk. She brushed aside the guards and confidently walked out. From there she went to meet Martin and Jim. I have an excerpt from her account which describes the next stage of her ordeal from Bochnia to Slovakia and Hungary.

This will give you some idea of her steely determination and iron will, never giving up. It is translated from Polish. She writes:

The flight from Bochnia to Slovakia took two months in the most horrendous of circumstances. In the first stage, the smugglers left us in the forest for a few days. We ended up in gaol. The underground organisation secured our release by bribing the guard. The underground paid for us to go to Hungary. We lost our way in the forest and I lost the children in the dark of the night. The underground again came to our rescue and in tatters we arrived in Budapest on 24 January 1943.

They placed us in a hotel. We had to move because the Gestapo was looking for us. I dispersed the children and in the morning I collected them. I approached the underground party to arrange for my two nieces and their cousin to be smuggled from Kraków to Budapest. The girls arrived and I had a tremendous struggle with six children.

Franka continued to describe this unbelievable odyssey. She accomplished the impossible. She saved the lives of six children.

After the War ended, Franka received a certificate issued by the British Mission in Romania to travel to Turkey and to Palestine with the six children. At this critical juncture, her brother Ignac Feuer was instrumental in helping them to start a new life of freedom in Palestine. Then another miracle occurred. They found out that Samek was alive, one of the lucky people saved by Schindler. He joined them in Tel Aviv where eight years later and under Martin's initiative, they made their way to Australia. Then come three golden years for her. The first grandchild was born and was named after her mother, Lieba. Samek and Martin went into business and were very successful and Jim, the youngest, studied Medicine. Franka blossomed again. The War was never spoken about for the rest of her life.

Unfortunately Samek became ill. Jim, as a young medical student, took his father to New York to try to save his life, but to no avail. Franka was devastated. At this point all her children rallied around her and smothered her with love.

Franka decided not to give up and continued, together with Martin, to work very hard in the business.

Thirteen-and-a-half years ago, Franka became sick. I have never in my life seen such overwhelming love and deep affection as that shown to Franka by Aneta, Martin and Jim. It is indescribable. I don't like to single anybody out in particular, but her daughter-in-law Dahlia was absolutely magnificent to her.

What truly defines Mamusiu was her consistent and fierce devotion to her grandchildren. This bond she nurtured from the time each one was born. Not only was she the matriarch of the family, but she drew their respect, merely by her commanding presence. She was definitely not a typical grandmother. Grapefruit, yoghurt and kasha were recommended over cakes and sweets; 6am walks, open windows during winter and svelte figures were insisted upon for all visiting grandchildren. She encouraged perfection physically and mentally and stressed success through education.

Franka was charismatic. As a result, when she fell ill, anyone who came in contact with her tried their utmost to help her, starting from the wonderful staff at London Textiles, to the entire medical team and also her Polish carers.

Drogie Panie, Elżbieta, Krysia, Wandzia, Kasia.
W Imieniu Całej Rodziny,
Będziemy wam zawsze wdzięczni za tę niesamowitą opiekę, którą panie okazałyście pani baral. Bóg zapłać.

[Dear Ladies, Elizabeth, Krysia, Wandzia and Kasia,
In the name of the whole family, we will be always grateful to you for the incredible help you gave to Mrs Baral. May God reward you.]

I have known my mother-in-law for almost half of her life and I think in this particular instance I know the way she may have thought. She was independent and stoic and her entire being was devoted to her family. Nothing else in the world mattered to her and most importantly, she would not have wanted any of her family to feel sorrow and suffer because of her. She is leaving now on her last journey on this earth, but she is going to heaven and the angels are waiting for her with outstretched wings and she will take an honourable place with the righteous people and she will formally be reunited with her beloved Samek.

She will intercede on our behalf, before almighty God. I beg you, let go of her gently and in dignity. You have always done the utmost for her.

Chazak ve'Ematz
(Be strong and of good courage)

God, who is full of compassion, who dwells on high, God of forgiveness, who is merciful, slow to anger and abounding in loving kindness, grant pardon of transgressions, nearness of salvation, and perfect rest beneath the shadow of Your divine presence, in the exalted places among the holy and pure, who shine as the brightness of heaven's expanse to *FREIDA (FRANKA) BAT MATTITYAHU* who has gone to her eternal rest.

We pray, Lord of compassion, remember for good all her merits and the righteous deeds which she performed on earth. Open to her the gates of righteousness and light, the gates of pity and grace. Shelter her for evermore under the cover of Your wings; and let her soul be bound up in the bond of eternal life. The Lord is her inheritance; may she rest in peace. And let us say, Amen.

אֵל מָלֵא רַחֲמִים שׁוֹכֵן בַּמְּרוֹמִים ׳ הַמְצֵא
מְנוּחָה נְכוֹנָה תַּחַת כַּנְפֵי הַשְּׁכִינָה ׳
בְּמַעֲלוֹת קְדוֹשִׁים וּטְהוֹרִים ׳ כְּזֹהַר הָרָקִיעַ
מַזְהִירִים ׳ אֶת־נִשְׁמַת הַיֶּלֶד (הַיַּלְדָּה) פּ״ב״פ
שֶׁהָלַךְ (שֶׁהָלְכָה) לְעוֹלָמוֹ (לְעוֹלָמָהּ) ׳ אָנָּא בַּעַל
הָרַחֲמִים הַסְתִּירֵהוּ (הַסְתִּירֶהָ) בְּסֵתֶר כְּנָפֶיךָ
לְעוֹלָמִים ׳ וּצְרוֹר בִּצְרוֹר הַחַיִּים אֶת נִשְׁמָתוֹ
(נִשְׁמָתָהּ) ׳ יְיָ הוּא נַחֲלָתוֹ (נַחֲלָתָהּ) וְיָנוּחַ
(וְתָנוּחַ) בְּשָׁלוֹם עַל מִשְׁכָּבוֹ (מִשְׁכָּבָהּ)
וְנֹאמַר אָמֵן :

GLOSSARY OF NAMES

Name	Relationship to Aneta	Notes
Aneta Baral (Annette, Anula, Anna, Anetka)		
Akavia, Miriam	Aneta's Auntie Ela's husband's niece	Celebrated author
Anna Sr (Ancika, Ancika cudna, Anna Körmendi Ottóné)	Aneta's Hungarian savior Ilonka Nemes' granddaughter	Received the Medal for Bravery from the Hungarian government and a medal for the Righteous Among Nations from Yad Vashem on behalf of her grandmother, Ilonka Nemes
Anna Jr	Aneta's Hungarian saviour Ilonka Nemes' great granddaughter	Anna Sr's daughter
Auntie Ela (maiden name Baral)	Aneta's auntie	Samuel Baral's younger sister
Baral, Juda (Yehuda)	Aneta's paternal grandfather	Wife: Jenta Schullehrer (maiden name)
Baral, Antonieta (Jenta)	Aneta's paternal grandmother	Juda Baral's first wife
Baral, Rachela Brawmann (Rachel, Rosa, Rózia)	Aneta's paternal grandmother	Juda Baral's second wife
Baral, Samuel (Samek, Staszek, Tato Samek)	Aneta's father	Number 41 on Schindler's List
Baral, Franka (married name) (Frania, Frieda, Franciska)	Aneta's mother	

Name	Relationship to Aneta	Notes
Baral, Aneta	Aneta's maiden name	Mother is Franka and father is Samek. Brothers are Marcel (Martin) and Janek (Jim)
Baral, Marcel (Martin)	Aneta's older brother	
Baral, Dahlia	Aneta's sister-in-law, married to Martin	
Baral, Steven	Aneta's nephew	Martin and Dahlia Baral's oldest child
Baral, Naomi	Aneta's niece	Martin and Dahlia Baral's second child
Baral, Liane	Aneta's niece	Martin and Dahlia Baral's youngest child
Baral, Janek (Jim, Jakob, Jacob)	Aneta's younger brother	
Baral, Leonie (maiden name Whitmont)	Aneta's sister-in-law	Jim Baral's first wife
Baral, Jonathan	Aneta's nephew	Janek's (Jim's) eldest son
Baral, Randolph	Aneta's nephwew	Janek's (Jim's) middle son
Baral, Edward	Aneta's nephew	Janek's (Jim's) youngest son
Ben-Gurion, David	Aneta employed in his office in Tel Aviv, Israel	Prime Minister of Israel
Ber, Milus	Aneta's cousin, Auntie Tosia's son	Franka's sister's son
Ber, Tosia (maiden name Feuer)	Aneta's auntie	Franka's sister
Bisping, Adam Benedykt	Aneta's close Polish friend	

Name	Relationship to Aneta	Notes
Bisping, Barbara	Aneta's close Polish friend	Wife of Adam Benedykt Bisping
Bleicher, Pola	Aneta's childhood friend, saved by Franka	Brother is Henek Bleicher (known later as Zvi Bar Lev)
Bleicher, Godek	Aneta's childhood friend, Pola's uncle	
Bleicher, Henek (Zvi Barlev)	Aneta's childhood friend, Pola's brother	Sister is Pola Bleicher. Ada and Olga's cousin
Bleicher, Sala	Aneta's childhood friend, Pola's mother	
Brodaty, Prof. Henry	Aneta's mother's doctor, a dementia specialist	
Ehrlich, Motek (Marcus)	Aneta's mother's brother-in-law	Married to Hela, Franka's sister
Ehrlich, Hela (maiden name Feuer)	Aneta's auntie	Franka's fourth sister and Ada and Olga's mother
Ehrlich, Ada (maiden name)	Aneta's cousin	Daughter, Hila and son, Ronen
Ehrlich, Olga (maiden name)	Aneta's cousin	Son, Yoav and daughter, Anat
Ezekowitz, Lilian (married name)	Aneta's daughter	
Ezekowitz, Dr Michael	Aneta's son-in-law	
Ezekowitz, Carol	Aneta's son-in-law's sister	
Ezekowitz, Ida	Aneta's son-in-law's mother	
Faust, Dorcia	Aneta's auntie	Dorcia's sister is Toduś (Toni)

Name	Relationship to Aneta	Notes
Feuer, Matias	Aneta's maternal grandfather	Son Jacob from a previous marriage
Feuer, Lieba (married name from her second marriage to Matias Feuer)	Aneta's maternal grandmother	She had a son, Motek Matzner from a previous marriage
Feuer, Mina (married name Susskind)	Aneta's auntie	Franka's oldest sister. Mother of Tusia and Bubek
Feuer, Bala (married name Hirsch)	Aneta's auntie	Franka's second oldest sister
Feuer, Franka (Frania, Frieda, Franciska) (married name Baral)	Aneta's mother	Franka's siblings from oldest to youngest: Mina, Bala, Franka, Hela, Tosia, Emil, Ignac. Half brothers: Jacob Feuer and Motek Matzner
Feuer, Hela	Aneta's auntie	Franka's fourth oldest sister
Feuer, Tosia (Toska) (married name Ber)	Aneta's auntie	Franka's youngest sister, husband Schlomo Ber
Feuer, Emil	Aneta's uncle	Franka's younger brother
Feuer, Mina	Aneta's auntie	Franka's brother Emil's wife
Feuer, Jasiu	Aneta's cousin	Emil and Mina's son
Feuer, Ignac (Ignacy, Ignaz)	Aneta's uncle	Franka's youngest brother, Marie and Lillie Feuer's father
Feuer, Toduś (Toni) (maiden name Wilner)	Aneta's uncle's wife	Ignac's wife

Name	Relationship to Aneta	Notes
Feuer, Marie	Aneta's cousin	Ignac and Toduś (Toni's) daughter
Feuer, Lillie	Aneta's cousin	Ignac and Toduś (Toni's) daughter
Feuer, Jacob	Aneta's uncle	Franka's half brother from Matias Feuer's first marriage
Feuer, Toni	Aneta's uncle's wife	Jacob Feuer's wife
Feuer, Gisele (Gisela/Tova)	Aneta's cousin	Jacob Feuer's daughter, sister of Tova and Yechiel, mother of Kuti
Feuer, Charlotte (Yafa)	Aneta's cousin	Jacob Feuer's daughter, sister of Tova and Yerchiel
Feuer, Aki (Yechiel, Yehiel)	Aneta's cousin	Jacob Feuer's son, brother of Tova and Yafa
Friedman Dr	Aneta's doctor	
Hirsch, Salo (Salomon)	Aneta's Auntie Bala's husband	
Hirsch, Bala (maiden name Feuer)	Aneta's auntie	Franka's second oldest sister and mother of Mela, Hesiu, Menachem
Hirsch, Mela	Aneta's cousin	Daughter of Bala and Salo
Hirsch, Hesiu	Aneta's cousin	Son of Bala and Salo
Hirsch, Menachem	Aneta's cousin	Son of Bala and Salo
Kamińska, Edzia	Aneta's Auntie Ela's sister-in-law	Good friend of Franka Baral in Kraków before the War
Kasia	Aneta's family housekeeper	In Kraków before the war

Name	Relationship to Aneta	Notes
Katalin (Catherine Vaskó Beci)	Aneta's Hungarian savior Ilonka Nemes' great niece	
Kołodziej, Elżbieta	Aneta's Polish savior Bronka Porwitowa's niece	Was given the title of Righteous Among Nations and received the medal from Yad vashem on behalf of her Auntie Bronka Porwitowa
Künstler, Moniek	Aneta's Auntie Ela's first husband	Brothers Liebish, Hirsch and Alfred
Laub, Anka	Aneta's childhood friend in Poland before the War	
Lemek, Hania	Aneta's auntie Hela's housekeeper	Ada and Olga lived with her in the countryside during part of the War
Maly (Marysia) (maiden name Schenker)	Aneta's life-long friend from Tel Aviv, Israel	
Matzner, Motek	Aneta's mother's step-brother	Son from Lieba Matzner's first marriage and brought this son to her second marriage to Matias Feuer
Matzner, Ethel	Aneta's mother's step-brother's wife, wife of Motek	
Milecki, Rabbi Ben Zion	Aneta's mother's Memorial Service Rabbi	
Mumusiu or Mumushu	Franka's name of endearment used by all the grandchildren	

Name	Relationship to Aneta	Notes
Muri, Erzsébet Margaret (Elizabeth)	Aneta's Hungarian savior Ilonka Nemes' niece	Ilonka's sister Elizabeth Vasko Muri moved to Canada in 1956. Elizabeth's daughter is Erzsébet (Elizabeth) Margaret Muri
Nagymama (grandmother in Hungarian)	Aneta's Hungarian savior Ilonka Nemes' mother	Ilonka Nemes' mother's full name is Anna Vaskó
Nagypapa (grandfather in Hungarian)	Aneta's Hungarian savior Ilonka Nemes' father	Ilonka Nemes' father's full name is János Vaskó
Nemes, Ilonka (name of endearment; real name is Ilona)	Aneta's family's Hungarian savior	
Nyugen, Lucy	Aneta's employee of over 30 years in Sydney, Australia	
Pfefferbaum, Hela (Helen)	Aneta's step-grandmother Rachel's niece	
Pfefferbaum, Manes	Aneta's step-grandmother Rachel's niece's husband	
Pfefferbaum, Bibi	Aneta's step-grandmother Rachel's niece's daughter	
Pfefferbaum, Zvika (Zvi)	Aneta's step-grandmother Rachel's niece's son	Wife Sylvia
Plessner, Moniek (Moshe)	Aneta's Aunt Ela's second husband in Israel	

Name	Relationship to Aneta	Notes
Plonka, Aniela	Aneta, Marcel and Janek's nanny in Kraków before the War	
Pogacz, Pola	Aneta's mother's midwife	
Porush, Rabbi Dr Israel	Aneta and Joseph's marriage Rabbi	
Porwitowa, Bronka (also known as Bronisława Porwit)	Aneta's family's Polish saviour	Worked for Motek before the War
Roth, Peter	Aneta's son-in-law	Michelle's husband
Roth, Michelle Rachel (maiden name Weinreich)	Aneta and Joseph's daughter and mother of Zoe and Max	
Roth, Zoe	Aneta's granddaughter	Michelle and Peter's twin daughter
Roth, Max	Aneta's grandson	Michelle and Peter's twin son
Schullehrer, Josef	Aneta's paternal great-grandfather	Daughter Antonieta
Schullehrer, Jenta (Antonieta)	Aneta's grandmother	Married to Juda Baral and is Josef Schullehrer's daughter
Seidler, Harry	Aneta's renowned architect for her home at Olola Avenue, Sydney	
Shehabi, Dr Yahya	Aneta's ICU doctor, Sydney	
Sliwa, Edward	Aneta's longstanding Polish friend	

Name	Relationship to Aneta	Notes
Sliwa, Sieprawska Ursula	Aneta's longstanding Polish friend	
Sofer-Schreiber, Simche	Aneta's husband's maternal grandfather	Joseph's grandfather
Stern, Itzhak	Aneta's father's friend	Chief advisor and accountant for Oscar Schindler. He typed the list of names known as 'Schindler's List'
Stern, Suza	Aneta's father's friend Itzhak's wife	
Susskind, Chaskiel	Aneta's auntie Mina's husband	
Susskind, Mina (maiden name Feuer)	Aneta's auntie	Franka's sister, married to Chaskiel
Susskind, Bubek	Aneta's cousin	Son of Mina and Chaskiel
Susskind, Tusia (Esther, Toska)	Aneta's cousin	Daughter of Mina and Chaskiel
Ung, Lee	Aneta's employee of over 30 years in Sydney, Australia	
Vaskó, Ilona	She connected Aneta and family to Ilonka Nemes' descendants	No relation to the Vaskó family of saviours
Weinreich, Abraham	Aneta's husband's paternal grandfather	Joseph's grandfather
Weinreich, Chaim	Aneta's father-in-law, Joseph's father	
Weinreich, Freidl (Fanny, Frania)	Aneta's mother-in-law	Joseph's mother
Weinreich, Moshe	Aneta's brother-in-law	Joseph's brother

Name	Relationship to Aneta	Notes
Weinreich, Joseph (Josele)	Aneta's husband	
Weinreich, Aneta	Aneta's married name. Mother of Lilian, Michelle and Henry	Grandmother of Zoe and Max Roth. Mother-in-law of Dr Michael Ezekowitz and Peter Roth
Weinreich, Lilian Helen (maiden name)	Aneta's older daughter	
Weinreich, Michelle Rachel (Malka) (maiden name)	Aneta's younger daughter	
Weinreich, Henry Samuel (Chaim)	Aneta and Joseph's son	Also known professionally as Henry Roth
Whitmont, Leonie	Aneta's sister-in-law, Jim Baral's first wife	
Wright, Judy	Grand-niece of Ilonka Nemes, Aneta's Hungarian saviour	Daughter of Erzsébet Margaret Muri (married name Szatlóczky)

Made in the USA
Monee, IL
24 November 2019